"This book is transformational. You  ı you
faith and fall more in love with youı e
uniquely created *you* to love Him. I and
read this book!"

John Trent, Ph.D.
President of The Center for StrongFamilies, coauthor of *The Blessing*, and author of
Breaking the Cycle of Divorce

"Myra has an astounding capacity to understand the full range of hearts
God has made and is redeeming, as seen in her brilliant exercises for the
nine spiritual temperaments. I recommend this book enthusiastically and
will make great use of it in my ministry of preparing pastors."

Darrell Johnson
Associate professor of pastoral theology, Regent College, Vancouver

"If you always suspected God tuned your heart to connect with Him in
a particular way, *What's Your God Language?* is a must-read book. It will
show you how to listen to the way you're made. It will give you permission
to express your heart for God in the shape of the longings He's given you.
Myra Perrine's book is a real gift to the body of Christ."

Paula Rinehart
Author of *Strong Women, Soft Hearts* and *Sex and the Soul of a Woman*

"*What's Your God Language?* provides a freeing and practical process
for discovering how we most deeply love and connect with Jesus. By
honoring the uniqueness of every spiritual journey, Myra Perrine helps
us understand that there is no one-size-fits-all spirituality."

Adele Calhoun
Pastor of spiritual formation, Christ Church of Oak Brook, Oak Brook, Illinois

"The best thing about *What's Your God Language?* is the integrity with
which it is written. Myra Perrine's passion to help people be intimate
with God flows from the life she lives. When you read this book, you'll
find yourself feeling validated, not criticized; challenged, and yet warmly
assisted by pages of practical instruction. I expect this book to bring a
great sense of relief to many people."

Sarah Sumner
Author of *Leadership above the Line*

"How we as human beings relate to God is no cookie-cutter process, and Myra Perrine's book is a wonderful contribution to understanding that diversity. This volume is freeing. It liberates us to explore God in ways that are rich, deep, and unique to how He has distinctly wired us."

Dr. Sam Metcalf
President of Church Resource Ministries

"Myra Perrine has personally blessed me with her openness to hear from God and engage in a risky, heart relationship with Him. God has used her to revolutionize my tired, habitual walk with Him. As a casualty of 'mechanized religion,' I found *What's Your God Language?* to be water on dry and thirsty ground. I cannot recommend it highly enough."

Dave Jackson
Church Resource Ministries, Canada

WHAT'S YOUR GOD LANGUAGE?

Connecting with God through
Your Unique Spiritual Temperament

DR. MYRA PERRINE

FOREWORD BY GARY THOMAS

SALT**RIVER**®

AN IMPRINT OF
TYNDALE HOUSE PUBLISHERS, INC.

Visit Tyndale's exciting Web site at www.tyndale.com

TYNDALE and Tyndale's quill logo are registered trademarks of Tyndale House Publishers, Inc.

SaltRiver and the SaltRiver logo are registered trademarks of Tyndale House Publishers, Inc.

What's Your God Language?: Connecting with God through Your Unique Spiritual Temperament

Copyright © 2007 by Myra Perrine. All rights reserved.

Cover photo copyright © by Veer. All rights reserved.

Author photo copyright © 2006 by Cynthia Stamatis. All rights reserved.

Designed by Beth Sparkman

Unless otherwise indicated, Scripture quotations are taken from the *Holy Bible*, New International Version®. NIV®. Copyright © 1973, 1978, 1984 by International Bible Society. Used by permission of Zondervan. All rights reserved.

Scripture quotations marked NASB are taken from the NEW AMERICAN STANDARD BIBLE®, Copyright © 1960, 1962, 1963, 1968, 1971, 1972, 1973, 1975, 1977, 1995 by The Lockman Foundation. Used by permission.

Scripture quotations marked TLB are taken from *The Living Bible* copyright © 1971. Used by permission of Tyndale House Publishers, Inc., Carol Stream, Illinois 60188. All rights reserved.

Scripture quotations marked NLT are taken from the *Holy Bible*, New Living Translation, copyright © 1996, 2004. Used by permission of Tyndale House Publishers, Inc., Carol Stream, Illinois 60188. All rights reserved.

Scripture quotations marked "*THE MESSAGE*" are taken from *THE MESSAGE*. Copyright © by Eugene H. Peterson 1993, 1994, 1995, 1996, 2000, 2001, 2002. Used by permission of NavPress Publishing Group.

Scripture quotations marked NKJV™ taken from the New King James Version.® Copyright © 1982 by Thomas Nelson, Inc. Used by permission. All rights reserved.

Scripture quotations marked KJV are taken from the *Holy Bible*, King James Version.

Scripture quotations marked Weymouth are from the Weymouth New Testament in Modern Speech, Richard Francis Weymouth, 1913. Public domain in the United States.

Library of Congress Cataloging-in-Publication Data

Perrine, Myra.
    What's your God language? : connecting with God through your unique spiritual temperament / Myra Perrine.
        p. cm.
    Includes bibliographical references.
    ISBN-13: 978-1-4143-1322-1 (sc)
    ISBN-10: 1-4143-1322-5 (sc)
    1. Spiritual life—Christianity. 2. Temperament--Religious aspects--Christianity. I. Title.
BV4597.57.P47 2007
248'.4--dc22   2006101640

Printed in the United States of America

13   12   11   10   09   08   07

7   6   5   4   3   2   1

CONTENTS

DEDICATION

To Dan, whose love, support,
and prayers have deepened
and widened my journey
and given me "double Jesus,"
and always to You, Lord.

ACKNOWLEDGMENTS

I am indebted to Gary Thomas, whose original work on the spiritual temperaments laid the foundation for this book, and to the many people who helped me transform my doctoral project into a book. I would like to thank my doctoral mentor, Dr. Stephen Peisner, who encouraged me to pursue publication; Dr. John Trent, who assisted me with the proposal; Lee Hough, who gave good advice in the early stages; and Dr. Sarah Sumner, whose supportive friendship I treasure and who introduced me to Jan Harris from Tyndale. I would also like to thank Lisa Jackson, my editor, whom I think of as my "makeup artist," because she beautifies my words with exquisite grace, and Church Resource Ministries and my Staff Development and Care Team, who prayed for me and gave me time to do the writing. And to the many friends, intercessors, and supporters who have loved and encouraged me along the way . . . thank you.

FOREWORD

You are about to do yourself a great favor.

There is no greater joy in life—absolutely none—than to grow in intimacy with the God who created us, who loves us, and whose grace sustains us. And I can't think of a better way to grow in this intimacy than to spend some time in the able and gentle hands of a wise spiritual director such as Dr. Myra Perrine.

Myra's book reaches the rare air of literary achievement: It is at once practical and profound, comforting and convicting, theoretical and instructive. With an experienced hand and an obvious passion for God, Myra leads us into a deeper understanding of what we can do to respond to our Creator's marvelous grace. She takes us far beyond the one-size-fits-all mentality of so many popular books and helps us embrace the unique relationship into which God calls each one of us.

While her initial thoughts were in part inspired by the temperaments I lay out in *Sacred Pathways*, Myra has done me "one better" by not only offering a fresh rendering of these pathways, but also creating very practical exercises that make understanding them a much more life-changing realization.

There is no higher study than learning what it means to love and be loved by God, which puts Myra's work in the highest realm of importance. I am honored to recommend her work to you, and I am thankful that so many will have their hearts' passion renewed as Myra takes all of us on a journey of spiritual renewal.

Gary Thomas

December 2006

PREFACE

Stuck. Frustrated. Dry. Confused. These are a few of the descriptors—
along with bored and guilty—I hear as I speak to Christians about their
relationship with the Lord. In my work with Church Resource Ministries,
I often see people who are hungry to connect with Jesus, yet they simply
aren't connecting, and what brings life to one doesn't automatically bring
life to another. Just recently, a woman approached me and announced,
"I don't fit into the prescribed Christian 'box,' and when I see how *other*
Christians worship God, I truthfully feel like I have to pretend." Her
dilemma is not unique. I meet people like this all the time who are looking
for answers about how to more authentically love and serve God.

This book grew out of that desire and a conviction that, although
life can be difficult, loving God ought not be! After all, He is the One
who initiates and ultimately is in charge of the process. As we respond
to His lead, a partnership with Him emerges—a rhythm of grace that
flows freely in and through the spiritual journey.

This is a truth I didn't understand when I first became a Christian
in 1970. Back then, I learned a simple acrostic for *growth* that worked
pretty well:

> **G**o to God in prayer daily.
> **R**ead God's Word daily.
> **O**bey God moment by moment.
> **W**itness for Christ by your life and words.
> **T**rust God for every detail of your life.
> **H**oly Spirit—allow Him to control and empower your daily life and
> witness.[1]

Those in our college ministry were taught to use this in our daily
spiritual lives. Early-morning quiet times consisting of prayer and Bible
reading were encouraged, and we upheld those standards faithfully. In

fact, I remember wondering if I was rising early enough after hearing that Billy Graham was first attracted to his not-yet-wife, Ruth, because she arose before dawn each day to pray. (Not being an early-morning person, I wondered how I would ever find a husband!)

Those initial years as a young believer were wonderful ones, a time when foundational truths and habits in the Word were being established. Yet over time, it became necessary for me to expand my approach in order to give God ample space to do *His* part in the dance, to unveil more of His mystery and transcendence—in His own way and at His own time. As I've progressed with Jesus for more than three decades, my way of relating to Him has broadened and deepened as well . . . in the midst of difficult situations that brought heartache and disappointment, and through experiences that challenged my faith to the core and required my roots to go deeper. Yet through it all, my connection with God developed new colors and nuances. And rightly so. Life necessitates change and growth—in knowing the Lord and in knowing oneself. For as Richard Foster says in his book *Celebration of Discipline,* "The desperate need today is not for a greater number of intelligent people, or gifted people, but for deep people."[2]

This book is the result of that ever-deepening process as I've listened to the navigational challenges forged in my own life and in the lives of others. It is also the result of the research gathered during my doctoral project as I explored spiritual formation through the lens of the spiritual temperaments. By studying how people best and most naturally relate to God—and offering them a series of specially designed spiritual practice exercises—I found quite fascinating results. As I surveyed and interviewed more than seventy ministry leaders about their spiritual preferences and practices, I noticed some interesting patterns:

1. The more closely someone's spiritual preferences matched his or her spiritual practices, the more spiritually "satisfied" that person reported to be in his or her relationship with God. In other words, greater spiritual satisfaction was experienced when people pursued God in ways they enjoyed and found most life giving.[3] Conversely, when spiritual preferences were not given expression—when people were solely doing what they

were taught to do rather than what they enjoyed—spiritual satisfaction was seen to decline, as did their sense of closeness to God.

2. The broader the spiritual practice scores across all nine spiritual temperaments, the more "hungry" people reported to be for God. In other words, the more experience and exposure people had in connecting with God in a variety of ways, the stronger their desire for Him became.

As I thought about this outcome, I remembered an old church-planting motto I'd once heard: "If Denny's were the only restaurant in town, would more people eat at Denny's, or would fewer people eat out?" This saying originally referred to the fact that different churches attract different people, but I wondered if it is also true that when people who had been taught that there is only one *right* way to "feast on the Lord," they simply grew tired of that one spiritual diet. It seemed that when people had tasted many different spiritual practices—habits of the heart handed down through the centuries—their appetites for knowing Jesus remained hearty and even increased.

But my findings went even further. As I spoke with pastors about the different spiritual temperaments of the people in their churches, they began to see their congregants through a useful grid that clarified why some were growing and others were not, and even why some were leaving their churches—not because of theological discrepancies (which had often been the presumed problem) but because of simple differences in spiritual preference. Pastoral teams now had a better handle on how to create more meaningful opportunities for worship and service within their churches so that all the "love languages" of God would be included.

This book has been developed as a result of my findings, not only to help individual Christians grow in their love for God, but also to assist pastors, small group leaders, church boards, missionaries, Christian school teachers, university professors, organizational leaders, husbands, wives, and parents foster spiritual growth by using the spiritual temperament grid to understand themselves and others. As Henri Nouwen said, until we are in touch with our own belovedness, we cannot touch the sacredness of another.[*] Until we embrace who God has made us to be, we will continually try to make others over in our own image.

This book will be a highly interactive tool to guide you through an important self-discovery process. Thus, it is not intended to be merely informational or inspirational, but *transformational* in its construction, providing practical "next steps" for you through offering ten weeks of spiritual practice exercises for each of the spiritual temperaments, which are located in part 2 of the book. The intermediate and advanced exercises are located at www.ChristianBookGuides.com.

My hope is that this book will bring increased unity and celebration within the body of Christ, promoting personal growth and maturity for all who read it.

INTRODUCTION
THE GREAT INVITATION

My husband and I recently received an unusual card in the mail. On the front was a picture of a friend standing right next to the president of the United States! Yes, it was a real photograph, but I was actually a little surprised because our friend is neither a political figure nor one who would typically strive to be seen with a person of prominence. Upon closer inspection, I noticed that the card was actually an invitation to a banquet being held for my friend's "important people," and the insinuation was that, while the president wouldn't be with us, we were among those just as valuable to our friend as the leader of the free world!

Moments after I put the card down, it hit me: The wording on the invitation was profoundly true. As children of God, we *are* just as valuable as those in places of political power and influence . . . at least to our heavenly Father. Then I began to ponder the Lord's staggering invitation for us to come to the banquet *He* is preparing!

> He said to his servants, "The wedding banquet is ready. . . . Go to the street corners and invite to the banquet anyone you find."
>
> *Matthew 22:8-9*

Yes, it is true. At the center of life is an invitation, preceded by a desire and a longing. God desires relationship with humankind—He invites us to come be with Him—and within us a longing resides to respond to that invitation.

> The Lord longs to be gracious to you, and therefore He waits on high to have compassion on you. For the Lord is a God of justice; how blessed are all those who long for Him. *Isaiah 30:18 (NASB)*

xiii

God is a *longing* God, and every longing of His heart has been placed within us, too . . . a longing for beauty, for love, for closeness with Him. In the beginning, Adam and Eve had total access to God, walking and talking with Him face-to-face in the cool of the day. God Himself instructed them and gave them creative, meaningful work crafted just for them—subduing, ruling, naming—the very work that He does. There were animals for them to enjoy, perfect health without pain or aging, splendor galore, green grass, and massively colorful flowers, as well as all the fruits and veggies they could ever eat, which were being watered effortlessly by surrounding rivers and a constant mist. Adam and Eve were in perfect communion with one another, naked and unashamed, totally comfortable with their passion and purity, feeling safe in undisturbed love and trust.

Then came the big snafu. Though humans were intended to live in the Garden, Adam and Eve had to leave that place of communion with God for less-than-pleasant reasons. As they departed, they carried with them the inherent longing they'd been given to have what they'd always known of God and His world—the world for which they'd been created. And all these years later, we still carry that same longing in our hearts, for deep inside we are homesick for our initial Garden-life with God. I'm guessing God is homesick for that life with us as well.

Many years after the first Garden had been closed to humankind, Jesus came to earth, expressing His longings:

> Oh Jerusalem, Jerusalem! . . . How often have I desired to gather
> thy children to me, just as a hen gathers her chickens under her
> wings, and you would not come!   *Matthew 23:37 (Weymouth)*

Though God wanted us to know the abundant, rich life He had designed for us to enjoy with Him (see John 10:10), people had found other ways to satisfy their desires. Our hearts had become occupied with a myriad of things, and we were pretty distracted and unreceptive to God's invitation. Because sin and the enemy had spoiled our original Garden place, we gradually lost touch with our own longings for home. Yet in spite of our reluctance, as Adam and Eve's offspring, we are still hungry to taste what they experienced in the Garden.

We cannot escape the truth: We were made by God, for God, and we bear His image on our hearts. His trademark has been permanently woven into the fabric of every human soul. The very fact that we have been created in the image of our Creator assumes our need for connection with Him. We are incomplete without our God-connection, for our natures and destinies as those created in His image call us to glorify and enjoy Him forever (see Genesis 1:26-27). This yearning for communion with our unseen, present Lord, who comes to us as Father, Son, and Spirit, is in every son of Adam and daughter of Eve.

According to a parable I once heard about the Creation, in one moment of time, God looked into a mirror and saw His own image. Then He broke the mirror and scattered it into a million pieces, each piece becoming a human soul, and each soul bringing something of the image of God to the world.[1] Now—whether we know God or not—the call to be God's image bearers remains. Our lives are shaped by our original purpose, and inwardly we hunger to come home to that place where we are fully known and loved. Oh, we can ignore that longing, masking it or trying to reconfigure it, but we cannot escape its reality, nor the perpetual summons reminding us that the great invitation has been extended personally to *us*.

This invitation is actually not dependent upon us at all, or upon our response. Even now, most days I live in oblivion to God's perpetual inviting, yet there are moments when the Lord breaks in. It is then that I find myself in what the Celts called the "thin place," where the veil that separates the eternal from the temporal becomes so thin and permeable that—through a vibrant sunset or a child at play—I get a whiff of celestial air. And there it is again: God's invitation, always beckoning, pressing, even disturbing me, reminding me of His consistent longing for . . . *me*. He has created me for Himself. Oh, the Inviter is astonishingly long-suffering in His love!

Yet when we choose to respond, we taste once again a rich morsel of what our first parents knew so well. When we say yes and come to God, we find once more that *He* becomes our greatest reward.

> *In this secluded place I meet a King.*
> *He comes alone to drink reality*
> > *With me. Sometimes we talk, sometimes we sit*
> > *And sip a life that passes by the crowd.*

As inwardness is born—a felted thing
Of power—a commonality—of grace
A union where unmended hopes are knit
Where silence roars as quiet sings aloud.
Oh Christ, I love it here! It is our place.
Speak Lord or not. Touch me or not. Show then
Your will or bid me wait in patient grace.
Fill all my hungry need with joy again.
With simple loaves of bread and chaliced wine
    Heaven, earth, and all of God are mine.[2]

We were meant to walk with our God in the cool of the day, in an ongoing relationship, just as our first parents did.

In the seventh century, John of Damascus, a Syrian theologian, described this love relationship as "the circle dance of God," referring to the interaction of the Trinity as *perichoresis. Choros* is an ancient Greek round dance performed at banquets and festive occasions. John of Damascus envisioned the Godhead as a holy community, a circle where there exists an all-out sense of joy, freedom, song, intimacy, and love, and we are invited in. George Cladis said it this way: "Within the nature of God there is community. God the Father, Son, and Spirit are in relationship with one another and yet are one God. A unity of community exists between persons who love each other and live together in harmony."[3] Astonishingly, we have been invited to join this holy dance!

This dance is one that includes family rights (see Galatians 3:26; 4:5), an inheritance (see Colossians 3:24), a never-ending life (see John 3:16), and an invitation to know our "Abba" personally (see Galatians 4:6). Dallas Willard describes it like this:

> We have received an invitation. We are invited to make a pilgrimage—into the heart and life of God. The invitation has long been on public record. You can hardly look anywhere across the human scene and not encounter it. . . . God's desire for us is that we should live in Him. . . . In its deepest nature and meaning our universe is a community of boundless and totally competent love.[4]

This invitation is an intimate one; we are asked to know and be known. The biblical authors described this relationship as more than sonship, even more than friendship; they called it betrothal (see 2 Corinthians 11:2). When God says He knows us, we are not surprised; after all, He is God. But when He invites us to *know Him*, that call to mutuality nearly knocks us off our feet! It makes us a bit uneasy, for surely God is God and we are not. How can this mutual knowing even be possible?

But Jesus restated the invitation when He said that knowing Him was the very essence of life.

> This is eternal life: that they may *know* you, the only true God, and Jesus Christ, whom you have sent.   *John 17:3 (emphasis added)*

The Old Testament authors wrote similar statements:

> Oh, that we might *know* the LORD! Let us press on to *know* him. He will respond to us as surely as the arrival of dawn or the coming of rains in early spring.   *Hosea 6:3 (NLT, emphasis added)*

The Hebrew word used here is *yada*, which means "to clearly understand by experience, to know as an intimate friend, to have relations with" (as Adam *knew* Eve and she conceived a child). Yes, this is a close relationship indeed.

And though we are at the same time compelled and frightened by this invitation, we often find we are most ready to receive God's offer during times of difficulty; it is then that we are most willing to turn toward God—our Source of Living Water—and drink deeply. As we cry out to Him, we look into His face with all our sin exposed and see that Jesus doesn't look away. Instead, He says,

> Fear not, for I have redeemed you; I have summoned you by name; you are mine. . . . You are precious and honored in my sight, and . . . I love you. . . . Do not be afraid, for I am with you.   *Isaiah 43:1, 4-5*

> Arise, my darling, my beautiful one, and come along.
> *Song of Solomon 2:10 (NASB)*

I have heard this intimate relationship defined as "in-to-me-see," and surely that is a good explanation. But I have constructed my own description. I see intimacy as growing in one's capacity to stand progressively (not perfectly) "exposed"—spirit and soul—in the presence of another with diminishing fear. All known defenses relax because we have confidence that the other will act with our best interests in mind, that this person will guard our dignity and never intentionally shame or hurt us.

In other words, intimacy grows when we feel so loved, so safe with someone that we can be open about ourselves, even disclosing things we normally wouldn't tell others—our doubts, our fears, and our failings. And because we've experienced a kind of "sanctuary of the soul" when we're together—truly wanting the best for each other: wholeness, emancipation from bondage, and contentment in Jesus—we find that we are at ease when we're together. We feel confident that when something needs to be said, it will be said, and in the best possible way. And because love covers a multitude of sins (see 1 Peter 4:8), I can rest knowing that as I uncover myself, the other will cover me.

This intimacy is actually all about the heart; a grace-filled, self-aware, ever-healing heart is a safe heart. And though intimacy doesn't come easily or automatically, one of the great things about it is that it's not static; it's dynamic. It can grow! With commitment and effort, intimacy develops as we learn to be honest and vulnerable with one another, saying the hard thing in gentleness and love—even when it's easier to remain silent.

The requirement for developing intimacy with God is quite similar: being honest, vulnerable, and saying the hard thing to Jesus—exposing my true self to the One whose character and goodness I'm coming to know and trust more fully day by day—as He also speaks the truth to me, making Himself vulnerable, saying the hard thing to me. It is a dialogue of mutual, loving honesty. And this is how it works: My bills are due, and as I talk to God, I grow to *know* and *trust* Him as *Jehovah-Jireh*, my Provider. I need to nurture and guide my children, and as I listen for His instruction, I learn to *know* God as my wise *Jehovah-Raah*, the One who shepherds me. I make mistakes and my life becomes cluttered and messy, but as I speak with the Lord about my muddles, He forgives and corrects me with words of truth and grace, and I come to *know* Him as *Jehovah-Shalom*, the Lord my peace. Every decision, situation, or hardship becomes an opportunity to grow in *knowing* and *trusting* the Lord, because the Almighty God Himself offers intimacy—sanctuary—in His love, as we *in-to-Him-see.*

Over the years I have come to realize that intimacy can only be experienced in the present moment, and unfortunately, many of us have trouble living in the present. We worry about the future; we mull over the past. But God only shows up in the *now,* and if I am willing to live there, He will indeed meet me. To be present in the moment is to arrive just as we are and open ourselves to someone else. With God, whenever we arrive, He is already present and waiting for us. He always arrives before we do and is consistently ready to connect; we don't have to over-come any reluctance on His part, for He created us for this connection.

The intimate life is, therefore, one of ongoing response to God's heart of passion for us—a response to His invitation to commune and partner with Him . . . now. He calls us to an eternal love relationship with Himself, the God of truth and grace, who—no matter what we've done—invites us to come and begin again with Him in the sacred dance. It is not so much about *what we do with God*—having a quiet time, spending time in prayer, serving—because it is not a perfunctory thing. It is more about *who we are with God*—being open, letting Jesus in, allowing ourselves to engage with Him heart to heart, trusting Him in the moment—because it is a relational thing. And even more impor-tant, in the final analysis it is not about what or who we are with God but what and who God is with us. He is the One who both initiates and sustains the invitation in this relationship.

Yes, God wants more from us than what we do for Him. He wants us, our hearts, our all. *We* are what He is after.

God's great invitation is still extended to us today—to come, to learn, to know, to dance. And what a dance it will be! I remember being asked one time to dance at a wedding reception by an attractive man named Joe. My mistake was that I simply said, "Sure," because later I learned that Joe had once been an Arthur Murray dance instructor. As we walked onto the floor, I soon realized that I was in way over my head! Joe was swinging me (alas, it was a "fast" dance), twirling me, and dipping me, and my goal quickly became to just remain vertical! But I eventually noticed that if I kept my eyes on Joe's face and just relaxed in his arms, he was a strong enough leader that I could follow him without

God Is Intent upon Our Hearts

It is wonderful to realize that the Lord longs to be connected with us—heart to heart. Though there is much talk today about our Christian behavior, the Lord is intent upon our *hearts* (a word used more than 850 times in the Bible). We are told to come to God humbly, with vulnerable and repentant hearts, with sincere and undivided hearts. Here are a few of the things God says about our hearts.

The LORD does not look at the things man looks at. Man looks at the outward appearance, but the LORD looks at the heart.   *I Samuel 16:7*

Let your heart therefore be wholly devoted to the LORD our God, to walk in His statutes and to keep His commandments, as at this day.
I Kings 8:61 (NASB)

Guard your heart above all else, for it determines the course of your life.
Proverbs 4:23 (NLT)

Blessed are the pure in heart, for they will see God.   *Matthew 5:8*

The good man out of the good treasure of his heart brings forth what is good; and the evil man out of the evil treasure brings forth what is evil; for his mouth speaks from that which fills his heart.   *Luke 6:45 (NASB)*

The goal of our instruction is love from a pure heart and a good conscience and a sincere faith.   *I Timothy 1:5 (NASB)*

Since you have in obedience to the truth purified your souls for a sincere love of the brethren, fervently love one another from the heart.
I Peter 1:22 (NASB)

Dear children, keep away from anything that might take God's place in your hearts.   *I John 5:21 (NLT)*

falling down or breaking something. I realized I didn't even need to know what was coming next because Joe knew, and he was leading. At one point, I even began to have fun, feeling as if I were Ginger Rogers being elegantly finessed around the dance floor by Fred Astaire himself!

As the dance ended, I saw that everyone had cleared off the floor and all eyes were on us. I hadn't seen this before; I was too busy focusing on Joe and surrendering to his lead. The crowd applauded as we walked to our seats, and as I looked into the eyes of the people who were smiling widely at me, I realized they didn't know the truth. They didn't know that I was a novice who was struggling just to stay upright, and it was Joe who deserved all the credit. Partnering with Joe actually made me look really good!

And so it is with Jesus. When we were first invited to dance, many of us began with a simple response. Since then, we may have wondered if we've gotten in over our heads. But somewhere along the line, we began to notice that things become easier when we fix our eyes on our Partner's face and relax in His arms; He is a strong Leader, and He can keep us upright. In this dance, there are points of exhilaration and joy like we've never known before, and we actually don't really need to know what's ahead. Our Partner knows, and He is leading. All we need to do is stay engaged in the dance and keep our eyes on Him in full surrender.

Of course, there is another way we can respond to His invitation. We can go to the dance floor not fully engaged with Jesus, spend most of our time looking around at what others are doing, learn the "right" steps, try to look cool, and now and then glace at our Partner with a nod. I've been there and done that. A dance like this isn't a tandem act; it's more of a solo performance. And this dance, of course, gets old. We find that we are constantly working to improve our style and do the steps better. But deep inside, we know this isn't the abundant dance Jesus invited us to. He wants us to be fully present to Him as He is fully present to us—leading, guiding, moving us across the floor with exhilaration. His dance is new every morning, and in our Partner's presence there is fullness of joy (see Psalm 16:11).

Perhaps you are reading this today feeling as fully engaged in the dance as you know how to be. For you this book may be a place to find new ways to deepen your connection with your Partner. For others, this book may serve as a reminder that there is Someone on the dance floor who awaits you even now. You will discover that though the spiritual temperaments may cause the dance to look different for each of us, one thing is clear: We all have to choose to respond. When the Lord invites us to "come and talk with [Him]," our hearts will respond with, "Lord, I am coming" (Psalm 27:8, TLB).

Do you sense His summons even now? And if you do, how will you respond to His invitation? Will you step onto the dance floor and see what happens next? It will be exhilarating! For just as one songwriter said:

> *I hope you never fear those mountains in the distance,*
> *Never settle for the path of least resistance. . . .*
> *Give the heavens above more than just a passing glance,*
> *And when you get the choice to sit it out or dance,*
> *I hope you dance*
> *I hope you dance*
> *I hope you dance.*[5]

PART ONE

THE GOD LANGUAGES

1

WHAT IS A
SPIRITUAL TEMPERAMENT?

Beth and I sat together in her living room drinking glasses of iced tea. Young parents of three, Beth and her husband were leading a large inner-city mission team, and Beth had asked if I'd come to help her sort out her spiritual life. Since I'd arrived, she'd told me about her recent move to the neighborhood, her freshly painted bedroom, and a bit about the kids. But I knew that once we settled down to tea, the spiritual concerns that were heaviest on her heart would begin to unfold.

On that hot summer day, Beth apprehensively told me her story. She said she felt dry spiritually, distant from God, that it had been a long time since she'd sensed God's presence or His leading in her life. Then she reluctantly confessed, "I actually haven't had a significant time with the Lord in months. My husband can sit at his desk, read his Bible, and journal for hours, but honestly, the only time I even feel *close* to God is when I'm in my garden."

Her garden. Beth continued to talk, but somehow I wasn't tuned in to what she was saying. My mind was riveted on the word *garden*. Vaguely picturing another garden, I found myself speculating about Eden, the setting where the Creator first interacted with His creation. Not a desk or a book or a journal. A garden.

A tiny bubble of sadness rose from my heart and burst on the surface of my thinking as I wondered what had happened. When did the very place the Lord first chose (and the Son selected in His most desperate hour) become so unacceptable? What had happened to narrow us so?

I stopped Beth midsentence and asked if we could go back and talk more about her time in the garden with God. Then we pondered together the Garden of Eden, deciding that since the Lord Himself initially chose it, perhaps the garden was indeed a sensible place to meet with Him. In fact, it may even be the optimal place for intimacy to occur, amid the earth, the plants, and the beauty of growing life. As we thought about the mystery of what is natural and organic, we both affirmed God's original choice.

Then with a bit of uncertain delight, I added my support of Beth's meeting place, sanctioning it as her very own "sacred space." With affirmation from me, Beth's eyes softened and the embarrassment faded from her face. A daughter of Eve had been given permission to meet with her Maker—genuinely, honestly, truly—in the place she felt most comfortable being herself.

That day as I got into my car, I wondered if I was feeling the same thing Peter felt long ago when he heard the Lord say, "Do not call something unclean if God has made it clean" (Acts 10:15, NLT). Something significant happened in my heart as I encouraged my friend to relate with God more authentically—in the breadth and depth of His creation. I saw in a more fundamental way my own need to help the Lord's people fully appreciate their own uniqueness, especially since diversity is one of God's core values. (After all, creating millions of distinct galaxies was His idea!) I longed for those who love the Lord to experience Him in His expansiveness, knowing firsthand that there is ample room for all to love Him—Father, Son, and Spirit—in a variety of ways.

MY ROLE AS A SPIRITUAL DIRECTOR

That summer day with Beth was just one of many days I've spent listening to the stories of people who love Jesus. There is Jillian, a particularly sensitive young woman whose style of loving Jesus is best expressed in caring for troubled youth. And Della, who is moved heavenward most powerfully when reading a theology book written a lifetime ago. And Tim, who connects best with God while sitting on his noiseless balcony at one o'clock in the morning.

Dealing with spiritual differences has become an important

ON YOUR OWN

*Consider the following questions about spiritual diversity,
and write your thoughts in your journal or notebook.*

Do you really believe spiritual differences are okay?

*People connect with Jesus differently, and God actually designed it that
way.* Do you agree or disagree with this statement? Why?

John Wesley, a renowned leader in England's evangelical revival
in the eighteenth century, believed that Scripture, tradition,
reason, and experience were complementary sources of religious
authority. Each was meant to confirm, illuminate, and make vital
the truths of the Christian life. Using each of these sources to
support your answer, how do you respond to this restatement of
the above assertion: *Considering Genesis 1 and God's universe (with its
vast variety, breadth, and depth), people connect with Jesus differently—
and God actually designed it that way.*

element of what I do. In fact, everywhere I go people ask how they
might find more meaning in their relationship with Jesus, feeling their
churches are not teaching them enough of what they need for their
personal lives and struggles. Leaders often come for help, because
in spite of their real need for spiritual connection, they simply aren't
connecting! We talk about their spiritual dissatisfaction—how they
hunger to know the Lord in His fullness, yet they just don't know how
to make that happen for themselves. They know how to serve God, and
they feel pretty good about that. But they realize there is more depth to
this journey, and many just can't find their way.

Interestingly, some of these people have already turned to
sources outside the evangelical church to find answers. The growing
popularity of Henri Nouwen and Thomas Merton demonstrates the

hunger for more than what is now being offered in many evangelical circles.[1] As Sam Metcalf, president of Church Resource Ministries, observes:

> One of the interesting phenomena that we see among the emerging generation of leaders in our post-modern world is a renewed interest in the liturgical. What I have noticed is a fascination, search, and even longing for a sense of historicity, rootedness, and tradition. There is too often a shallowness and even triteness that characterizes Western evangelicalism. Awe, grandeur, and a sense of transcendence gets lost sometimes in our groping for relevance.[2]

It seems that even among those who have walked with God for a long time, it is still uncertain territory knowing how to move into deeper communion with Him. We are hungry—not for more to do, but for more of God Himself. The generic "one size fits all" formula for spiritual growth simply isn't cutting it. Serving as a pastoral counselor and spiritual director, I've observed that there is a real need for permission among those who are serious about Jesus to meet Him in ways that don't exactly correspond with how others are meeting Him in their homes or communities of faith. In fact, this theme continually emerges in my conversations: "I want to connect with God more deeply, but I don't know how. And the way someone else does it isn't working for me. Can you help?"

Thankfully, there is help for these people. Our God—who is so vast and broad and wide—*does* want to meet us, and He seems intent upon doing that in a variety of ways. We don't have to worry when the book our friend finds helpful doesn't help us. Nor do we have to wonder why we feel most alive having a hearty discussion about theology in our Sunday school class while others prefer sitting in the congregation singing hymns. Because God created us differently, judgmental thoughts and misunderstandings don't have to accompany disparities between Christians. Yes, part of these differences in our spiritual wiring can be attributed to spiritual gifting, but when it comes to enjoying God, some things cannot be explained simply by the spiritual gift categories.

THE "ONE GOD, MANY RELATIONSHIPS" PHENOMENON

While "wiring" may be a catchword born of modern thinking, the idea of nuanced differences in knowing the one true God has been evident throughout Christendom. What moves one person toward loving and serving God is often very different from another's approach, and some have described these differences as the "one God, many relationships" phenomenon,[3] recognizing that what inspires, fills, and provokes us spiritually is often not the same. Bill Hybels discusses this in his book *Courageous Leadership*:

> Years ago I began to notice that various leaders whom I respected went about their walks with God in vastly different ways. The variety was stunning to me. I started keeping a mental list of all their different approaches. Then I came across a book called *Sacred Pathways*, written by Gary Thomas, which further pushed my thinking on this subject. . . . Sacred pathways are like doors that open into a room where we can feel particularly close to God. Just as different leaders have many different personalities and combinations of gifts, so they have many different spiritual pathways.[4]

I, too, have become aware of these differing spiritual pathways in my work. But spiritual variations took on new texture and meaning during my doctoral work in spiritual formation. As I began surveying ministry leaders for my doctoral project, discussing with them their spiritual preferences—their most fundamental, natural, and intrinsic ways of knowing and loving God—I began to see that greater spiritual passion resulted when people were pursuing God in ways they enjoyed and found most life giving. Often these spiritual preferences were not given expression; instead, people seemed to be doing what they were taught to do, almost afraid of what they enjoyed. When this occurred, I noticed that spiritual satisfaction declined, as did a person's sense of closeness to God. Even spiritual hunger waned when a person was not relating to God as he or she was wired to do. The relationship I saw between spiritual preferences and spiritual practices intrigued me as well, especially when I noticed that by matching preferences with practices, a person's passion for God might actually increase.

I also found that many times people need to be *invited* to do what they enjoy most in their relationship with God. Without that permission—that freedom—Christians can become stuck in old patterns, even though these patterns are not working for them. Thus, I saw the importance of activating that which flows most naturally from our hearts to God's, namely, knowing our spiritual temperaments and how we are uniquely wired.

THE SPIRITUAL TEMPERAMENTS

When we talk about the spiritual journey, we don't often hear about "spiritual temperaments." We may hear folks discussing their spiritual gifts or how their personalities affect their prayer lives,[5] but we find little language to explain the most central issue of our lives—how we most deeply love and connect with Jesus. While one person may recognize that his heart for God grows stronger when he is taking a stand against evil, and another might sense that her passion for God rises most while she is sitting in a cathedral before a life-size statue of her Savior, we may not realize that these differences are not arbitrary or random; they are the result of our spiritual temperaments.

When we use the language of spiritual temperaments to describe our spiritual preferences, we are talking about how our inclinations and distinctions fall into identifiable categories, groupings that help us understand others and ourselves more readily. Gary Thomas, the originator of the spiritual temperaments concept, has described these innate spiritual pathways in his book *Sacred Pathways: Discovering Your Soul's Path to God.*[6] He discusses nine ways to draw near to God:

- The Activist—loving God through confrontation with evil
- The Ascetic—loving God through solitude and simplicity
- The Caregiver—loving God through serving others
- The Contemplative—loving God through adoration
- The Enthusiast—loving God through mystery and celebration
- The Intellectual—loving God through the mind
- The Naturalist—loving God through experiencing Him outdoors
- The Sensate—loving God through the senses
- The Traditionalist—loving God through ritual and symbol

I used these descriptions in my own doctoral work and found them to be helpful and enlightening. The Naturalist, for example, senses God's nearness when he or she is outside, while Ascetics find their love for God most stimulated in a simple environment of silence and solitude. Of course, the ways people relate to God may surpass these nine, but the categories provide a good starting place for assessing our spiritual wiring. Each of these spiritual temperaments will be described in detail later, in chapter 3.

ON YOUR OWN

Consider the following questions about your own knowledge of spiritual temperaments:

List all the things that you currently know about spiritual temperaments. Where did you learn these things, and how has this knowledge affected your own connection to God?

What would you like to learn about spiritual temperaments? How do you think gaining this new knowledge will affect your connection to God?

Answering Some Basic Questions

Since the concept of spiritual temperaments has not been widely discussed, let's look at a few common questions.

What exactly is a spiritual temperament?

A spiritual temperament is the way we best relate to God, namely, our most natural and meaningful approach to connecting with God, knowing God, and loving God. A spiritual temperament serves as an entry point into greater awareness of Jesus—His presence and His love. It is that place where we almost effortlessly find what some have referred to as our "sacred space." Our spiritual temperaments influence where and how we are quieted inside, and where and how we most often sense God speaking to us, refreshing us, and stirring our passion for Him. We might say it is where we most often hear "the gentle invitation of Jesus to dwell with Him."[7] Our spiritual temperament serves as our "default mode" spiritually, the style we fall back on when we want to be with God and are not intentionally pursuing Him another way.

Just as one person may prefer football to golf, or skiing to mountain biking, so a spiritual temperament is a preference in the spiritual realm. While a personality temperament identifies our preferences when interacting with people and the world around us on a horizontal plane, a spiritual temperament identifies how we interact with God and the spiritual realities on the vertical level. Unlike other mere preferences, however, when we neglect our spiritual temperaments, we often feel dry and lifeless spiritually.

It's important to note that spiritual temperaments are not intended to be neat little boxes that conveniently explain everything about us. Instead, they are ways to help us understand how and why we do things a certain way. They are simply pieces of the puzzle of our complex makeup and are not meant to function as permanent labels that completely define us.

ON YOUR OWN
Consider the following:

How do you respond to this question raised by Henri Nouwen: "Where is it that you most often hear the gentle invitation of Jesus to dwell with Him?"

Do we choose our spiritual temperaments?
Just as our personalities seem to come as part of the birth package, so our spiritual temperaments seem to be God-given, not something we select. Indeed, we see differing spiritual temperaments within the same family, and spiritual preferences can be observed in a child even at an early age. As soon as spiritual likes and dislikes appear, a spiritual tempera-

ment may be revealing itself. But throughout life, we all have choices, and these choices play into the equation of who we become, even in the spiritual realm. For example, though I may enjoy praying in solitude, it is my choice whether to join a monastery or simply become a member of a prayer group in my local church. Although initially my preferences may have been innate, my choices—along with the choices of others who influence me—will certainly play a role in the person I become.

Why does God give us spiritual temperaments?

I like to think of a spiritual temperament as a genre, a way that God is using to tell His story to us. As Ken Gire explains in his book *Windows of the Soul*, in the beginning of time there was God and humankind. Then came a great temptation, a great Fall, and a great hiding.[8] Perhaps God knew that we would continue to hide unless He found a way to communicate with us, to break into our distracted lives and penetrate our hearts with the reality that we are loved by Someone outside ourselves, Someone who is constantly watching and waiting for us to step into life with Him. So He crafted a way to remind us that He is always there, desiring to connect, and then He hardwired that reminder into our souls.

Do you ever find that no matter what your relationship with God is like at the moment, the sight of a mountain range or the vastness of the ocean can literally stop you in your tracks and take your mind to the One who created this beauty? Or maybe the face of a child becomes a reminder of God's love, or some majestic piece of music calms your soul, directing your thoughts heavenward. We need these cues—prompts that stir our hunger for the divine, unseen realities—to point us to the Lord.

So God uses our spiritual temperaments to draw us to Himself?

Yes. In the beginning, humankind was created with a deep hunger for God and a propensity to worship Him. But in our fallenness, our hunger became obscured, our propensity to worship clouded. While the world continues to distract us from our God-hunger—especially as we worship at the throne of the created rather than the Creator—God offers a higher invitation. In the midst of our busy, cluttered lives, His clarion call can still be heard: "I am here. Come to Me. Draw close to

Me and let Me love you." Through our spiritual temperaments, God keeps reaching out to us, even when our hearts have become dull and we have gotten lost in our overcommittment. He is unmistakable in these moments as we find ourselves involuntarily ushered into His presence. Something in us is quieted and hushed, and suddenly we are aware that He is there.

Do those who don't know Jesus have spiritual temperaments?

I'm not sure I can fully answer that question. But I do know that long before I came to Jesus, I was drawn to a God of beauty whose name I didn't know. When I walked along the beach, I knew that there must be a Creator behind all the beauty and vastness of the creation, and this Creator was surely more powerful than I. Intuitively I recognized that this God must desire some sort of response from me. Perhaps God was, even then, using my spiritual temperament to invite me to see the Unseen. Perhaps it is through our spiritual temperaments that we find ourselves involuntarily responding to the Transcendent, and in turn, getting a glimpse of the Savior who waits for us all our lives.

Why do so many differing spiritual temperaments exist?

The Lord of creation—whose universe displays an endless breadth of diversity—gave His children many ways of enjoying Him and expressing love for Him. In creation, we see that God did not create just one type of anything, whether it was a flower or a fingerprint or an animal or a solar system. Why, then, should we expect there to be only one way for God's people to love and worship Him?

Likewise, those who physically walked with Jesus didn't all love Him identically. While John the Beloved enjoyed spending time in reflection with Jesus (see John 13:23), Peter was a man of action who, at times, was bold to confront the evil threatening his Lord (see John 18:10). Andrew seemed to be the practical type who wanted to serve Jesus by helping feed the hungry (see John 6:8-9), while James was indignant about those who did not receive his Master, offering to call down fire from heaven (see Luke 9:54). When it comes to loving God, there are certainly a lot of ways to express that affection.

In addition, God is so vast, so deep, and so broad that it takes many expressions of love to affirm the multiple facets of His Person; just *one* picture is not enough! In fact, when it comes to worshipping God, even multiple venues fall short of His magnificence and beauty—whether dancing before Him, serving the poor, or experiencing Him in nature. Indeed, our spiritual hunger is greater than just one expression can accommodate.

And God Himself doesn't come in the same way to all those who seek Him. He humbles Himself and meets us where we are, calling astronomers from the East through a star and a Scripture (see Matthew 2), while sending a whole host of angels to sing His Son's birth announcement to some shepherds (see Luke 2). God is never contained in our little boxes.

Each spiritual temperament displays a distinct aspect of God's character—His justice, His care, His beauty, and His changelessness. Together we are like a diamond, each showing the world a distinct facet of who God is through our unique expressions of love for Him. It's almost as if God has many "love languages."[9] His heart is moved when each of us speaks to Him in the language of the heart, whether that be quiet meditation or robust song or speaking out against tyranny to defend the poor. Each language thrills God's heart a bit differently.

Do most people have only one spiritual temperament?

None of us function with only one spiritual temperament, but we all have a primary way that we find most meaningful when relating to God—one or two ways that help us encounter Him *best.* I use three terms to divide the temperaments into subsets, depending upon the strength of each spiritual temperament: Our *passionate* temperaments are those that are strongest and stir our passion for God most readily; our *pleasurable* temperaments are those that we enjoy and that nurture our relationship with God; and our *potential* temperaments are those that are relatively unused and undeveloped, almost foreign to us. The ways the spiritual temperaments interact with one another also create configurations that help define who we are.

Can my spiritual temperaments change over time?

Just as people's tastes in food change with time as they grow and age, so differing experiences can modify our spiritual temperaments. Although a

13

person will most likely retain the same core temperament, the strength of his or her preferences can certainly shift, especially as new spiritual experiences are added and new practices utilized. Thankfully, we are never limited by our preferences when it comes to knowing and loving God!

Though I have maintained the same two passionate spiritual temperaments throughout the time I have known the Lord, my other spiritual preferences—those falling within the pleasurable and potential ranges—seem to be more seasonal in their strength. For example, when I was a new Christian, my activism was higher. When I went through a time of near burnout in ministry, my Naturalist temperament became more prominent because I needed to get away from the people part of ministry and just be nurtured by God in the outdoors. I have found that my secondary preferences seem to evolve somewhat during different stages of life, while my primary spiritual temperaments remain the same.

Interestingly, some people conclude that as we age, we tend to find our "true home" with God in terms of how we most prefer to know and love Him. It is conceivable that when we were younger, we were more influenced by our families' preferences or the style of loving God prescribed by our communities of faith. But over time, we become restless and less willing to bother with anything that does not really bring deep, authentic connection with Jesus. I have seen this same phenomenon among young people, too. Unwilling to simply go through the motions, they want to relate to God in ways that truly fit them and bring a genuine spiritual bond, in spite of what they have been taught or shown by others.

Will knowing my spiritual temperament help me in my intimacy with Christ?

Knowing ourselves—including the preferences and inclinations we have in seeking God—is an important way we honor the Lord, who made us. Coming to God authentically, "as we are," is essential. James Houston, renowned author, professor, and spiritual director, says that when we come to God, we must always begin where He is creating desire for Himself within us. I have a friend who likes to sit by the fireplace and pray, especially when her baby is asleep and her husband is out of the house. She senses God's presence in these moments, and her desire to be with the Lord is often strongest then.

Houston goes on to say that we can't simply meet God as others meet Him, because God will only meet us in the "authentic place"[10]—that place within ourselves that is unprocessed, candid, and sincere. In other words, God will meet us when we come to Him authentically, with honest and open hearts. And we can be certain that He will meet us when we come to Him in an unsimulated, genuine way.

ON YOUR OWN

Consider the following questions:

Describe a time when you felt especially close to God. What were the circumstances surrounding that connection?

In what kind of setting do you most enjoy communing with God?

I like to think of the "authentic place" as that home in my soul where I can truly be myself with God—with nothing feigned—and let what is in my heart flow to Him naturally. Because God loves me unconditionally, I can afford to be honest with Him about my true identity. I can share my feelings and thoughts openly, and my spiritual temperament permits me to love God from that authentic place where I take delight in being with Him.

But what if I haven't known my spiritual temperament all these years? Many people have worshipped and loved God in ways that best suit them for as long as they have known Jesus, yet they've done this almost intuitively. Others have stayed closer to the tradition in which they were raised, trying to live out their spiritual lives "by the book." But as we continue in our spiritual journeys, we sometimes find ourselves in a place where things sort of stop working for us spiritually. It is then that greater self-awareness becomes vital.

A problem results, however, when self-awareness is not permitted and one's spiritual temperament is not affirmed as a gift from God— first by the individual and then by the body of Christ. As John Colborne says:

> If being spiritual is limited to the practice of the spiritual disciplines in ways narrowly defined by specific practices carried out in specific ways, we will continue to frustrate people who are doomed to seek spirituality in ways completely unnatural to them. Such an approach fails to recognize that God has made us all in his image, as spiritual beings with the capacity to grow and express our spirituality in many different ways.[11]

In other words, while spiritual disciplines are important, listening to your inclinations and desires is also essential in guiding you deeper into knowing and loving God.

Is the ultimate goal to know and understand my spiritual temperament? While understanding one's spiritual temperament is crucial, it is not the ultimate objective. This is not about narcissism, self-actualization, or the kind of spiritual self-absorption that occurs when we make ourselves the center of the equation. Rather, it is about knowing ourselves so that we can not only feed our own souls but also "know God in a new way, love him with every cell of our being, and then express that love by reaching out to others."[12] The spiritual life is not simply about what goes on inside of us; it is about loving God and those around us. As Jesus said, "You shall love the Lord your God with all your heart, and with all your soul, and with all your strength, and with all your mind; and your neighbor as yourself" (Luke 10:27, NASB).

The ultimate goal, then, is to know the Father as the Son knows Him, to trust the Father as the Son trusts Him, to love the Father as the Son loves Him, and to allow His Spirit to fill our lives so that we grow into the "measure of the stature which belongs to the fullness of Christ" (Ephesians 4:13, NASB). That is how God ultimately designed us to function in this life.

When He is our portion and we are delighting in Him, we will not be so tempted to partake of the "junk food" around us, because finding fulfillment in God is the most powerful antidote to sin.[13] Thus, the outcome of knowing our spiritual temperaments is a life of ongoing communion with God, which draws us "toward the love of God, the character of Christ, and daily obedience to His leading as God draws us into greater, loving intimacy with the Trinity. . . . It impacts character development, but it is more than any character trait or skill; it encompasses the believer's whole-life response to the Triune God."[14]

IN SUMMARY

Putting it all together, a spiritual temperament is God's *gift to you*. It is how He designed you to best connect with Him. Perhaps God gives spiritual temperaments as directly as He gives spiritual gifts, or perhaps they come, in part, via the experiences that shape our lives. However our spiritual temperaments are formed—whether by nature or nurture or a combination of both—they become God's gift to us.

Secondly, a spiritual temperament is your *gift to God*—it is how you best express love to Him and where your passion for Him is stirred. God derives pleasure as we love Him and receive His love, and the way He made us is the way He knows we will most readily find our joy and delight in Him.

Thirdly, a spiritual temperament is your *gift to the body of Christ*. Who you are and how you best know and love God are the gifts you bring to others who are different from you. We model these gifts for those around us as we live out our faith. The body needs what you bring, just as you need what it brings. When the Bible commands us to "stimulate one another to love and good deeds" (Hebrews 10:24, NASB), this includes letting others see the way we love and serve Christ. The faith of others grows as they see us expressing our love for God.

Lastly, a spiritual temperament is your *gift to a lost world*. As others see the joy and satisfaction you derive from knowing and loving God, they will witness the reality of a God who is worth knowing, loving, celebrating, and serving. That will make others hungry for Jesus. As you identify your spiritual temperament and claim it as God's gift, others are also blessed.

Now let's take a look at how God has uniquely wired *you!*

For Further Reflection and Discussion

1. As you reread the excerpt below, paraphrased from James Houston's words, what do you think is meant by the "authentic place"?

   When we come to God, we must always begin where He is creating desire for Himself within us. We can't meet God as we would meet someone else, because God only and always meets us in the "authentic place."

2. Describe *your* authentic place with God.

3. Pay special attention this week to your "authentic place," and ask yourself the question, "Where do I sense desire for God occurring?" Try to notice when, where, and what is happening when desire for God is present. Then sit with that desire a few minutes; pay attention to it and let it settle in you. Later record your experience.

2

HOW AM I
SPIRITUALLY UNIQUE?

As we mature in our faith, we find that intimacy with God becomes intricately linked with our self-knowledge. Just as Socrates said, "Know thyself," so our early church father Saint Augustine said, "Let me know myself, let me know Thee!" Thus, knowing our spiritual temperaments becomes a valuable piece of the self-knowledge that can enhance our relationship with God.

Recently my church offered a class on how to develop an ever-deepening walk with Jesus. Several of my pastors shared how that depth was happening for them, and interestingly, each one said something quite different. One introduced us to a slew of his commentaries, while another described how several of the spiritual disciplines worked for him. My favorite story came from Pastor Travis, a godly man, who openly admitted that he finds a formulaic quiet time too confining and has never been able to sit still for an hour to pray or read his Bible. Instead, he talks with God best while he walks, and he is more attentive to Scripture while listening to the Bible on tape as he drives. Yet he is a man who knows the Lord in profound ways—perhaps partly because he knows himself. He has learned to avoid the guilt and frustration that come from trying to mimic another's way of knowing and loving God. And thankfully, he is able to be honest with himself about this and discover what works best for him.

Of course, the Word of God is absolutely essential for all the spiritual temperaments, yet the *way* we approach the Word may be different. So, too, there is a valuable place for the spiritual disciplines in every life with God, though when we see the disciplines as tools that foster greater spiritual desire, we begin to realize even the disciplines need to be applied in a variety of ways (which we will discuss more in chapter 4). But for now, it is good to remember that a "one size fits all" formula is not the best way to partner with the Holy Sprit in this life with Him. For just as we would not prescribe one medication for every illness or one exercise plan for all body types, so we must begin to acknowledge the differences in people and how they connect with Jesus or express their love for Him. And why should we all be expected to love God the same way, anyway? "We would think it absurd to insist that newly evangelized Christians in Moravia create an identical worship service to Presbyterians in Boston or Baptists in Georgia. Yet we prescribe the same type of spirituality for both the farmer in Iowa and the lawyer in Washington, D.C."[1]

Thus, if we want to help others mature in their faith, as well as grow ourselves, it is important to understand and teach the spiritual temperaments—in our churches and home groups and all the places where Christians congregate. Jesus is our model for this as we learn to trust the Father in ways that are both familiar and unfamiliar—allowing our souls to be transformed by Him. As Adele Ahlberg Calhoun says, "Transformation happens as you keep company with Jesus. . . . And wanting to keep company with Jesus has a staying power that 'shoulds' and 'oughts' seldom have."[2]

SPIRITUAL PASSION, PLEASURE, AND POTENTIAL

So how do *you* best express your love for God? What fuels your desire to know the Lord more deeply? When is it that you feel closest to Jesus? As we have already discussed, our spiritual temperaments influence the way each of us responds to these questions, revealing our most natural entry points into a more genuine connection with God.

Before we get into the descriptions of the nine spiritual temperaments in chapter 3, let's begin by using the following spiritual inventory to find out more about our own individual preferences and practices. Then, as you read about the nine temperaments, you will see more clearly how God has uniquely wired you.

The Spiritual Temperament Inventory is intended to help you discover your unique spiritual temperament or spiritual preferences.

Remember, the word *inventory* means "to take stock," so as you answer the questions, allow them to help you take stock of your spiritual life and see where you may want to go from here. After you read the descriptions of the nine spiritual temperaments in chapter 3, you may want to retake the inventory using a pencil or a different color pen to update your answers.

The Spiritual Temperament Inventory*

As you read the following statements, please circle the number that *most closely* reflects how you feel and think. There are no right or wrong answers, so please be as honest as possible. Usually the first answer that comes to mind is the most accurate response. If one part of a question is strongly true for you but another part is not, mark one of the answers in the middle.

> 4 = *Very true*
> 3 = *Often true*
> 2 = *Sometimes true*
> 1 = *Rarely true*
> 0 = *Never true*

1. Taking a stand for what is right in this world and opposing what is wrong causes me to draw closer to God; therefore, I think it's important to stay current on issues and urge others to do so also.	4 3 2 1 0
2. I would enjoy having several hours to spend alone in silent prayer.	4 3 2 1 0
3. I sense God's pleasure when I am caring for others, e.g., helping a friend who's in need, giving a ride to someone without a car, or working in the soup kitchen in my community of faith.	4 3 2 1 0
4. I would enjoy reading about or talking with someone who knows God deeply so that I could learn how to have a more intimate friendship with Jesus.	4 3 2 1 0

*Gary Thomas's book *Sacred Pathways* and Fraser Venter's insights into activism inspired some of these questions.

5. I would like to go to a workshop that teaches how to worship God through dance or how to praise Him at home through music.	4 3 2 I 0
6. I think it is imperative for Christians to study the essential doctrines of the faith, while letting their feelings and experiences with God be a peripheral matter.	4 3 2 I 0
7. I usually feel closer to God when I am out in nature than when I spend time indoors in church.	4 3 2 I 0
8. I find pleasure in worshipping God as I gaze at a beautifully translucent stained-glass window in a church where some aspect of my Lord is depicted.	4 3 2 I 0
9. I would enjoy following a Christian calendar with my family during our prayer times, or even using the *Book of Common Prayer*.	4 3 2 I 0
10. The suffering and evil in this world really bother me, and I feel strongly that the apathy of the masses must be challenged.	4 3 2 I 0
11. Praying alone or worshipping God in silence is usually more meaningful to me than seeking Him in a group setting.	4 3 2 I 0
12. Being a caring servant of God who puts faith into action is very important to me.	4 3 2 I 0
13. I feel close to God when He speaks words of love to me as if He were my dearest friend.	4 3 2 I 0
14. God is an awesome God, and during worship at church, we need to express our enthusiasm in song, as opposed to sitting uninvolved as if we were bored, reading the church bulletin, or just passively watching others as they sing.	4 3 2 I 0

15. I buy a lot of Christian books because I appreciate thought-provoking reading that challenges me to think more deeply and broadly about aspects of my faith.	4	3	2	1	0
16. I derive great joy from praying or communing with God as I sit beside a brook, walk outdoors, or see His handiwork in nature.	4	3	2	1	0
17. When I enter a stunningly beautiful church, just the loveliness around me lifts my heart to God, increasing my passion for Him.	4	3	2	1	0
18. The Christian faith—rooted in centuries of godly tradition—must continually find its expression in the corporate life, which always takes precedence over individualized worship.	4	3	2	1	0
19. When I see or read about someone who is confronting evil or taking positive action to change the unjust conditions in the world, my love for God is stirred.	4	3	2	1	0
20. When I am alone with God, I feel closer to Him, since I can most readily focus on His presence in quiet settings.	4	3	2	1	0
21. I am not pleased when I see Christians who love God yet walk right past a sick neighbor or a family in need without helping them.	4	3	2	1	0
22. I would enjoy having uninterrupted time each day to sit alone with Jesus, gazing into His face, listening to His voice, or simply basking in the warmth of His love.	4	3	2	1	0
23. I would like to learn more about how God uses dreams to lead His people.	4	3	2	1	0
24. Knowing the truth and having a mind ordered by "right thinking" is very important to me.	4	3	2	1	0

25. I would be thrilled if our church held a service on the beach or in a wooded glen—somewhere outside in God's creation.	4	3	2	I	0
26. A High Church service with formal Communion or the Eucharist is something I would enjoy.	4	3	2	I	0
27. I value greatly the idea of having a prayer ritual (or rule), especially as it connects me with other believers who are observing the same practice.	4	3	2	I	0
28. It is essential that injustice and the status quo be confronted, and it's the Lord who compels me to take action when it comes to poverty, prostitution, slavery, the conditions in our local schools, or the neglect/oppression of the aged.	4	3	2	I	0
29. I would enjoy reading about the monastic life and learning how God calls some of His people to live a very simple life for His glory.	4	3	2	I	0
30. When I am helping those in need, I experience God's love, whether they are weak, poor, sick, or imprisoned.	4	3	2	I	0
31. In my heart, I desire for God to be my closest friend and most intimate companion.	4	3	2	I	0
32. I like listening to worship music at home or in my car, because almost nothing brings life to me like praising God.	4	3	2	I	0
33. My love for God grows when I take an extended period of time to study His Word using rich sourcebooks, such as well-documented commentaries.	4	3	2	I	0
34. If I could go to a garden or a lake to be with God, I would be very happy.	4	3	2	I	0

35. How I wish I could have experienced the wonderfully sensuous Old Testament style of worship, with its poignant smells and colorful regalia.	4 3 2 1 0
36. A seminar describing the meaning of symbols and liturgy in the church is something I would enjoy attending.	4 3 2 1 0
37. I can't identify with Christians who lack compassion or fail to take action when they see wrong occurring in their immediate contexts.	4 3 2 1 0
38. The thought of spending a few days at a monastery to pray and meditate upon the Lord in solitude sounds delightful.	4 3 2 1 0
39. I feel like I am showing my love for God when I am helping "the least of these" by meeting practical needs, e.g., fixing a meal or helping with a household repair.	4 3 2 1 0
40. When I am with God, I tend to picture Him as my Shepherd, Abba, or Friend.	4 3 2 1 0
41. When I worship God in the congregation, my heart is so filled to overflowing with love for Him that I just want to stand up, clap, or raise my hands.	4 3 2 1 0
42. Hearing a renowned speaker present solid research about historical, biblical truth would really interest me, and it would be delightful to discuss this content with a group of informed thinkers.	4 3 2 1 0
43. When I am in the beauty of God's creation, I find myself spiritually refreshed because being with the Lord in the outdoors is so inspiring.	4 3 2 1 0
44. I love being in a church where all my senses come alive so that I can almost see, smell, hear, taste, and touch the majesty of God.	4 3 2 1 0

45. One of the best parts of my relationship with the Lord is worshipping Him in familiar ways, using the meaningful traditions I remember from childhood.	4 3 2 1 0
46. A presentation by Gary Haugen on "God's Heart of Justice: Why Do Bad Things Happen and Good People Just Watch?" is something I would like to attend.	4 3 2 1 0
47. Living an ordered life that utilizes the spiritual disciplines is very important to me.	4 3 2 1 0
48. I would like to improve my skills in lay counseling to be better equipped to help those in need.	4 3 2 1 0
49. When spending time with God, I enjoy contemplating His love and affection.	4 3 2 1 0
50. Praising God is meant to be a joyous and jubilant experience!	4 3 2 1 0
51. Many of my closest moments with God are when I'm learning something new or my mind is stimulated about some important aspect of His Kingdom.	4 3 2 1 0
52. I would be delighted to see a picturesque movie in church entitled *Worshipping God through Creation*.	4 3 2 1 0
53. I like the thought of using art or drawing in my worship of God or when I journal or pray.	4 3 2 1 0
54. The history of the faith and its age-old rituals move me greatly.	4 3 2 1 0

Your Spiritual Temperament Scores

Now that you've taken the Spiritual Temperament Inventory, tally the numbers you recorded for each of the following answers to find your *spiritual temperament*:

							Total	H M L
Activist	1 ___	10 ___	19 ___	28 ___	37 ___	46 ___	_____	_____
Ascetic	2 ___	11 ___	20 ___	29 ___	38 ___	47 ___	_____	_____
Caregiver	3 ___	12 ___	21 ___	30 ___	39 ___	48 ___	_____	_____
Contemplative	4 ___	13 ___	22 ___	31 ___	40 ___	49 ___	_____	_____
Enthusiast	5 ___	14 ___	23 ___	32 ___	41 ___	50 ___	_____	_____
Intellectual	6 ___	15 ___	24 ___	33 ___	42 ___	51 ___	_____	_____
Naturalist	7 ___	16 ___	25 ___	34 ___	43 ___	52 ___	_____	_____
Sensate	8 ___	17 ___	26 ___	35 ___	44 ___	53 ___	_____	_____
Traditionalist	9 ___	18 ___	27 ___	36 ___	45 ___	54 ___	_____	_____

Write today's date here to remind you of when you first took the Spiritual Temperament Inventory: _____

Now look at your scores. Write an **H** (for **high**) by those scores that fall between 18 and 24. These are your strongest or most *passionate* spiritual temperaments. How many *passionate* spiritual temperaments do you have? _____

Write an **M** (for **moderate**) by those scores that fall between 12 and 17. These are your moderate or *pleasurable* spiritual temperaments. How many *pleasurable* spiritual temperaments do you have? _____

Write an **L** (for **low**) by those scores that fall between 0 and 11. These are your least developed or *potential* spiritual temperaments. How many *potential* spiritual temperaments do you have? _____

DISCOVERING MORE

Once you've taken the Spiritual Temperament Inventory, you'll need to take the Spiritual Practices Inventory, which will help you determine your current spiritual habits or usual spiritual practices.

The Spiritual Practices Inventory

After totaling your spiritual temperament scores, identify your current spiritual practices to see how they match your spiritual preferences. As you read the following statements, please circle the number that most closely describes your *current practice*. There are no right or wrong answers, so be as honest as possible. Usually, the first answer you give is the most accurate response. If one part of the question is strongly true for you and another part is not, mark one of the answers in the middle.

4 = I do this **two or more times a week.**
3 = I do this **one or more times a month.**
2 = I do this **several times a year.**
I = I do this **once or twice a year.**
0 = I **never** do this.

I. I have a regular pattern or ritual of prayer.	4 3 2 I 0
2. When I pray, I focus my heart by lighting a candle, holding a cross, looking at a picture of Jesus, or in some way utilizing my senses in worship.	4 3 2 I 0
3. I walk or sit outside when I pray, appreciating the presence of God in the beauty of His creation.	4 3 2 I 0
4. I study the Bible with tools: a concordance, a Bible dictionary, a commentary, etc.	4 3 2 I 0
5. I listen to music that emphasizes praising and worshipping God while I am at home or driving in my car.	4 3 2 I 0

6. When I read my Bible, I dialogue with Jesus or think deeply about what He is saying to me through the passage for at least ten to fifteen minutes at a time.	4 3 2 1 0
7. I help people in need in practical ways: by visiting shut-ins, assisting those in crisis, or lending a hand to someone who needs help.	4 3 2 1 0
8. I spend time alone with God in solitude for a day or more at a time.	4 3 2 1 0
9. I get out and talk to people, carry signs, write articles or letters, or do whatever is necessary to help others engage with the culture and right the wrongs in the world.	4 3 2 1 0
10. I worship within the community of faith, knowing that—throughout history—the Lord has been most accurately represented there.	4 3 2 1 0
11. I attend a church service where incense and beautiful icons are a part of worship.	4 3 2 1 0
12. I spend time with God in His creation (for example, by watching birds or other animals, listening to the sound of the wind or rain, or sitting outside or beside a stream in the mountains).	4 3 2 1 0
13. I read theology books and other works that challenge my spiritual thinking and provide stimulating mental and spiritual food for thought.	4 3 2 1 0
14. I dance before the Lord, sensing His pleasure as I enter into worship—body, soul, and spirit.	4 3 2 1 0
15. I sense God telling me He loves me and conveying His affection in little ways.	4 3 2 1 0

16. I make time to help those in my community, church, or family who need an extra pair of hands or a listening ear.	4 3 2 1 0
17. I spend an hour or more at a time in prayer, partly sitting in silence with the Lord.	4 3 2 1 0
18. Because it's important for me to see individual lives and/or society change, I sign or circulate petitions, attend meetings, or get involved on the Internet regarding issues about which I feel strongly.	4 3 2 1 0
19. I participate in the liturgy and take the sacraments at church because the familiar traditions of the faith are an important part of my life with God.	4 3 2 1 0
20. I look at beautiful architecture, stained-glass windows, lovely paintings, or marble statues in a church because I sense God's majesty there.	4 3 2 1 0
21. I get out into nature by going to the ocean or mountains, sitting in the sun, or taking a walk to meet with God.	4 3 2 1 0
22. I get involved in intellectual discussions on biblical topics that are relevant and interesting to me.	4 3 2 1 0
23. I experience such enjoyment when I worship the Lord that I sometimes stand, laugh, or cry in response to God's Spirit.	4 3 2 1 0
24. I sense God's presence and compassionate love when we talk together.	4 3 2 1 0
25. I am involved with the poor or those less fortunate than I.	4 3 2 1 0
26. I practice the spiritual disciplines in my life (e.g., fasting, silence, solitude, and simplicity).	4 3 2 1 0

27. I speak up when with people who don't seem to care or do anything about the moral offenses that are harming the youth of our nation, such as pornography on the Internet.	4 3 2 1 0
28. I participate in the Communion of the saints using the symbolic rituals of the faith.	4 3 2 1 0
29. I experience deep peace in the Lord when I am working with my hands, moving as I pray, or holding a small cross or something tangible while spending time with God.	4 3 2 1 0
30. I see lessons about God and His ways when I am out in creation.	4 3 2 1 0
31. I enter into dialogue with others about tough spiritual questions.	4 3 2 1 0
32. I pay attention to my dreams as the Lord speaks to me in mystery.	4 3 2 1 0
33. I gaze lovingly into the Lord's face and am caught up in Jesus' love for me.	4 3 2 1 0
34. I do whatever it takes—as unto the Lord—to help people feel safe, welcomed, and cared for.	4 3 2 1 0
35. I meet God in my simple environment of stillness, obedience, and prayer.	4 3 2 1 0
36. I am outspoken about sin and ungodly behavior that breaks the heart of God.	4 3 2 1 0
37. I observe the sacred days that help the body of Christ honor the historical influence of the church.	4 3 2 1 0

38. I go to museums and get pleasure from the great spiritual classics, or attend concerts in my church or community where lovely choral and chamber music are featured.	4	3	2	I	0
39. I am changed when I am in nature: I find great soul rest there as I slow down and get more in sync with God's rhythms.	4	3	2	I	0
40. I read books about somewhat complex subjects such as apologetics, missiology, ethics, or other theological topics.	4	3	2	I	0
41. I experience a "party" in my soul when I worship God in the congregation.	4	3	2	I	0
42. I adore God as I meditate on His tenderness and goodness in my life.	4	3	2	I	0
43. I volunteer my time in a soup kitchen, pregnancy clinic, literacy program, prison ministry, or other places of need.	4	3	2	I	0
44. I discipline my life—even going without food—to awaken my hunger for God.	4	3	2	I	0
45. I pray for God's intervention while watching the news, reading the newspaper, or walking down city streets.	4	3	2	I	0
46. I practice a "rule" or "habit" of prayer, which includes regular Bible reading and a prayer routine.	4	3	2	I	0
47. I meet with God in places where beautiful art, magnificent structures, or grand cathedrals lift my heart and eyes heavenward.	4	3	2	I	0
48. I pray and think more clearly about problems and most of life when I am in the out-of-doors.	4	3	2	I	0

49. I read great authors who cause me to grow spiritually and mentally in my relationship with God.	4 3 2 1 0
50. As needed, I pray for miraculous healing and other supernatural works of God.	4 3 2 1 0
51. I practice contemplative prayer as I sit quietly before God, not reading or speaking, but simply being in God's loving presence.	4 3 2 1 0
52. When I see people who look like they need help, I ask if I can be of assistance to them.	4 3 2 1 0
53. I spend time alone with God and my own thoughts in places of austerity and solitude.	4 3 2 1 0
54. I talk about my faith with those who don't yet know the Lord so that people will come out of darkness and into the light of Christ.	4 3 2 1 0

Your Spiritual Practices Scores

Now that you've taken the Spiritual Practices Inventory, tally the numbers you recorded for each of the following answers to find your spiritual practice scores:

							Total	H M L
Activist	9 ___	18 ___	27 ___	36 ___	45 ___	54 ___	_____	_____
Ascetic	8 ___	17 ___	26 ___	35 ___	44 ___	53 ___	_____	_____
Caregiver	7 ___	16 ___	25 ___	34 ___	43 ___	52 ___	_____	_____
Contemplative	6 ___	15 ___	24 ___	33 ___	42 ___	51 ___	_____	_____
Enthusiast	5 ___	14 ___	23 ___	32 ___	41 ___	50 ___	_____	_____
Intellectual	4 ___	13 ___	22 ___	31 ___	40 ___	49 ___	_____	_____
Naturalist	3 ___	12 ___	21 ___	30 ___	39 ___	48 ___	_____	_____
Sensate	2 ___	11 ___	20 ___	29 ___	38 ___	47 ___	_____	_____
Traditionalist	1 ___	10 ___	19 ___	28 ___	37 ___	46 ___	_____	_____

Write today's date here to remind you of when you first took the Spiritual Practices Inventory: _____

Now look at your scores above. Write an **H** (for **high**) by those scores that fall between 18 and 24. These are your strongest or most well-developed spiritual practices. How many **high** spiritual practices do you have? _____

Write an **M** (for **moderate**) by those scores that fall between 12 and 17. These are your moderately developed spiritual practices. How many **moderate** spiritual practices do you have? _____

Write an **L** (for **low**) by those scores that fall between 0 and 11. These are your lowest or least developed spiritual practices. How many **low** spiritual practices do you have? _____

Now that you've taken these two inventories, you are ready to read about the nine spiritual temperaments in chapter 3. As you do, remember that these nine categories are simply descriptions of how a person best meets God and grows closer to Him. Later in the book, we will compare your spiritual temperament scores with your spiritual practices scores to determine what your next steps might be. But first, let's discover more about your spiritual temperament and how you have been uniquely wired.

ON YOUR OWN
Consider the following questions:

Our early church fathers believed that an awareness of who we are is fundamentally linked with a growing relationship with God. In fact, they said that an unexamined life was due to "moral sloth." This statement from John Calvin, which is sometimes called the "double knowing," reinforces this principle: "Man never attains to a true self-knowledge until he has previously contemplated the face of God, and come down after such a contemplation to look into himself."

Why might this be true?

Why could the "double knowing"—knowledge of oneself coupled with a knowledge of God—be important in the life of a Christian? in your own life?

ON YOUR OWN
Consider the following:

In *Renovation of the Heart*, Dallas Willard says, "We usually know very little about the things that move in our own soul, the deepest level of our life, or what is driving it. Our 'within' is astonishingly complex and subtle."

What do these words mean to you?

Rephrase Willard's words as you speak them back to God as a prayer.

For Further Reflection and Discussion

1. For many people, the results of these two inventories might feel confining—like being put into a box. But it's important to remember that these findings are the simple beginning of a self-discovery process. What is it about the category of your highest-scoring spiritual temperament (Activist, Ascetic, Caregiver, Contemplative, Enthusiast, Intellectual, Naturalist, Sensate, or Traditionalist) that seems most accurate in your life?

2. As you look at your spiritual temperament scores and the categories in which your numbers are the highest, what do you realize about yourself? What new questions arise?

3. Just as Socrates said, "Know thyself," our early church father Saint Augustine added, "Let me know myself, let me know Thee!" How might increasing your own self-knowledge assist you in your relationship with God?

4. Today in many Christian circles, we are not encouraged to think about the interior life. Much of our teaching is about what to do as Christians and how we should behave. In his book *The Table of Inwardness*, Calvin Miller says, "We shrink to step across the threshold to ourselves." Do you find that looking within is difficult in your own life? What would you ask for from God in the way of courage, insight, humility, or perspective as you consider stepping "across the threshold" to a better understanding of your own unique wiring?

3

HOW IS MY GOD LANGUAGE SIGNIFICANT?

Years ago on a glorious day in June, I walked down the aisle and became Mrs. Daniel Monroe Perrine. That day, everything seemed perfect—the weather, the flowers, the radiant faces of old friends who'd come from far away to see us, and obviously, my handsome groom. Dan and I wrote our own vows, so even the words we spoke to one another overflowed with meaning. Everything about that day made me feel more lavishly loved than I'd ever imagined!

Our wedding marked a new chapter in our lives, but Dan and I both knew that our marriage did not consist of that one "I do." We knew it would take "as long as we both shall live" to develop the kind of love that would deepen only from living each day together. Of course, on that June day, we both thought we knew quite a bit about love. After all, we weren't young pups, so we didn't think that loving each other would be all that difficult.

Then . . . surprise! It took about two months of "wedded bliss" before we had our first "conversation" about the fact that the way Dan communicated love was different from the way I communicated love. I had read Gary Chapman's book on the five love languages—the differing ways people express love to one another. And so it was on a hot summer day while heading to Rome that Dan and I first began to realize we did not speak the same language!

As time passed, we saw more clearly that even though Dan and I both communicate love through spending quality time with one another, I interpreted quality time to mean face-to-face soul talk, while Dan's concept of quality time was more about shoulder-to-shoulder togetherness and doing activities with one another—companionship. Not that I minded companionship; in fact, I really enjoyed it, but the *dialect* of my love language was different. Interestingly, Dan's first wife, Kathy, who had gone to heaven after losing her battle with leukemia, had enjoyed the same shoulder-to-shoulder variety of love as Dan, so my request for deeper soul connection was a bit foreign to him. Thus, after years of speaking one love language with Kathy, Dan found himself needing to learn a whole new language: mine! (Dan often points out that this was easier said than done!)

As we began to tackle this new challenge, a friend explained to Dan that my needs were actually God's invitation for him to know Jesus better. I'm not sure how comforting that was to Dan, but the words were true: My desire for greater intimacy caused Dan to better understand God's desire for greater face-to-face closeness with Him. Likewise, I realized that Dan's quieter version of togetherness was bringing me to a place where I could truly enjoy more extended periods of silence with the Lord. As the Contemplatives of old used to say, silence is the highest form of prayer, and I realized that when Dan had something to say to me, he would say it (not just when I asked him a question or started a conversation). Through Dan, I was growing more satisfied in God's presence, enjoying Jesus in wordless rest, knowing that He, too, would speak when He had something to say.

Dan and I have since been settling into our own wonderful "bilingual" marriage. We've found that just as we have differing ways of giving and receiving love, we also have dissimilar ways of loving God. The Lord, unlike us, never needs to learn a new dialect because He is fluent in every language. But when we speak to Him, we each come with a language all our own.

I've found that spiritual temperaments are a lot like love languages. My spiritual temperament is my way of loving God; yours is your way. And while no language is unfamiliar to our omni-lingual Creator, each of us comes to Him speaking a dialect that is uniquely characteristic to how we were created, a language that is fundamental to the way we draw life from Him. For we were created with a capacity to receive life and faith, wisdom and direction, strength and boldness from our union with Christ, and the language we speak with Him becomes the starting point for how that happens. Each challenge we face is a new opportunity to trust God and see His goodness and wisdom at work in our lives; as we know Him and trust Him more, we are able to accomplish more in our partnership together. What was once a huge, scary prospect for us faith-wise now seems like a small, doable event because we've seen God come through for us time after time, giving us all we needed when we needed it—in what we recognize as ever-enlarging doses of grace. As servants of the living God, all our gifts, abilities, and efforts will amount to nothing without that abiding connection with Jesus, and knowing as much as possible about this connection is truly important. Bill Hybels says it this way in his paraphrase of 1 Corinthians 13:

> *If I cast vision with the tongues of men and angels, but lead without the love of God at my core,*
> *I am a ringing cell phone or worse, a clamoring vacuous corporate type.*
> *If I have the gift of leadership and can provide direction, build teams, and set goals,*
> > *but fail to exhibit Christ-like kindness or give Christ the credit for my accomplishments,*
> *In the eyes of God, all my achievements count for precisely nothing.*
> *If I give my salary to the poor, my reserved parking space in the church lot to a summer intern, or my deacons' bodies to be burned,*
> > *but neglect to relate and work in a manner worthy of the one whose name I bear,*
> *In the final analysis, it all counts for precisely nothing.*
> *A close, humble walk with Christ never fails. It strengthens the heart, redirects the will, restrains the ego, and purifies the motives.*
> *It never fails.*
> *When I was a young leader, independent and too busy to pray,*
> *I blew stuff up and wounded every third person I led.*
> *But now that I am mature and have left my childish ways . . .*
> *I do that somewhat less!*
> *And now these three remain:*
> > *the faith to follow God boldly,*
> > *the hope to press on even when my heart is breaking,*
> > *and the love to enrich the hearts of all those I lead.*
> *But the greatest of these is love—the love that only comes from a quiet, close, daily walk with Christ.*[1]

Nurturing this daily walk is our primary calling, and while connecting with the Lord is critical, *how* we connect is a matter of preference.

As you read the following descriptions of the nine spiritual temperaments, try to think of each one as a "God language," a way of being with God that helps you know Him better and love Him more. Remember, your spiritual temperament is also your gift *to* God—your way of worshipping Him. Plus, our spiritual temperaments, or "God languages," are our gifts to one another—how the multiple facets of God's character and attributes are displayed through us to the world.

A look at the life of Jesus reveals not only breadth and depth but a multiplicity of styles in expressing His love for His Father: Jesus often chose *silence* and *solitude* to be alone with God; He demonstrated consistent *adoration* and *love* for His Abba; He knew how and when to gather with others and enter into *celebration*; and Jesus also used *ritual* and *symbol* in worship. The Savior often went *outdoors* to be with His Father and, using spittle and mud to make clay for a blind man's eyes, employed the *sensory* as a part of His ministry. Christ obviously used his *intellect* to study and utilize Scripture, and He actively *confronted evil and injustice* with power. Jesus readily *cared* for others through a life of continual service. Hence, the breadth and depth of Jesus' spiritual life is indeed a model for us in all aspects of our faith.

As you read about each of the nine spiritual temperaments, record your spiritual temperament scores found on page 27. Your highest spiritual preference score will indicate your strongest or most passionate spiritual temperament.

Again, my thanks to Gary Thomas for creating and detailing these nine spiritual temperament categories.

ACTIVISTS: LOVING GOD THROUGH CONFRONTATION WITH EVIL

Record your spiritual temperament score for the Activist from page 27. _____
Is it high, medium, or low? _____

One day as I was walking into my office, I saw a group of junior high students standing on the corner smoking cigarettes. These kids were definitely not old enough to buy tobacco, and as they flicked the ashes with an "Ain't I cool?" attitude, something rose up within me that truthfully doesn't appear very often. I recognized it as "holy concern, holy compassion, and holy commotion!"

I walked up to the group and used my "Hi, kids!" people skills to start a conversation. About thirty seconds into the dialogue, the discussion turned to the pitfalls of smoking. I told them about my father, an avid smoker who had died at the age of sixty-five of a heart attack, expounding on the harmful effects of cigarette smoking on the heart and lungs, and explaining how difficult it was to lose my dad at such an early age. These kids—a rather captive audience—seemed to be listening. Then I pushed the envelope a little further and began to ask a few questions of them, such as why they smoked, how they'd gotten started, and who had helped them obtain this illegal substance. (With that last question, all cigarettes were promptly snuffed out!) I was basically trying to dismantle the glamour of this addictive vice.

While the whole drama lasted less than five minutes, the kids seemed open to my concern. As we parted, I mentioned that the same God who created them also loved and died for them, and He had a plan for their lives. They were really paying attention now. As we said goodbye, I prayed for these kids, hoping that their attraction to cigarettes would undergo a marked decline, and that their sense of dignity, self-esteem, and spiritual curiosity would be raised.

Characteristics of the Activist

Although not an Activist by temperament, that day I became one by practice. The Activist is often quite bold in his or her desire to see evil confronted and good prevail. In fact, the Activist will often get involved in spite of the personal cost. And there will be a personal cost, because whenever light confronts darkness, there are ramifications; darkness doesn't give up without a fight. As Jesus told us in Matthew 5:10, "Blessed are those who are persecuted because of righteousness, for theirs is the kingdom of heaven." For an Activist, wanting to be liked is not as high a priority as standing up for the widow and orphan in their distress (see James 1:27).

The Activist, therefore, is wired by God to courageously come against evil and rally for the good. Although God commands all of us

to hate evil and take action when we encounter injustice in our midst
(see Jeremiah 7:5-7), the Activist is literally energized and rejuve-
nated by this. When the Activist is confronting wrong, the result is
a greater sense of solidarity and fellowship with the triune God. For
just as Jesus confronted the Pharisees and spoke directly to people
about the error of their ways, so also is the Activist able to challenge
others, not because of personality, but because of perspective—he
or she sees the good and upright heart of God and cannot avoid
proclaiming it.

Identifying the Activists in a crowd is not difficult. These people
are often a prophetic voice in their generation, speaking out against
wrong and causing discomfort at best or hostility at worst. Activists
may frequently share the gospel with those who do not yet know Jesus,
or they can be found leading prayer walks or attending marches while
also urging others to do the same. You might recognize an Activist
as one who works with the poor or stays current on issues relating
to prostitution, slavery, or the neglect and oppression of the aged.
Compelled to challenge apathy and the status quo, these people take
action when they see wrong occurring in the world around them.
They might attend a seminar by Gary Haugen called "God's Heart of
Justice: Why Do Bad Things Happen and Good People Just Watch?"
or engage the culture regarding moral offenses. When you hear an
Activist speaking out about pornography on the Internet or any kind
of behavior that breaks the heart of God, you can be sure that you are
in the presence of a gift from the Lord Himself—a person who will
help you see more clearly God's heart of justice and righteous. We need
Activists to remind us that we live in a fallen world and that if God's
Kingdom is to come on earth as it is in heaven, action and courage will
be required on the part of God's people.

I have known Activists who were so distraught over an issue
that tears came to their eyes when they spoke about it, and these same
Activists were surprised when others didn't see the problem with equal
black-and-white intensity. This can, at times, make Activists unpopular,
even in Christian circles. Always waving the flag of their particular
cause, Activists sometimes cause those around them to wish they would
give it a rest. This can leave Activists feeling lonely, misunderstood, and

isolated, like Elijah, who thought he was the only prophet left after his encounter with Jezebel (see 1 Kings 19). When exhausted, Activists can even believe that their zeal is greater than God's!

Activism takes a different shape for different people, depending upon the particular evil they are standing against. Bill Hybels describes himself as an Activist and says that these energetic types seem to operate best at Mach speed. "Because of their wiring they need—actually they *revel* in—a highly challenging environment that pushes them to the absolute edge of their potential. It's when they're right on that edge that they feel closest to God."[2]

Biblical Examples of Activists

We see activism throughout Scripture:

- Moses confronting (and then going overboard and killing) the Egyptian who was beating a Hebrew (see Exodus 2:11-12), rescuing the shepherd girls from being harassed (see Exodus 2:17), and confronting Pharaoh (Exodus see 4–11)
- Elijah challenging the prophets of Baal (see 1 Kings 18)
- Habakkuk prophetically calling out for justice (see Habakkuk 1–2)
- Nehemiah fasting and praying when he saw the condition of the city (see Nehemiah 1)
- Amos crying out, "Let justice roll down like waters and righteousness like an ever-flowing stream" (Amos 5:24, NASB)

The Messiah Himself was an Activist. Consider these words that were spoken about Him even before He was born:

With righteousness He will judge the poor, and decide with fairness for the afflicted of the earth; and He will strike the earth with the rod of His mouth, and with the breath of His lips He will slay the wicked. Also righteousness will be the belt about His loins, and faithfulness the belt about His waist.   *Isaiah 11:4-5 (NASB)*

A throne will even be established in lovingkindness, and a judge will sit on it in faithfulness in the tent of David; moreover, he will seek justice and be prompt in righteousness.   *Isaiah 16:5 (NASB)*

Truly Jesus confronted evil boldly when needed (see Matthew 23). We see the fulfillment of these prophetic words as Jesus walked the earth, actively confronting the religious system of the day and, of course, paying the ultimate price for His standoff with evil.

In our history books, we see other Activists whose names are synonymous with the good they ushered in. Among them are David Livingstone, Susan B. Anthony, Florence Nightingale, Albert Schweitzer, Dorothy Day, Mother Teresa, and Martin Luther King Jr.—just to name a few. One of my favorite Activists was the Quaker John Woolman (1720–1772), who tirelessly, sacrificially, and peacefully stood against slavery. Whenever I'm tempted to think, *What can one person do?* I remember the relentless determination of Woolman, who helped abolish slavery in his own denomination and ultimately throughout the Western world.[3]

Over the centuries, Activists have been known for proverbially biting off more than they could chew—and sometimes doing it with high velocity. Yet the church would not be what it is today without John Wesley (a ministry go-getter), George Whitefield (who nearly preached himself to the point of collapse), and D. L. Moody (who always kept folks wondering how he could do so much). Activists often are like rocket launchers, igniting passion for Jesus wherever they go. Hybels says that Activists feel closest to God when they have "wrung out every last drop of . . . emotional, physical, and spiritual potential for a worthy kingdom cause."[4] Sometimes they might even feel guilty about the way they love to throw themselves completely into ministry (I'm sure others feel guilty around them too, but for different reasons). Hybels's counsel to Activists is to accept the way God made them and come into God's presence boldly, even if it's with their hair on fire![5]

We owe a lot to the Activists. Many of the people who have started ministries or currently direct a Christian organization have an Activist temperament. Their vision, tenacity, drive, and vigor keep them moving forward without a lot of affirmation; indeed, they are able to progress even in the midst of antagonism. While appearing to be mere truth-tellers, they are actually more: They are justice-carriers. They see the world around them through a keen lens, and their hearts cannot rest with the injustice they see. In my doctoral work, when meeting young

Activists, I often noticed that they were not the sign-carrying, petition-circulating types of the former generation. These younger Activists were often a quieter sort, with a deep, less visible presence; yet their committed hearts and staunch actions were just as strong.

After reading this description of an Activist, check your spiritual temperament score on page 27. Do you agree with your Activist score? If not, review the spiritual temperament questions on pages 21 to 26 (particularly questions 1, 10, 19, 28, 37, and 46), and see how you might now answer these questions differently. Even though your exact score is not as important as the insight you've gained about yourself and your relationship with God, record your revised score here: _____

ON YOUR OWN
Consider the following:

Do other people come to mind who may be Activists? If so, list them in your journal.

Is there someone you might want to talk with this week about what you have learned about this spiritual temperament?

What have you learned about yourself from reading about this spiritual temperament?

If you are an Activist, thank God now for the gift He has given you of displaying His heart of justice and righteousness to a world that thinks of Him as absent and indifferent, even tolerant of evil. Thank Him, too, for the gift you are to Him and to others. Write out your prayer in your journal.

47

ASCETICS: LOVING GOD THROUGH SOLITUDE AND SIMPLICITY

Record your spiritual temperament score for the Ascetic from page 27. _____
Is it high, medium, or low? _____

Several years ago I decided to take a silent retreat. It was a few days before Easter, so I went to a beautiful monastery to focus on the events of Holy Week. I also took some important work I hoped to do and a few good books to read. The monastery provided a spiritual director, so—in my attempt to maximize the retreat experience—I decided to utilize Sister Ruth for the one-hour-a-day private meeting she offered.

The first day I met with Sister Ruth, she informed me that she did not want me to read any of the books I had brought along or do any outside work; she simply wanted me to meditate on a few selected passages from the book of Isaiah concerning the suffering of the coming Messiah. I noticed as I began the exercise that these passages were very sad and made me feel depressed, and after an hour or so of focusing on them, praying through them, thinking about them, and picturing them in my imagination, I was sure Sister Ruth would understand when I told her that I didn't want to do the exercises any longer. (I omitted telling her that I had already been reading ahead to some of the more triumphant sections in the book of Isaiah.)

To my surprise the next day, as I described my depressed plight to Sister Ruth, her eyes twinkled. She didn't evidence concern at all; in fact, she lit up. Not only did she want me to continue mediating on the "suffering servant" passages, she now instructed me to stay in my room all day—no walking around the lovely grounds or sitting outside in the beauty of nature, no smiling at other retreatants or enjoying secret rendezvous with friends from town who had driven out to see me. I was directed to come out of my room only for meals and was reminded that even mealtime was a occasion for strict silence and solitude to aid me in concentrating upon the suffering of my Lord. Obviously, Sister Ruth was an Ascetic to the core!

The good news about that retreat is that I made it through alive! I even experienced some breakthrough moments with Jesus that produced a change in me, and I believe that now I could do a retreat of this nature with much less angst. But for a true Ascetic, this retreat would have been made to order. For though I enjoy alone time with God, true Ascetics more than *enjoy* solitude—they *require* extended times of silence and solitude to recharge their spiritual batteries. For the Ascetic, it is in these quiet places of holy stillness that God's presence is more profoundly ushered in, and being nourished by regular times of apartness is crucial.

Characteristics of the Ascetic

The life of an Ascetic is fundamentally an internal one, and the Ascetic works hard to develop that inner life. Believing that silence is a gift, they sometimes view words as burdensome, dissipating one's energies and distracting one from giving total attention to God. The Ascetics of old used to take vows of silence for the purpose of purifying themselves so they could commune more fully with Jesus. As Jerome, a Christian in the fourth century, said, "To me the town is a prison, and solitude is paradise."[6] Stressing inner asceticism, Jerome noted that solitude is not so much a detachment from people as it is an inner disposition "quite compatible with proximity to other men."[7] A true Ascetic can find a lonely desert even in the midst of a busy city.[8]

Distracted by the senses, Ascetics appreciate a low level of sensory input. Simple living conditions and environments, as well as simplicity in dress and lifestyle, are usually valued. The mere act of walking into a barren, quiet room in a monastery can cause an Ascetic to begin to move toward worship. I recently attended a conference at a monastery with a friend. As we drove onto the grounds, she noticed that her breathing began to deepen and her pace slowed. She verbalized to me as only an Ascetic could that she sensed her spirit being lifted to God just by stepping into this environment of solitude.

Enduring hardship and suffering is also part and parcel for the Ascetic. This helps the Ascetic experience the "sacred romance" with Jesus more fully. Many of the missionaries I know who serve in rural areas have an Ascetic temperament, and they view the difficulties they face simply as instruments to mature their love for God and His people. Early Ascetics even slept on the ground or purposefully exposed themselves to adverse weather conditions to gain greater spiritual training.[9] Unlike masochists, Ascetics consider suffering and self-denial not ends in themselves but merely means to loving God more completely. Strictness is utilized as a way of expressing devotion to God, a way to deny the flesh so that deeper communion with the living God can be attained. According to German theologian Dietrich Bonhoeffer, who was eventually martyred by the Nazis, without an element of the Ascetic in us, we will find it difficult to wholly follow Christ.[10]

The Ascetic also values hard work. The very word *Ascetic* literally means "to labor" or "work." Consider that for 90 percent of Jesus' life, He was a common laborer. For the Ascetic there is no distinction between the sacred and the secular; all work done unto the Lord is an act of worship. Saint Benedict said, "The monk in his labor is celebrating a liturgy, the liturgy of creation."[11] For many of our forefathers, all work was considered prayer, and in all they did they were communing with God.

For Ascetics, food is not seen as something to give visceral pleasure as much as a means of sustenance, and going without it helps nurture greater hunger for God. Saint Francis of Assisi was said to devour fasting as a man devours food.[12] Not only does fasting allow the Ascetic to give to God time that would normally be used for fleeting matters, but it also permits one to give up the pleasures and consolations of this world for greater spiritual satisfaction.

Ascetics stress actions and conduct above words, which gives their words more authority when eventually spoken. Just as the Bible says, "In quietness and in confidence shall be your strength" (Isaiah 30:15, KJV), so Ascetics foster a tranquility of soul born of stillness. They are people of obedience, because for them, submission prevents self-indulgence while also assaulting human pride. In this rebellious world, the Ascetic believes that respect for human authority demonstrates an ultimate respect for God's authority. Unlike the religious leaders in the Bible who heaped heavy burdens on others while luxuriating themselves (see Matthew 23:4), the truly mature Ascetic is strict with the self while being tender toward others.

The Ascetic life has historically been associated with the mystical, or the Contemplative, but in modern times the two have been split apart.[13] While contemplation will certainly be among the practices of an Ascetic, the lifestyle of a true Ascetic has long been one that uses self-denial to become free from besetting sins.

Biblical Examples of Ascetics

In the Bible, we see several people who demonstrate Ascetic temperaments:

- John the Baptist going into the wilderness to be alone with God (see Matthew 3)
- Daniel fasting, praying, and sitting in sackcloth and ashes (see Daniel 9)
- Joel prevailing upon the leaders of Israel to wail and mourn (see Joel 1–2)

For sure, one of the greatest Ascetics we observe in the Bible is Jesus, who continually went away to be alone with the Father (see Matthew 14:23), fasted (see Matthew 4:1-2), and even prayed throughout the night (see Luke 6:12). Jesus lived a life of simplicity with few earthly possessions (see Matthew 8:20), learned obedience from the things he suffered (see Hebrews 5:8), and was willing to endure hardship for love of the Father (see 1 Peter 2:23).

The church owes a lot to those with Ascetic temperaments. Many of our spiritual disciplines have been made accessible through the writings of Ascetics who take the quest for godly transformation seriously. When the Bible tells us to work out our salvation with fear and trembling, the Ascetic is apt to see this as his or her principal life calling. And rightly so, for Ascetics remind us of the importance of simplicity and singleness of purpose. Ascetics have also taught the church that detachment—becoming indifferent to all created things—is necessary if we are to live with an increasing attachment to Christ Himself. This capacity for detachment has sustained the church for centuries, teaching us to choose God above all else, as Jesus did in the garden when He said, "Not my will, but thine, be done" (Luke 22:42, KJV).

If you are a person who feels closest to God during extended times of silent prayer, your spiritual temperament may be that of an Ascetic. If the monastic life of stillness, obedience, and simplicity is attractive to you, and you find an ordered life that utilizes the spiritual disciplines appealing, then your asceticism score might be rather high.

After reading this description of an Ascetic, check your spiritual temperament score on page 27. Do you agree with your Ascetic score? If not, review the spiritual temperament questions on pages 21 to 26 (particularly questions 2, 11, 20, 29, 38, and 47), and see how you might now answer the questions differently. Remembering that your score is not as important as the insight you gain about your relationship with God, record your revised score here: _____ .

ON YOUR OWN
Consider the following:

Do other people come to mind who may be Ascetics? If so, list them in your journal.

Is there someone you might want to talk with this week about what you have learned about this spiritual temperament?

What have you learned about yourself from reading about this spiritual temperament?

If you are an Ascetic, thank God now for the gift He has given you of seeing Him in the midst of simplicity. Thank Him, too, for the grace to be committed to careful obedience in a world where defiance, greed, and self-indulgence are the order of the day, and for the gift you are to Him and to others. Write out your prayer in your journal.

CAREGIVERS: LOVING GOD THROUGH SERVING OTHERS

Record your spiritual temperament score for the Caregiver from page 27. _____
Is it high, medium, or low? _____

I love to be around Diane. She's a volunteer in a pregnancy crisis clinic, and when she talks about the young girls she counsels, her face glows. When we are together, Diane takes good care of me, making sure I have something to drink and that I am well fed and content. She is a Caregiver par excellence, much like my husband, Dan, who works for an organization that empowers the poor in Africa. A consummate Caregiver, he would attend to every orphan, widow, and struggling farmer on the continent if he could. Dan has a huge servant's heart and is always mindful of ways to help others. Readily able to spot another's need, he often lends a helping hand before even being asked. That is the Caregiver's temperament—showing love for God by tangibly serving others.

Characteristics of the Caregiver

Caregivers see practical needs and move toward them. They are servants, doers of the Word, hands-on types whose spiritual pace is quickened when they are helping in concrete ways. Caregivers feel closest to God when they are laboring for Him in His Kingdom. In fact, I have seen Caregivers who were full of praise to God after being able to spend a whole day just helping someone. Even though Caregivers may look like others in a typical Christian setting, they feel most joy-filled and alive not during prayer or when they are studying theology but when they are serving, volunteering in ministry, or helping another person accomplish God's work. I once had a friend who was a hospice worker, and she told me she never felt God's presence more strongly than when she was washing the body of a person who was about to see Jesus face-to-face. It was at those times that she was most aware that the Lord Himself was in the room!

I find it interesting that the Caregiver and Activist can be doing the same things, yet one is taking action because of a wrong that needs to be righted (with God's justice in mind), while the other is taking action because he or she sees a practical need (with God's kindness moving him or her forward). What pastor wouldn't give his or her right arm for a truckload of folks with this spiritual temperament? I once heard about a man who took an early retirement so he could move right across the street from the church, because he never felt as close to God as when he was serving people who were advancing the Kingdom.[14]

Though many people feel close to God (and others, for that matter) when they are doing something for Him, for Caregivers these times markedly increase their awareness of God's presence. They also experience shouldering the burdens of others as a form of prayer. Mother Teresa taught us to look behind the eyes of the poor to see the eyes of God. Her love for the leper was not what drove her; it was her love for Jesus and her commitment to care for those He loves. She knew the real meaning of Jesus' words, "Whatever you did for one of the least of these brothers of mine, you did for me" (Matthew 25:40).

Interestingly, I have found that people with the Caregiver temperament often serve in the background, and sometimes they can be overlooked or feel inferior to those with more public spiritual temperaments. When the Intellectual is talking about theology or the Contemplative is sharing her or his latest encounter with God, the Caregiver may be working in the kitchen feeling a lot less important. And in some environments, Caregivers do receive less value than the more visible temperaments. Although we know we need Caregivers, those who are content to be in the background serving without notice are sometimes not lauded as much as those out in front stimulating our hearts and minds. Unless Caregivers are in environments where their spiritual temperaments are genuinely esteemed, their contributions can sadly go unnoticed.

Biblical Examples of Caregivers

In the Bible, we see several people who demonstrated a Caregiver temperament:

- Mordecai was a superlative Caregiver, and as we study his life, we notice that he gave to God by caring for Esther, an orphan, and even raising her as his own daughter (see Esther 2:7). Once Esther was grown, Mordecai continued to care for her by visiting her daily in the palace. But Mordecai was not codependent; he was not a lonely man who needed to care for someone of prominence to bolster his self-esteem. Mordecai was

a man with a caring heart who had clear convictions. He refused
to bow to Haman, making it clear that his caregiving was
merely an extension of his love for God. Though Caregivers are
shepherds at heart, they can be lions when it comes to carrying
out their mission.[15] The same spirit of care that Mordecai
showed Esther he also showed to the king when he overheard a
plot to harm him. Later Mordecai moved to save a nation when
all the Jews were being threatened. And at every turn, Mordecai
gave the glory to God, which is what the mature Caregiver does.

- Ruth was a Caregiver who vowed to look after her mother-
  in-law, Naomi, and served her by gleaning in the fields (see
  Ruth 1–2).
- The women who came to the tomb at dawn after Jesus' resur-
  rection and brought spices to anoint the Lord's body were
  Caregivers (see Luke 24:1).

Jesus was undoubtedly the most skilled Caregiver of all, perpetu-
ally looking after the sick, the demonized, the poor, and those with all
manner of needs (see Matthew 4:23-24; 9:35-36). And He taught His
followers—whether they had Caregiver spiritual temperaments or not—
to do the same. He took a towel and washed His disciples' feet (see John
13:4-12), then commanded them to follow His example and wash one
another's feet (see John 13:14). And He didn't just wash the feet of those
who were His greatest fans; He washed Judas's feet, knowing that within
hours Judas would betray Him. He taught the value of caring for those
who were His enemies as well as His friends when He told the parable
of the Good Samaritan, instructing His followers to be people who give
practical, hands-on help even to strangers in need. He expects those who
love Him to demonstrate that love by caring for those around them.

Biblical mandates for caregiving are plenteous. We are all
commanded to:

- Care for other believers. "Whoever has this world's goods, and sees
  his brother in need, and shuts up his heart from him, how does the
  love of God abide in him?" (1 John 3:17, NKJV); "Contribut[e] to
  the needs of the saints" (Romans 12:13, NASB); see also Philippians
  2:4; 1 Peter 4:10; Hebrews 6:10; and Romans 12:10.

- Care for orphans and widows. "Pure and undefiled religion in the sight of our God and Father is this: to visit orphans and widows in their distress" (James 1:27, NASB).
- Care for prisoners. "Remember the prisoners, as though in prison with them, and those who are ill-treated, since you yourselves also are in the body" (Hebrews 13:3, NASB).
- Care for the poor. "Jesus said to him, 'If you wish to be complete, go and sell your possessions and give to the poor, and you will have treasure in heaven; and come, follow Me'" (Matthew 19:21, NASB).
- Care for others through hospitality. "Practice hospitality" (Romans 12:13); see also Hebrews 13:2.
- Care for the interests of Jesus Christ. "I hope in the Lord Jesus to send Timothy to you shortly, so that I also may be encouraged when I learn of your condition. For I have no one else of kindred spirit who will genuinely be concerned for your welfare. For they all seek after their own interests, not those of Christ Jesus" (Philippians 2:19-21, NASB).

While the church today is mindful of Jesus' words to care for others, we're not as vigilant about following His example, especially when it involves relying on Him for supernatural love and power. In Matthew 11:5, when Jesus was asked if He was truly the Messiah, He offered indisputable evidence to confirm His deity: "The blind receive sight, the lame walk, those who have leprosy are cured, the deaf hear, the dead are raised, and *the good news is preached to the poor*" (emphasis added). Only by the supernatural power of God could the blind see, the lame walk, the dead come to life . . . *and* someone love God enough to care for the poor. Caregiving is clear evidence that God is in the house. Those with the Caregiver temperament are wearing signs around their necks that read, "Come watch God at work as I care for people." This is a powerful temperament indeed.

Caregivers are a great gift to the body of Christ because through their lives we see the kindness and sensitivity of God for His people in every situation. He says we can throw the whole weight of our burdens upon Him because He cares for us (see 1 Peter 5:7). Of course, no person can ever aid us like the Lord Jesus Himself, for though we are instructed to bear one another's burdens (see Galatians 6:2), we are also told to carry our own loads (see Galatians 6:5). When it comes to having our needs met, full dependence upon the Lord is mandatory because only He can always care for us adequately.

If you like to put your faith into action by helping others in need and in that service you sense God's pleasure, you may have a Caregiver spiritual temperament. If you experience God's love most readily when you are reaching out to help the weak, the poor, the sick, or the imprisoned, and if that's how you show your love for Jesus, your Caregiver scores may be quite high.

After reading this description of a Caregiver, check your spiritual temperament score on page 27. Do you agree with your Caregiver score? If not, review the spiritual temperament questions on pages 21 to 26 (particularly questions 3, 12, 21, 30, 39, and 48), and see how you might revise your answers. Even though your exact score is not as important as the insight you've gained about yourself and your relationship with God, record your revised score here: _____ .

ON YOUR OWN
Consider the following:

Do other people come to mind who may be Caregivers? If so, list them in your journal.

Is there someone you might want to talk with this week about what you have learned about this spiritual temperament?

What things have you learned about yourself from reading about this spiritual temperament?

If you are a Caregiver, thank God now for the gift He has given you of displaying His heart of compassion and kindness to a world that views Him as aloof and too busy for them. Thank Him, too, for the gift you are to Him and to others. Write out your prayer in your journal.

CONTEMPLATIVES: LOVING GOD THROUGH ADORATION

Record your spiritual temperament score for the Contemplative from page 27. _____
Is it high, medium, or low? _____

During my senior year in college as a fairly young Christian, I was
asked by my evangelistic team leader, Bill, to share with him my deepest
desire in life. I didn't hesitate to tell Bill that my greatest passion was to
really know God and love Him completely. Interestingly, after I spoke
these words, there was a long pause in the conversation. I looked at
Bill's face and could see that he wasn't all that pleased. In fact, when he
finally spoke, he began by giving me a mini-lecture on how that outlook
could preclude me from my higher calling of preaching the gospel to
a lost world. Since we were both very committed to sharing our faith,
I'm not sure why Bill felt the need to amplify the consequences of what
he deemed my "misguided infatuation" with the Lord, adding that Jesus
was much more interested in expanding His Kingdom than in simply
being adored, which is what heaven was for. And besides, Bill reminded
me that my attitude did not help our team's outreach, either!

Needless to say, I was surprised by Bill's response. After all, I
wasn't going to stop telling people about Jesus, nor did I have any
thoughts of becoming cloistered and unconcerned with others. I was,
however, sharing the longings of my heart, revealing a deeper love for
God than (dare I say?) the ministry.

Looking back, I now know that this conversation was pointing to
my spiritual temperament. A Contemplative to the core, I have since
seen firsthand the delights and limitations of loving God through
adoration, and I've also experienced how this spiritual temperament can often be misunderstood. While some may appreciate the
Contemplative's depth and approach, others may not like the fact that
this person seems to march to a different drummer.

> While other believers are joyfully filling their calendars with
> relational commitments or serving opportunities, these sincere
> Christians are carefully guarding their schedules, avoiding at all
> costs the patterns of busyness they see around them. For reasons
> they may not fully understand, these people are easily drained by

relationships and activities. . . . Give them a Bible, a good piece of literature, a poem and a journal, and they'll disappear for days. . . . They operate with sensitive spiritual antennae and can discern the activity of God wherever they are.[16]

This is the way of the Contemplative. Though Contemplatives can get a lot done out of love for the Lord, their preference—while others are out *doing* for God—is simply *being* with Him, much like Mary of Bethany, who sat attentively at Jesus' feet.

Characteristics of the Contemplative

Contemplatives enjoy basking in the warmth of God's love and spending extended time simply delighting in God's presence. Their first work is the work of adoring God,[17] and they see all of life as an opportunity to develop a deeper friendship with Jesus. Contemplatives may talk openly about intimacy with God—using the language of lovers—and they tend to be at home with their more mystical side.

Being "purpose driven" does not inspire Contemplatives; they are, instead, what I call "Person drawn." In fact, for them, all of life is primarily about growing in their intimacy with Jesus. When the Lord spoke about the woman who poured out the alabaster box of expensive ointment upon His head, the disciples immediately asked what the *purpose* was (see Matthew 26:8, KJV). They saw this as an inefficient, nonsensical gesture—a waste. But to God, whose grace to a prodigal son may have also seemed excessive (see Luke 15:11-32), love does not always need to be efficient and pragmatic. Jesus was pleased with this woman's lavish display of affection in light of His impending rendezvous with the cross. He said, "Why do you bother the woman? For she has done a good deed to Me" (Matthew 26:10, NASB). Jesus, who was about to pour out His life on Calvary, knew the value of sacrificing all for love.

Lest it be thought that the Contemplative spiritual temperament is primarily for the feminine gender, it was James Houston who described his times in prayer as holding hands with God while "two lovers do nothing but gaze into each other's eyes."[18] This kind of resting in God's presence is what keeps the Contemplative alive. Although imagery of this nature may make some feel uncomfortable (or even wonder if the

Contemplative is becoming too familiar with the Lord of lords), it's good
to remember that though Contemplatives may be a little out of step with
others, they are often the ones who compose the songs that stir our hearts
or write the books that make us think new thoughts about God.[19]

Richard Foster, author and founder of Renovaré, a nonprofit
organization committed to working for church renewal, is just such a
Contemplative. His books draw us with amazing insight to the Father.
He writes:

> Today the heart of God is an open wound of love. He aches over our
> distance and preoccupation. He mourns that we do not draw near
> to Him. He grieves that we have forgotten Him. He weeps over our
> obsession with muchness and manyness. He longs for our presence.
> He is inviting you—and me—to come home, to come home to where
> we belong, to come home to that for which we were created. His arms
> are stretched out wide to receive us. His heart is enlarged to take us
> in. For too long we have been in a far country: a country of noise and
> hurry and crowds, a country of climb and push and shove, a country
> of frustration and fear and intimidation. And He welcomes us home:
> home to serenity and peace and joy, home to friendship and fellowship
> and openness, home to intimacy and acceptance and affirmation. . . .
> The Father's heart is open wide—you are welcome to come in. . . .
> With simplicity of heart we allow ourselves to be gathered up into
> the arms of the Father and let him sing his love song over us.[20]

These are the musings and images of one with a Contemplative spiritual
temperament indeed!

Other great Contemplative authors have also brought us a wealth
of literature, including the late Thomas Merton, a Trappist monk;
Henri Nouwen, the late priest who wrote of being God's beloved; and
Dallas Willard, who says that God in Himself is a sweet society and we
are invited in. These Contemplative authors have helped us to know the
Lord more deeply, and it is important to consider this about someone
with a Contemplative spiritual temperament:

> If you know contemplative types, relate to them very carefully.
> Immature leaders usually think that contemplatives are wasting

time with all their deep thinking. "Get busy!" they want to say. "There's a hill to take. Let's go." But mature leaders understand that contemplatives need to spend considerable time outside the mainstream. They need to protect their thought life. Eventually their reflections will lead to something wonderful that will bless the whole church. Leaders whose primary pathway is contemplative need to give themselves an extra measure of grace. They need to give themselves permission to spend long hours in quiet reflection, even if others view it as inappropriate or strange, because for them that's the door that opens into the presence of God.[21]

Biblical Examples of the Contemplative

In the Bible, we see many people who displayed Contemplative spiritual temperaments:

- John the Beloved, who laid on the breast of Jesus and used the words *love, friend,* and *Bridegroom* more than any other biblical author
- Mary of Bethany, sister of Lazarus and Martha, who sat at Jesus' feet and later poured out sacrificial love upon Him (see Luke 10:38-42; John 12:1-7)

Jesus Himself, who called His Father "Abba," clearly demonstrated His Contemplative side. He talked openly about the love and closeness He and the Father shared, for to Jesus, a life of intimate association with the Father was the only one He'd ever known (see Matthew 3:17; John 17:23-26).

It is also important to note that in life, while most of our longings lead to a search that is designed to bring us to God, it is not only the Contemplative who must engage in this search of seeking and finding. We are all invited in—to seek Him, His Kingdom, and His righteousness (see Matthew 6:33; 7:7). We are promised that God will reward the diligent seeker—with *Himself* (see Hebrews 11:6). Thomas Merton said that only the one who truly seeks God with real desire finds Him, not those who remain at a distance and confine life to a "few routine exercises or external acts of worship and service."[22] Seeking God must be a priority for us all, as M. Basil Pennington reminds us:

> I have run into a situation in marriage counseling a number of times. The couple is unhappy. The wife is dissatisfied and the husband cannot see why. He goes into a long recital of all he is doing for her. He is holding down two or three jobs, building a new house, buying her everything. But to all this, the wife quietly replies: "If only he would stop for a few minutes and give me himself!" I sometimes think that God, as He sees us rushing about in all our doing of good, says to Himself: If only they would stop for a few minutes and give me themselves![23]

Contemplatives are passionate lovers of God who remind us that the Creator in Genesis—the One who spoke the worlds into existence—also became the baby in the manger, entering time to cohabit with His creation. The transcendent One whom Isaiah saw high and lifted up is also the imminent One who welcomed a sinful woman as she kissed His feet, washing them with her tears and wiping them with her hair (see Luke 7:36-50). Contemplatives astound us with their freedom to draw close and experience the God who comes near (see Psalm 34:18), receiving the affection of the One whose love is better than wine (see Song of Songs 1:2).

If you are a person who finds joy in your intimate friendship with Jesus, or if you come alive when you sense God's Spirit speaking words of love to you as you sit gazing into your Beloved's face, chances are you have a Contemplative spiritual temperament. And if you tend to pray using images of God as your Friend, Abba, or intimate Companion, your Contemplative scores may be very high.

After reading the description of the Contemplative, check your spiritual temperament score on page 27. Do you agree with your Contemplative score? If not, review the spiritual temperament questions on pages 21 to 26 (particularly questions 4, 13, 22, 31, 40, and 49), and see how you might revise your answers. Even though your exact score is not as important as the insight you've gained about yourself and your relationship with God, record your revised score here: _____ .

ON YOUR OWN

Consider the following:

Do other people come to mind who may be Contemplatives? If so, list them in your journal.

Is there someone you might want to talk with this week about what you have learned about this spiritual temperament?

What things have you learned about yourself from reading about this spiritual temperament?

If you are a Contemplative, thank God now for the gift He has given you of displaying His heart of affection and nearness to a world that thinks of Him as cold and distant. Thank Him, too, for the gift you are to Him and to others. Write out your prayer in your journal.

ENTHUSIASTS: LOVING GOD THROUGH MYSTERY AND CELEBRATION

Record your spiritual temperament score for the Enthusiast from page 27. _____
Is it high, medium, or low? _____

As we walked into the concert, I saw an entire stadium of people standing on their feet, hands raised, praising God. Some were singing; others were clapping or shouting or literally dancing in their places. The air was alive with celebration, and as I looked at many of the faces in the crowd, I leaned over to my husband and said, "Honey, tonight we are surrounded by a great crowd of Enthusiasts!" Indeed, the Spirit of

God was moving in that place, and everyone around us was excited to move too!

Characteristics of the Enthusiast

The Enthusiast loves God with gusto. These cheerleaders of the faith often feel closest to God when they have gathered as a group to sing and worship.[24] Deeply inspired by joyful celebration, Enthusiasts are usually quite comfortable expressing emotion when praising God. You may see them cry or kneel or even lie prostrate during worship as they feel the Spirit's leading.

I find Enthusiasts easy to spot in a crowd, not only because they seem to feel at home with many different types of spiritual expression, but also because they are often playful and have a childlike spirit toward the things of God.[25] Enthusiasts tend to live lives of expectancy, seeing church and other Christian gatherings as times of spiritual recreation. They like to pray and be creative, and they are known for keeping things alive. I once heard a charismatic pastor say jokingly that some of the people in his church may not be in heaven because they will be so excited that they'll run right past it! Of course, not all Enthusiasts are charismatic, but the charismatic will most likely enjoy the Enthusiast's zeal. Nor are all Enthusiasts extroverts; I know some quiet Enthusiasts, yet when it comes to worshipping God, they are fully alive, showing great openness for God's Spirit to have His way.

When it comes to the things of God, Enthusiasts are rarely shy about expressing their love for God publicly. Others may wonder how Enthusiasts can display their feelings with such abandon, but Enthusiasts are not likely to be thinking about anyone looking on; they are simply lost in love for God. A person who does not share this spiritual temperament might find it easy to judge such outward expressions, but Enthusiasts don't desire to draw attention to themselves (though they would not object to being a signpost pointing the way to God). They simply refuse to let anyone or anything stand in the way of their conveying love to the Majestic One. If others catch the spirit of worship from them, all the better, since worship is considered "party time," and all are invited.

Unlike Contemplatives, who express love to God in intimate

words, Enthusiasts express love to God in open displays of affection within the congregation, which is often where their hearts experience a torrent of praise!

Like those with Contemplative spiritual temperaments, the Enthusiast also feels right at home with spiritual mystery. Enthusiasts in the Old and New Testaments welcomed the supernatural work of the Holy Sprit, including giving merit to dreams as a way of receiving direction from God.[26] Because of their tendency and desire to explore the mystical, it is good when Enthusiasts remain in a community with mature, trusted Christians who can help them discern God's voice and movement in their lives in a wise, safe context.

Bill Hybels refers to the Enthusiast temperament as the "worship pathway." He tells the story of a friend who had been a Christian since childhood but had only attended a very formal church that left him feeling empty. When he became an adult, this man visited a congregation on the other side of town where worshipping "in the Spirit" was the norm. Suddenly this hard-core businessman began to bawl like a baby, and his tears continued throughout the entire worship service. He had no clue what was happening to him and wondered if maybe he'd "blown a midlife gasket."[27]

Eventually, Bill's friend realized that his heart had been so starved for expressive, lively worship that when he finally experienced it, it was like a dam breaking inside him, and a new wave of the Holy Spirit's activity flooded his life. This businessman listens to worship CDs and worships for hours when he yearns to feel the presence of God or when he simply has a joy-filled heart and wants to express thanksgiving.[28] We certainly need the freedom and exuberance of those with the Enthusiast spiritual temperament in our churches today.

Biblical Examples of Enthusiasts

In the Bible, we see many Enthusiast spiritual temperaments:

- King David gives us one of the greatest examples of an Enthusiast in the Bible when he danced before the Lord with all his might. When the Ark of the Covenant was being carried into Jerusalem, David was so lost in gratitude and celebration that he danced wearing only an ephod, a small linen garment something like an apron. A consummate worship leader, David led the whole house of Israel in shouting and loud praise music. But David's wife, Michal, judged him quite harshly for his lack of restraint, and when she saw him leaping and dancing before the Lord, she despised him. Apparently she thought Israel's king was not behaving with the dignity he should display. But this was David's response to her criticism: "I was dancing before the Lord. . . . So I am willing to act like a fool in order to show my joy in the Lord" (2 Samuel 6:21, TLB). David went on to write many psalms that call us to worship God wholeheartedly:

Bless the LORD, O my soul, and all that is within me, bless His holy name. Bless the LORD, O my soul, and forget none of His benefits; who pardons all your iniquities, who heals all your diseases; who redeems your life from the pit, who crowns you with lovingkindness and compassion; who satisfies your years with good things. . . . Bless the LORD, you His angels, mighty in strength, who perform His word, obeying the voice of His word! Bless the LORD, all you His hosts, you who serve Him, doing His will. Let everything that has breath praise the LORD.

Psalm 103:1-5, 20-21; 150:6 (NASB)

- Miriam danced and sang before the Lord with all her might after the Lord delivered her nation from the Egyptians (see Exodus 15).
- The Samaritan leper, being healed, ran to Jesus, falling on his face and glorifying God with a loud voice (see Luke 17:15-16).
- Children praised God and shouted in the Temple, "Hosanna to the Son of David" (see Matthew 21:14-16).

Jesus Himself showed enthusiasm as He entered Jerusalem riding on a donkey, affirming the crowds as they yelled, "Blessed is the king who comes in the name of the Lord!" (Luke 19:38). Jesus was a great Man of praise.

Enthusiasts often lead the congregation to the throne of God— whether they are standing in front of the church or simply worshipping

ON YOUR OWN
Consider the following:

Do other people come to mind who may be Enthusiasts? If so, list them in your journal.

Is there someone you might want to talk with this week about what you have learned about this spiritual temperament?

What have you learned about yourself from reading about this spiritual temperament?

If you are an Enthusiast, thank God now for the gift He has given you of displaying His joy and celebration to a world that thinks of Him as a straitlaced killjoy. Thank Him, too, for the gift you are to Him and to others. Write out your prayer in your journal.

among the people. Their devotion becomes the model, and others around them can feel inspired to follow suit. Many of the people who are producing our popular worship music today are Enthusiasts. We owe a lot to these worshippers who lead us to Jesus through their songs and concerts, and whose gift of celebration helps us be aware on earth of the big shindig awaiting us in heaven!

The world has been given a marvelous gift through those with Enthusiast spiritual temperaments. Not only do they give us wonderful worship music, they also add a sense of fun, optimism, and zest to any group. These faith-loving, glass-half-full types remind us of what heaven will be like when all the saints meet at the throne to adore the triune God. They help us get our eyes off ourselves and onto Jesus, and through their candor remind us that God delights in receiving our unself-conscious, childlike affection. Without a few Enthusiasts in the group, our Christian gatherings would truly be dull.

If you take great pleasure in praising God with others and find worship such a joyous experience that you often want to stand, clap, or raise your hands to God, you may have an Enthusiast spiritual temperament. Or if you like to listen regularly to worship music at home or in your car because this music brings life to you like nothing else, you're probably an Enthusiast. If you have a strong interest in the mystical, including how God uses dreams to lead His people, you also might find your Enthusiast score quite high.

After reading this description of the Enthusiast, check your spiritual temperament score on page 27. Do you agree with your Enthusiast score? If not, review the spiritual temperament questions on pages 21 to 26 (particularly questions 5, 14, 23, 32, 41, and 50), and see how you might revise your answers. Even though your exact score is not as important as the insight you've gained about yourself and your relationship with God, record your revised score here: _____ .

INTELLECTUALS: LOVING GOD THROUGH THE MIND

Record your spiritual temperament score for the Intellectual from page 27. _____
Is it high, medium or low? _____

As I sat next to Nelson in church one Sunday morning, I noticed that while the pastor was preaching, Nelson had put the sermon in outline form, taken more than a page of notes, and filled in each point with several questions—including the names of books for the pastor to consider that both reinforced and challenged his message. Since it didn't seem like a particularly special sermon, I was surprised by Nelson's motivation and ability to listen fully while also recording all his corollary thoughts. Of course, I couldn't help but wonder how the pastor would feel when Nelson walked up after the message and handed him a sermon critique along with several pages of additional items to be considered!

Thankfully, in this case, Nelson is a respected elder in the church, plus the pastor is a very secure person. Perhaps you have known people like Nelson who seem to thrive on mulling over spiritual concepts. Whenever you mention something you have recently learned about God, these people immediately suggest three or four books for you to read, sometimes reciting an exact quotation from one of the authors. If so, you have most likely encountered individuals with Intellectual spiritual temperaments, people who actually feel closest to God when they are actively and vigorously engaging with God with their minds.

I recall one encounter I had with an Intellectual more than a decade ago when I was speaking to a group about intimacy with God. I asked those present when it was that they felt closest to the Lord and what was happening in their lives at those times. After several answered, I noticed the leader wasn't giving a reply, so I invited him to respond. With a smile he said shyly, "I know this is going to sound funny, but when I read theology or ecclesiology, I really begin to worship. Reading and pondering deep truths moves me toward God like nothing else!" Here was a person with an Intellectual spiritual temperament indeed.

Characteristics of the Intellectual

In the spiritual realm, the Intellectual temperament does not necessarily describe someone who is more intelligent than others, nor someone with a formal education or an academic degree. Rather, these people love God best through using their minds to ponder Jesus and His truths. By understanding Scripture and being involved in all forms of cognitive activity, they see faith as something to be understood as much as experienced. For them, right thinking is essential, and they love learning new things about God and His Kingdom. In fact, they get bored when their minds are not fully stimulated.

Bill Hybels notes that people who connect best with God through their intellects are often those who must be using their minds in order to make significant spiritual progress. When Intellectuals attend a testimonial service in which people are describing God's activity in their lives, they often think, *Where's the beef? These heartwarming stories are all well and good, but where's the substance? Where's the theological data? I need something to chew on. I'm dying here!*[29] It helps to know that Intellectuals are neither coldhearted nor snobbish; they simply use their cognitive abilities to love God.

If you know any Intellectuals, you might see them having morning devotions with an open commentary or two. They may be reading challenging books, taking Bible classes, attending lecture series, or being pulled toward people and conversations that challenge their thinking. In essence, Intellectuals' minds always seem to be considering truth so that their hearts can be engaged. My friend is married to an Intellectual, and after attending a spiritual seminar she had thoroughly enjoyed, her husband began pointing out logical errors in the presentation as they were leaving the auditorium. While this was annoying to my friend (who just wanted to feel blessed by what she'd heard), her husband was not trying to be critical or find fault; he's simply wired to question anything that cannot be integrated into his mental and spiritual grid.

Intellectuals can be intimidating to others in the body of Christ because they seem skeptical, and they definitely know what they believe. It's good to be prepared if you want to discuss ethics, theology, apologetics, or any details of the Bible with Intellectuals, who will most likely have all their mental ducks in a row. Some Intellectuals come across adversely to those who readily express their feelings or rely heavily upon spiritual experience, because to the Intellectual, that sort of Christianity appears mindless or irresponsible if not backed up with well-reasoned facts. Intellectuals, who are dedicated to grappling with the truth, often assume others ought to be wrestlers with faith issues as well.

While I was doing my doctoral research, I found that some who scored high as Intellectuals did not particularly like their spiritual temperament; in fact, one I interviewed asked if he could exchange his spiritual temperament for a different one. Of course, spiritual practices can be broadened, and that is a good and necessary goal (which we will discuss later in chapter 4), but our spiritual temperaments are gifts from God. Therefore, it is more than okay to enjoy delving deeply into study and research. You don't have to apologize for wanting to spend time reading and learning new things, for just as the Ascetic needs extended periods of solitude and silence and the Contemplative needs time to rest in the Father's arms, so the Intellectual needs to come to God with an inquiring mind.

Of course, some with Intellectual spiritual temperaments do not feel at all bad about their cognitive inclinations. Quite the contrary, they think everyone who loves Jesus ought to study like they do, read broadly like they do, and be able to debate like they do. I have known Intellectuals who project an attitude of haughtiness and elitism, acting as if theirs is the only *credible* spiritual temperament, the only legitimate way to really know God. That attitude, needless to say, is not one that the Lord hands out with any of the spiritual temperaments.

Again, if we compare ourselves to the way God wired others, we will likely feel either superior or inferior. We may erroneously assume that the way God wired us is the way He has made everyone, and if others are not functioning in their spiritual lives the way we do, something must be wrong—with them or with us. The Intellectual may also conclude that those who are not delving into deep spiritual waters are simply lazy or superficial. This, obviously, is an untrue and unfortunate assumption.

Hybels tells of someone on his staff who has an Intellectual spiritual temperament. This man researched Christianity for two years before making a commitment to Christ. "His mind needed to be convinced before he could open his heart. Now, years after his conversion, he reads theology, archaeology, philosophy, and history recreationally. It feeds his soul."[30] This leader gets excited when an archaeologist in the Middle East makes a significant discovery confirming the Bible. And that is a wonderfully good thing, as those with Intellectual temperaments need this kind of consistent stretching and challenging.

Biblical Examples of Intellectuals

When we look for Intellectuals in the Bible, several immediately come to mind:

- Solomon was given such vast wisdom, understanding, and knowledge that no one could match his comprehension; he composed three thousand proverbs and more than one thousand songs (see 1 Kings 4:29-34).
- Once the apostle Paul was fully convinced about something in the spiritual realm, his heart and life quickly followed; he recognized that spiritual transformation is something that happens primarily through the renewing of the mind (see Romans 12:2).

71

- Gamaliel, a Pharisee and teacher of the Law, was Paul's instructor (see Acts 5:34; 22:3).
- Apollos from Alexandria was a mighty orator of the Scriptures (see Acts 18:24-25).
- Aquila and Priscilla coached Apollos when they heard that he was only acquainted with the baptism of John and needed further spiritual instruction (see Acts 18:25-26).

Of course Jesus Himself demonstrated an Intellectual spiritual temperament through being well-versed in the Scriptures. He had memorized large portions of the Pentateuch and was able to speak boldly and astutely about complex theological matters with everyone from the religious leaders of the day to Pilate himself (see Mark 1:22; John 18:33-38).

We also see Intellectuals throughout the history of the church and observe what they have been able to accomplish for the Kingdom of God. Augustine, Aquinas, Calvin, and Pascal were great Christian thinkers, even though they disagreed with one another.[31] Then we have Martin Luther, whom nothing could stop once he realized the truth of the gospel; C. S. Lewis, who was set on fire once he became convinced of God's truth; and Chuck Colson, who came to Christ and began a ministry when he comprehended the intellectual supremacy of the Christian worldview.[32] Francis Schaeffer, the Intellectual who founded L'Abri in Switzerland, used to invite anyone who wanted to access God through the mind to come study with him. He summoned seekers to use their intellects to discover a well-reasoned faith. I have known several founders of ministries who are Intellectuals, and when they lead, it becomes obvious that God has given them this spiritual temperament for greater Kingdom influence.

Just as Jesus told us to love the Lord our God with all our minds and strength (see Luke 10:27), God has also given the Intellectual spiritual temperament as a gift to the body of Christ. The church has been greatly enhanced by those who are willing to study for long seasons in order to write a commentary, prepare a lecture series, or expound on the essential doctrines of the faith. We are grateful for those who work to maintain ordered minds so that they can anchor the tenants of the

ON YOUR OWN
Consider the following:

Do other people come to mind who may be Intellectuals? If so, list them in your journal.

Is there someone you might want to talk with this week about what you have learned about this spiritual temperament?

What have you learned about yourself from reading about this spiritual temperament?

If you have an Intellectual spiritual temperament, thank God now for the gift He has given you of loving truth, and for your commitment to relentlessly hold on to the God of the Bible, who is both reasonable and rooted in history. Thank God, too, for your part in displaying His truth to a world that believes in a deity who can be morphed into anything humankind imagines him or her to be, and for the gift you are to Jesus and to others. Write out your prayer in your journal.

faith in historical fact, or who are willing to tackle difficult subjects or teach church history, ethics, apologetics, missiology, or other theological topics. We would not have most of our Christian colleges, authors, or teachers and preachers without this spiritual temperament.

If you prefer to study the Bible with a concordance, dictionary, or commentary, or if you read great authors of the faith in order to learn and be challenged spiritually, you may have an Intellectual spiritual temperament. If you get involved in Intellectual discussions or enter into dialogue with others regarding tough spiritual questions, you may find your Intellectual temperament scores to be quite high.

After reading the description of the Intellectual, check your spiritual temperament score on page 27. Do you agree with your Intellectual score? If not, review the spiritual temperament questions on pages 21 to 26 (particularly questions 6, 15, 24, 33, 42, and 51), and see how you might revise your answers. Even though your exact score is not as important as the insight you've gained about yourself and your relationship with God, record your revised score here: _____ .

NATURALISTS: LOVING GOD THROUGH EXPERIENCING HIM OUTDOORS

Record your spiritual temperament score for the Naturalist from page 27. _____
Is it high, medium, or low? _____

Sometimes after a hard day when I am depleted and emotionally spent, nothing rejuvenates my soul like sitting on my back porch watching the hummingbirds drink from the bird feeder, or literally stopping to smell the roses. One afternoon when I was particularly fatigued, I spotted a beautiful red rose blooming in my backyard, and something inside just leaped for joy. I ran out to cut the rose and put it in a vase, feeling as excited as a child with a new bike. That is the power of God's beauty in nature to those with Naturalist spiritual temperaments.

Characteristics of the Naturalist

Naturalists feel closest to God when in the outdoors. Something inside their souls comes alive when they are surrounded by God's splendor in nature, be it the mountains, the desert, the plains, or the beach. For Naturalists, just being outside can dramatically increase their awareness of God, since witnessing the Lord in nature comes easily. They might see a massive rock formation and be moved to reflect upon the rock-solid faithfulness of God, or they might see His gentleness as a breeze blows through the trees, or they might sense while hiking in the heat of the day that God is an oasis who restores our dry, dusty souls.[33]

If given the choice to have coffee with a friend at Starbucks or meet outside in a park, the Naturalist would have no trouble selecting the latter. As one of my Naturalist friends once said, "When I look up and see the moon and stars, I feel strengthened. Instantly, I know I am not alone; God's creation refreshes me because I find *Him* there!" This needn't be surprising, since when God first created Adam and Eve, He put them in a Garden. Perhaps Naturalists are just getting back to their roots.[34] For the Garden is where God initially met with His people, and the Bible even describes *us* as the garden of the Lord (see Song of Songs 4:12-16; Isaiah 51:3; 58:11). Because the Bible talks so much about nature—green pastures, lilies of the field, and a land flowing with milk and honey—some have suggested that the Bible is even understood best when read outside.[35]

I have several friends who are dyed-in-the-wool Naturalists. One likes to go to the park and watch the ducks. There she feels God smile as she observes the little ducklings waddling toward the pond, their mother prodding them along with her beak. At these times my friend senses the Lord saying, *I care for you just like that mother duck cares for her ducklings; sometimes I prod you along too, even though you don't always like my gentle nudges.* God consistently manifests His heart to her through nature.

For the Naturalist, seeing detail in what God has made is like receiving little love notes from Him. As Naturalists observe the scenery around them, their souls open to receive from the Lord through His beauty. Annie Dillard, who has been called an "exegete of creation," tells this story about just such an experience:

> One day I was walking along Tinker Creek thinking of nothing at all and I saw the tree with the lights in it. I saw the backyard cedar where the mourning doves roost charged and transfigured, each cell buzzing with flame. I stood on the grass with the lights in it, grass that was wholly fire, utterly focused and utterly dreamed. It was less like seeing than like being for the first time seen, knocked breathless by a powerful glance.[36]

God's creation is like that; it reaches down into the soul of the Naturalist, becoming a classroom to teach about God's rhythm, timing, and the seasons of life and death. In a world where humans can try to push and manipulate to make things happen, the Naturalist knows that within God's design, time belongs to Him. Humans are put in their place, humbled by what we cannot make or control. "Since the creation of the world God's invisible qualities—his eternal power and divine nature—have been clearly seen, being understood from what has been made" (Romans 1:20). God reminds us here that He is the Creator and we are not. Nature doesn't ask our permission to carry on; it doesn't check our schedules. The weather doesn't care what we have planned. Naturalists know this, and they find comfort in being smaller than the One who created them. All of nature becomes a place to study the Creator. Dillard says this about the thrill of learning from creation:

> It's all a matter of keeping my eyes open. . . . I analyze and pry. I hurl over logs and roll away stones; I study the bank a square foot at a time, probing and tilting my head. . . . But there is another kind of seeing that involves a letting go. When I see this way, I sway transfixed and emptied.[37]

At a spiritual retreat I once attended, the leader gave us an assignment to go outside and take a reflective walk, letting the Lord lead us and speak to us through His creation. My Naturalist friend later sent me what she wrote during her time outdoors:

> I found a stream I hadn't noticed before and followed it. This stream was very small and I could have skipped right by it or seen the whole thing in a few minutes, but instead I walked the entire length, every inch, down to the pond at the end. Noticing the rocks at the bottom and how many times the flow of the stream was blocked by leaves and high rocks, I realized several things, like how easy it is for me to go through life taking shortcuts and missing important pieces. As I walked the stream, the rocks seemed to signify people . . . people whom I will never meet unless I choose to take the long way around . . . people I *have* met because I've taken the time. It is so tempting to hurry so I can "get on to the good stuff" in my life. That is how I think of my work for the Lord. But God doesn't want my work if He can't have my soul, too. His economy says, "Slow down . . . let me articulate your heart to you . . . let me show you where I will take you over time."

That is how God gently speaks to us when we listen to Him through the sounds and sights of nature. Perhaps that is why so many Naturalists are poets. These authors find inspiration in the intricacy of God's creation. While Loren Wilkinson writes about the spirituality of creation,[38] Anne Morrow Lindbergh speaks of finding God on the seashore.[39] In this poem, one Naturalist looks around and is stirred to record what is seen:

THE SALMON CREEK TRAIL

I come down early to the trail to walk the wetland's forged travail.
The air is brisk and biting cold
But solitude's undaunting call draws me to the wooded fall.
Towering Fir and Maples frail shed their leaves upon the trail.
Colors swirling, drifting down, soon imbed the cold, drenched ground.
Though alone upon the trail, heron, duck and geese prevail.
Quacking clatter, fluttering wings, creatures argue, scurry, sing!
The Creator whispers through,
"Can you see Me, too?"
My soul drinks deep along the trail as my heart captures each detail.
Tall grass bows beneath the frost
Once bent with sparkling spiderwebs, now yields to winter's creeping ebb.
Flooding rains without restrain will soon submerge this wet terrain.
The time will come to rest, renew,
Reminding me, I need this, too.
Perspective clears as I head home, no longer on the trail alone.
Life's concerns and questions fade, new foundations have been laid.
The early morning sun climbs high, now springing, playful dogs trot by.
Mothers mitted with mugs of brew make me smile and think of You.[40]

One day another Naturalist friend was telling me about her frustration with her spiritual life. Blaming herself for not spending enough time reading the Bible, she said she probably needed to join a study group at church or maybe enroll in a seminary class. Her solutions surprised me since she is clearly a Naturalist. When I told her about her spiritual temperament and asked if she'd ever considered meeting God at the beach or reading her Bible in her backyard, she responded, "Well, that must be why I've been so frustrated all these years!" Sometimes Naturalists need permission to recharge their spiritual batteries outdoors, enjoying the living Word through all He created. They think that being with God in a lovely outdoor place doesn't count as a quiet time. If more Naturalists felt okay about praying in nature, they'd probably have a greater awareness of the Lord's presence and feel more rested and refreshed—body, soul, and spirit.[41]

Biblical Examples of Naturalists

In the Bible, we see many Naturalists:

- As a young man, when David was outdoors tending his sheep, he no doubt saw God's handiwork and knew God more intensely by being surrounded by His creation. Later David wrote:

  The heavens declare the glory of God; the skies proclaim the work of his hands. Day after day they pour forth speech; night after night they display knowledge.   *Psalm 19:1-2*

  I lift up my eyes to the hills—where does my help come from?
  Psalm 121:1

  The LORD is my shepherd, I shall not want. He makes me lie down in green pastures; He leads me beside quiet waters.
  Psalm 23:1-2 (NASB)

- Isaiah also could have been a Naturalist. Consider his response to God's creation:

  God, the LORD, created the heavens and stretched them out. He created the earth and everything in it. He gives breath to everyone, life to everyone who walks the earth. *Isaiah 42:5 (NLT)*

- John the Baptist, of course, lived in the outdoors and sought God in the wilderness (see Mark 1:3-6).

Jesus, too, often went to the mountains to pray and spend time with His Father. He got away from the crowds by being in the outdoors, and in His darkest hour He went to gather strength from His Father in a garden.

We are grateful for Naturalists, who remind us that it is necessary

ON YOUR OWN
Consider the following:

Do other people come to mind who may be Naturalists? If so, list them in your journal.

Is there someone you might want to talk with this week about what you have learned about this spiritual temperament?

What have you learned about yourself from reading about this spiritual temperament?

If you have a Naturalist spiritual temperament, thank God now for the gift He has given you of loving the outdoors and seeing His hand in the smallest detail of what He's created. Thank Him, too, for fashioning you to call others to slow down and notice His handiwork. And in this busy world where people often rush right past all that the Creator has given us in the natural beauty around us, thank Him for the gift you are to God and to others. Write out your prayer in your journal.

to take time to smell the flowers. The Naturalist helps us keep in mind that we are not in control—of the sky, the weather, the elements, or life itself. While we may talk about being the captains of our fate and the masters of our ships, the Naturalist scoffs and points out that even the biggest and best vessels are subject to the powerful impulses of ocean waves. They help us worship the God of detail and design, the God of true ecology and order.

If you are a person who feels closer to God out in nature than indoors, and if you get great joy from praying and communing with

God as you observe His handiwork, you may have a Naturalist spiritual temperament. If you find your heart involuntarily moved heavenward by being at the beach or in a wooded glen, or if you readily see lessons about the Almighty as you observe what He has made, your Naturalist score is probably rather high.

After reading the description of the Naturalist, check your spiritual temperament score on page 27. Do you agree with your Naturalist score? If not, review the spiritual temperament questions on pages 21 to 26 (particularly questions 7, 16, 25, 34, 43, and 52), and see how you might revise your answers. Even though your exact score is not as important as the insight you've gained about yourself and your relationship with God, record your revised score here: _____ .

SENSATES: LOVING GOD THROUGH THE SENSES

Record your spiritual temperament score for the Sensate from page 27. _____
Is it high, medium, or low? _____

There is a place of worship I've heard about in Southern California that was designed to attract those who don't regularly attend church: young artists and people who think outside the box (or those who say, "What box?"). This church is also a place that accommodates people with Sensate spiritual temperaments—those who love the Lord through utilizing their God-given senses. Those who attend are invited to taste, touch, and smell as they enjoy the Lord. Instead of pews, they sit at round tables where food and coffee are available; there are stations in the sanctuary where people can draw or paint during the service, including a sand tray for those who want to create something with their hands. Many of the people I know who attend here have Sensate spiritual temperaments and find it a wonderfully alive place to meet with God and one another.

Throughout the ages, we've used the five senses to know and experience God. Gary Thomas says, "Christianity without beauty becomes a disembodied religion of the mind."[42] Human artistry and beauty have long been employed to mediate the loveliness of God. C. S. Lewis wrote that beauty was a pathway to God, and as early as the first century, the Russian emissaries of Prince Vladimir penned their experience of the

Greek Orthodox Church, saying that as they entered the place, they knew not whether they were in heaven or on earth. "For on earth there is no such splendor or such beauty, and we are at a loss to describe it."[43]

Characteristics of the Sensate

Those with Sensate spiritual temperaments use all their senses—taste, touch, smell, sound, and sight—to focus more fully on Jesus. Easily lost in the awe and splendor of God, Sensates find themselves particularly drawn to God when they are in the presence of beauty, such as intricate architecture, classical music, formal language, incense, icons, or stained glass. Just as the Naturalist enjoys God's creation in the outdoors, so the Sensate enjoys the splendor of what humankind—made in the likeness and image of God—creates to reveal and illustrate God. I found this to be true when I visited the Sistine Chapel in Rome. As I sat there staring at Michelangelo's amazing depiction of the Kingdom of God—from Creation through the Fall to the final glory—I'd never quite *experienced* the spiritual battle as vividly in all the reading I'd done, and I was mesmerized by the visual details that enabled me to more fully grasp the subtle truths unveiled in paint. As I studied the walls and ceilings of that chapel, I thought of all the people who might never pick up a theology book and realized how limiting we are when we believe that the primary way to learn about God is through printed words on a page. How wonderful it was to study biblical truth through image and vision. I walked away thinking, *That Michelangelo was quite a theologian!*

Today, I meet quite a few Sensates who see spiritual meaning come alive on the screen, through movies such as *The Lord of the Rings* or *The Matrix*. For the Sensate, visual imagery has become a mediator of the invisible Kingdom of God.

Biblical Examples of Sensates

To say that God is the God of the Sensate is an understatement, for the Bible is brimming with instances in which the Lord Himself employed all the senses to give His people greater knowledge of Himself:

- He gave the Israelites a land flowing with milk and honey (see Numbers 13).

- He descended in visible glory on Mount Sinai (see Exodus 24:16-17).
- His glory fell on and engulfed the Tabernacle and the Temple (see Exodus 40:34; 2 Chronicles 7:1-3).
- He commanded a burnt offering of bulls and lambs that must have smelled like a barbecue (see Leviticus 3:5; Deuteronomy 33:10).
- He gave His people intricate details about how to make the Temple, including beautiful art forms of gold, silver, bronze, and wood, with fine linen embroidery (see Exodus 35:31-35).
- He invites us to worship Him with thunderous cymbals and other instruments (see Psalm 150).
- He came to Ezekiel in a vision, allowing him to *feel* the wind and the cloud filling the Temple; *see* the flashes of lightning, the brilliant light, and the magnificent throne of sapphire; *hear* the roar of rushing water, the sound of wings, and a loud rumbling; and then *eat* the sweet-tasting scroll (see Ezekiel 1:4, 26-27; 3:1-3, 12-15).[44]

Jesus Himself used the senses when He spat in the dirt to make mud, putting it on the eyes of the blind man (see John 9:6), touched a leper and a blind man to heal them (see Matthew 8:3; 9:29), and revealed Himself with vivid white hair, a golden girdle, eyes of flaming fire, glowing feet of bronze, and a voice that was like the sound of many waters (see Revelation 1:10-16).

As we look at the five senses, we can see how throughout time they have led us to experience a God of mystery and wonder.

Sound: In the Old Testament times, Scripture was always read out loud, as the words were said to be "spirated," or God-breathed. Thousands of years later, Martin Luther argued that Scripture was meant to be heard, not just silently read, and that listening to the Bible, along with the music of Bach or Handel was a great spiritual experience. Handel himself talked of "transcendental keys," any key signature with five to eight sharps, which he associated with heaven.[45]

Touch: Orthodox worship includes a cross, an altar, a holy instrument, and frequent kissing.[46] In Protestant churches, we touch during dedication ceremonies and baptisms. The Bible tells us in four different passages to greet one another with a holy kiss (Romans 16:16; 1 Corinthians 16:20; 2 Corinthians 13:12; 1 Thessalonians 5:26).

Taste: References to taste can be seen throughout the Bible. The psalmist said, "Taste and see that the LORD is good" (Psalm 34:8); "How sweet are your words to my taste" (Psalm 119:103); "You are the salt of the earth. But if the salt loses its saltiness, how can it be made salty again?" (Matthew 5:13); "Whoever is thirsty, let him come; and whoever wishes, let him take the free gift of the water of life" (Revelation 22:17). Jesus Himself invites us to taste the bread and drink the wine that represent His body and blood (see Matthew 26:26-28), and Jesus spent His last hours on earth preparing a meal for His disciples (see John 21:13).

Sight: Sight is probably our most powerful sense. Gary Thomas accurately states, "The use of sight in Christian worship and prayer is rooted in the incarnation."[47] The Word became flesh; Jesus came partly so we could *see* God in His fullness. "Creation itself is a great work of art, and all works after it are echoes of the original."[48] During the Renaissance, about the same time Martin Luther was posting his theses on the door of the Castle Church in Wittenberg, Raphael and other sculptors, painters, and architects were recording God's truths in marble, wood, and stone. Before the common person could read a religious manuscript, Michelangelo was constructing a textbook using canvas, walls, and marble, signifying that paint and stone have amazing power to bring spiritual truths alive. The great architecture of the Greek, Roman, Byzantine, Romanesque, Gothic, and Renaissance periods, with their magnificent icons, mediated a spiritual grandeur that has for years renewed those who love the Lord.

Smell: The sense of smell always reinforces our experiences. God's people have long used spices and incense to worship Him. God's Word says, "In every place incense and pure offerings will be brought to my name" (Malachi 1:11). Psychologically, our minds are sharpened and altered in the presence of incense.[49] In Eastern Orthodoxy, incense represents the prayers of the saints as they arise to heaven.[50] The apostle Paul even refers to God's people as a sweet fragrance of Jesus (see 2 Corinthians 2:14-16).

Kinesthetic: While doing my doctoral work, I stumbled across dozens of people who told me they connected best with God through movement, or the *kinesthetic* sense. Just as Jesus met the disciples while they were walking on the road to Emmaus, so, too, many people speak of meeting Jesus today while walking or being on the move. For example, in one class where I taught on the spiritual temperaments, Howard reported that he sensed God's presence most strongly when he was driving his car, adding, "Boy, can I pray when I get behind the wheel!" A woman in the same class told me that she connects best with God when she is vacuuming. Their comments confirmed what I had heard again and again—for some people, movement ushers in their "sacred space." Whether sewing, building something in a workshop, jogging, or walking, many individuals sense God's nearness most when they are in the midst of movement.

I could identify with this because some of my most meaningful times with the Lord have been while I'm swimming laps in the pool. The repetitive motion seems to unclog my soul, not to mention the way the water becomes a metaphor for God holding, surrounding, and carrying me. I am more able to focus when I swim because it's during those times that what's inside my soul comes out to the Godhead with the least amount of effort. When I swim, there are few distractions, allowing me to have a heightened awareness of God. Worship and oneness seem to flow. My friend says she often feels the Lord's pleasure when she runs (like Eric Liddell in *Chariots of Fire*). It's then that she tends to get her best ideas as well. This may be because during exercise, oxygen is flowing in full force to our whole bodies—including the brain—and since we aren't using our minds for anything taxing, all that oxygen allows us to think our best thoughts—and perhaps sense God's Spirit best too.

It actually makes sense that the kinesthetic—which literally means "to move"—would be a customary way of connecting with God, since so much of what God created moves, from the smallest cells to the largest stars. Since movement is part of God's design, it seems logical that a God of motion would meet His people through the kinesthetic sense.

If some of the following statements are true about you, God may be meeting you through the kinesthetic:

- "I try to sit still and be with God, but I connect better with Him when I am doing something with my hands."
- "I get antsy when I try to read the Bible in one spot, and I focus much better by using Scripture memory cards as I walk or run errands."
- "I feel stuck and can't get the words out when I sit or kneel in prayer, but when I get up and move, the communication begins to flow freely."

Certainly for some people, movement seems to free the mind and heart to engage with God; thus it is good to recognize that the kinesthetic sense is another way to love Jesus.

The church owes a great deal to those with Sensate spiritual temperaments who create objects of beauty that draw us closer to God. Much of Europe is filled with the paintings and architecture of masterful artisans who found great pleasure in creating tangible expressions of God's excellence and majesty. Today's evangelical churches would benefit greatly from using more of the visual and tactile to aid people in knowing and loving God.

If you like the thought of drawing in your journal as you pray or attending a church where all your senses come alive so that you can almost see, smell, hear, taste, and touch the majesty of God, the Sensate spiritual temperament may accurately describe you. And if you are a creative person who likes the thought of Old Testament worship, with its poignant smells and colorful regalia, or if you find a High Church service attractive, with its formal Communion and incense, you might find your Sensate score to be rather high.

After reading this description of the Sensate, now check your spiritual temperament score on page 27. Do you agree with your Sensate score? If not, review the spiritual temperament questions on pages 21 to 26 (particularly questions 8, 17, 26, 35, 44, and 53), and see how you might revise your answers. Even though your exact score is not as important as the insight you've gained about yourself and your relationship with God, record your revised score here: _____ .

ON YOUR OWN

Consider the following:

Do other people come to mind who may be Sensates? If so, list them in your journal.

Is there someone you might want to talk with this week about what you have learned about this spiritual temperament?

What have you learned about yourself from reading about this spiritual temperament?

If you have a Sensate spiritual temperament, thank God now for the gift He has given you of creating and appreciating beauty and form. Thank Him, too, for the part you play in displaying to a world that overemphasizes the cognitive just how important it is to worship God with our whole bodies by using all the senses, and thus for the gift you are to Jesus and to others. Write out your prayer in your journal.

TRADITIONALISTS: LOVING GOD THROUGH RITUAL AND SYMBOL

Record your spiritual temperament score for the Traditionalist from page 27: _____ .
Is it high, medium, or low? _____

When Father Mike invited me to attend his church, I was curiously interested. I'd never been to an Episcopal church before, so I was rather eager to see what it was like. That Sunday, I wasn't quite sure what to expect, but as the service began and a young person wearing a formal robe entered holding a large cross above her head, I felt an unexpected stirring. Then another person came in holding an open Bible. As she walked past me down the aisle, I began to tear up. Later during the Communion service, as Father Mike prayed, lifting the cup heavenward, I choked up again. Although I wasn't quite sure just why my emotions were bubbling up, as I knelt at the altar to take the Eucharist, I felt as though my soul was being fed more profoundly than I'd ever remembered. Something about the rituals, the liturgical patterns, and the symbols that day transported me into an awareness of the Holy Spirit's presence, filling me with an enormous appreciation for Jesus Christ.

Although I wasn't totally certain what had happened in my soul, the sense of God's sweet companionship lingered with me all the next week. I knew that I hadn't been stimulated by the upbeat praise music or three-point sermon I generally hear in the church I attend; instead, I'd somehow been carried to the transcendent God who is wholly Other. Perhaps Gertrud Mueller Nelson captures it best when she says that the age-old rituals and symbols help us move into the timeless stream of God:

> God proceeded to create a world of order with space, matter, time, life, and humans in his own image. Through ritual and ceremonies we people in turn make order out of chaos. In endless space, we create a fixed point to orient ourselves: a sacred space. To timelessness we impose rhythmic repetitions: the recurrent feast. . . . What is too vast and shapeless, we deal with in smaller, manageable pieces. We do this for practicality but we also do this for high purpose: to relate safely to the mysterious, to communicate with the transcendent.[51]

Author Von Ogden Vogt said that people can't understand the truth without a symbol, a sacrament, or a rite with which to express that truth. Others have noted that rituals and symbols give us a piece of the eternal, almost like a child at the beach trying to hold on to a bit of the vast ocean by digging a hole in the sand to catch some water as the current brings it to shore. As we attempt to contain the uncontainable, we are aware that "the power of the Almighty needs, sometimes, to be guarded against but it also needs to be beckoned, called forth and wooed."[52]

Such is the heartbeat of the Traditionalist spiritual temperament. The practices that have held our faith securely in place for centuries still serve as the entry point into knowing a timeless, changeless God. Indeed, it is through the age-old symbols and rituals of the church that Traditionalists experience God's majesty.

Characteristics of the Traditionalist

All of us, to some degree, like traditions: We bring gifts to weddings, sing songs while the candles are blown out on birthday cakes, and prefer to open our Christmas presents on Christmas Eve rather than Christmas Day—or vice versa. We may choose to hide Easter eggs or bake particular foods to observe specific holidays. For example, on our wedding anniversary, my husband and I always return to Morro Bay, California, where we spent our honeymoon. We stay at the same hotel, eat at some of our same favorite restaurants, and meander through the ocean in our red kayak just as we did that first year. Why? Because it feels good to recreate that celebration of love that we initially shared together by revisiting that familiar place. In a small way, it helps us relive how we felt about one another way back when, and it causes us to reflect on the ever-present meaning behind our love. Traditions help us to *remember*, and this remembering enhances our current joy.

Those with Traditionalist spiritual temperaments are simply taking this aspect of remembering and converting it to matters of the faith. God says that He remembers, and He instructs us to remember too: Remember the Sabbath; remember that He brought His people out of slavery in Egypt; remember the new covenant given by the Lord Jesus in Communion. Remembering is essential, and traditions help us to look back and remember.

Traditionalists enjoy worship, prayer, Communion, Bible reading, and other faith practices when they are done in familiar ways, realizing that these rituals help them join hands and hearts with the saints of old. Something about continuity and sameness ushers in the presence of God for the Traditionalist. Gary Thomas says, "Rituals, like sacraments, provide a way for us to enter into God's glory and still be protected from a force that is too great for human experience."[53]

I experienced this sense of glory and simultaneous connection with the history of the faith when I worshipped in Father Mike's church. That Sunday, as I heard the homily being given to his little congregation in California, I realized that Anglicans in every city all over the world were hearing the same Bible passage on the very same day. I remembered the Anglican church I'd attended in Jerusalem and was warmed by the sense of solidarity, feeling strangely present to that city and its people. That association elevated me above the here and now, and a piece of my heart was reconnected to those worshipping in that faraway place—both now and then.

Perhaps that sense of timelessness is what moves the Traditionalist most. I experienced it again when I visited a Presbyterian church one Sunday as the deacons and elders were being ordained. Suddenly it dawned on me that I had been ordained in a Presbyterian church years before on that same Sunday of the year. During the ceremony, all those in that church who had been previously ordained came forward to pray for the newly appointed elders and deacons. As I watched, more than fifty saints—most of whom had white hair—walked to the front to pray for the newly ordained, lingering to hug one another after prayer. Though I knew no one, I was unexpectedly moved by these gestures of continuity, support, accountability, and heritage. The past elders represented years of loving and serving God, and as the saints who had served before surrounded the new ordinates, I envisioned the greater crowd of witnesses spoken of in Hebrews 12 cheering them on from the heavenlies. That day I felt an unforeseen bond with those faithful witnesses who had gone before me to glory.

When I was a child, I enjoyed many of the customs in the church we occasionally attended. In fact, I liked knowing what was coming next during the service. We stood as the Word of God was read, bowed our heads for prayer, observed a moment of silence, and dressed up to show our respect for God and His house. Today I wonder if our lack of attention to detail fosters a casualness with God that undermines our adoration of Him. Gary Thomas says that if we are flippant toward God's symbols, we may also be flippant toward what they represent.[54]

When I was in Russia teaching the Bible, no Russian would ever place that sacred book on the floor, because they valued it so highly—often kissing it when it was given to them or holding it against their chests. For those just exiting Communism who had never laid eyes on a Bible before, to put that sacred book on the floor was an inexcusable act of disrespect for the God who was disclosed in its pages.

Of course, traditionalism goes beyond our personal enjoyment of symbols to that which is vitally more important: holding in place the historic truths of the faith, beliefs that were never intended to be morphed or changed or personalized so that their original meaning was lost. Traditions are utilized to guard against our tendency to make personal that which was initially communal—a faith given to a nation, a people, and an assembly now called the body of Christ. The Christian faith is only authentic and real when its people are united around a common belief in one Lord, one faith, and one baptism. And this is the safety and consolation of tradition. For long before individuals had access to Scripture, they repeatedly recited the essential doctrines of the faith through creeds, such as the Nicene Creed:

> We believe in one God, the Father Almighty, Maker of heaven and earth, and of all things visible and invisible.
>
> And in one Lord Jesus Christ, the only-begotten Son of God, begotten of the Father before all worlds, God of God, Light of Light, Very God of Very God, begotten, not made, being of one substance with the Father, by whom all things were made; who for us men, and for our salvation, came down from heaven, and was incarnate by the Holy Spirit of the Virgin Mary, and was made man, and was crucified also for us under Pontius Pilate. He suffered and was buried, and the third day He rose again according to the Scriptures, and ascended into heaven, and sits on the right hand of the Father. And he shall come again with glory to judge both the quick and the dead, whose kingdom shall have no end.
>
> And we believe in the Holy Spirit, the Lord and Giver of Life, who proceeds from the Father and the Son, who with the Father and the Son together is worshipped and glorified, who spoke by the prophets.

And we believe in one holy catholic and apostolic Church. We
acknowledge one baptism for the remission of sins. And we look
for the resurrection of the dead, and the life of the world to come.
Amen.

Without such creeds, which have been handed down for centuries,
the church would have lost the fundamental substance of her faith. If
you have ever sat through a sermon that was chock-full of error and
biblical distortion, you might be forever grateful to the Traditionalist
spiritual temperament, which could be needed more in our churches
today than ever before!

Obviously, rituals can be observed without any genuine connection
to the Lord, and symbols do not necessarily carry inherent meaning in
and of themselves. However, the Lord's people, the church of God, have
been attributing a common meaning and significance to these symbols
and traditions for centuries. Because significant worth has been passed
down with each tradition from generation to generation, the essence of
our faith is now embedded in the symbols themselves. I never understood
the significance of the cross to Catholic believers until I spent a week in a
monastery. The Catholic cross, which bears the image of a suffering Savior,
is immensely important, because seeing Christ's passion when looking at
the cross is a reminder of what our Savior went through, modeling the
cost of faith in today's narcissistic world. Just as Hebrews 12 exhorts us to
fix our eyes on Jesus so that we will not grow weary and lose heart, so we
can literally fix our eyes on Jesus every time we look at the Catholic cross,
knowing that His suffering models for us the capacity to endure. When we
see what He undertook for us, we are encouraged to trust God, no matter
what we experience.

Biblical Examples of Traditionalists

In the Bible, we see many examples of Traditionalists:

- Abraham and his family built altars to signify where God had
  met them, taking seriously those occasions when Jehovah
  had spoken His word to them. These altars symbolized their
  worship of a God who is faithful to His promises; they became
  stones of remembrance, memorials to commemorate what God

had done for Abraham and his family. The nation of Israel understood that God is not casual about how we worship Him. He gave the Israelites an exact pattern for building the Tabernacle, each item becoming a symbolic representation of a spiritual truth (see Exodus 25:40). The book of Leviticus gives specific instructions on how and when to make offerings to God, and the Israelites were instructed on the generational use of tassels to be sewn on their garments to help them remember the commandments of the Lord (see Numbers 15:37-40).

- Moses made a bronze serpent for the people to look at so that they could be healed (see Numbers 21:9).
- Ezra upheld the rituals and ceremonies of the faith when he proclaimed fasts, offered sacrifices, mourned for sin, made confession, and publicly read Scripture (see Ezra 7:16-17; 8:21).
- In the New Testament, the disciples observed Jewish feasts, and the early church remembered Jesus during the Lord's Supper (see Acts 2:42-47; 1 Corinthians 11:17-34).

Jesus Himself kept the traditions when He went every year to Jerusalem to observe the Passover with His parents, stood in the synagogue on the Sabbath to read the scrolls, and reclined at the table with the men going to Emmaus, blessing and breaking the bread (see Luke 4:16; 24:30). The word *remember* is used 170 times in the Bible, and whether we are Traditionalists by spiritual temperament or not, we are commanded to recollect the acts of God on behalf of His people (see Psalm 105:5; 143:5). Because our God is the same yesterday, today, and forever (see Hebrews 13:8), His character and goodness can still be trusted today.

The symbolism from the past continues to influence many modern churches in the twenty-first century. Initially, Sunday was set aside as the day of worship to represent the time Jesus rose from the dead. Communion was instituted as a regular occurrence to remember the covenant Jesus made with His people (see Mark 14:24; 1 Corinthians 11:25), and of course, the cross represents Christ's suffering and resurrection as well as our redemption from sin. In the early church (and in some denominations today), colors were also used as symbols: white signified the purity of Easter and Christmas; red spoke of the cross, and purple was used during Lent, Holy Week, and Advent, signifying the union of love and pain. Black was used only on Good Friday.[55]

Although Traditionalists are sometimes considered to be old-fashioned or thought of as stick-in-the-muds, they surely play an essential role today. Traditionalists serve as gatekeepers, guarding the slow erosion of the sacred that can occur through slight modifications to the truth. They call us back again and again to the tried-and-true tenets of the faith of our forefathers and mothers. As they remind us of the transcendence of the Almighty and of His awe-inspiring presence, beauty, and influence, they will not be inclined to yield easily to new fads or spiritual whims. When the "me" generation tries to personalize a faith that is first and foremost corporate, Traditionalists remind us that "sweet little Jesus boy" is also the wonderful Counselor, the almighty God, the everlasting Father, and the Prince of Peace (see Isaiah 9:6). They will not let us forget that Jehovah is now and always will be the holy One of Israel, and that though He is sometimes quietly present, He is still the Commander of the heavenly host (see Daniel 8:11). It is equally important that while the Contemplative is referring to God as Friend and Bridegroom, the Traditionalist is describing Him as the exalted One who is high and lifted up (see Isaiah 52:13), the King of kings and Lord of lords (see Deuteronomy 10:17). This God, who is active from the "beginning to the end of time, from every here to every there, from every now to every then,"[56] is indeed eternal and changeless. We are grateful for the Traditionalist spiritual temperament, which takes us back to these fundamental realities of our faith, and of our God!

If you enjoy following a Christian calendar during family prayer time, or if you like to use the *Book of Common Prayer* for a personal ritual (or rule) of prayer—especially if it connects you to other believers who practice the same rule—you may find that you have a Traditionalist spiritual temperament. If learning more about the meaning of symbols and liturgy in the church is appealing to you, or if you like to worship in a familiar way that reminds you of your childhood, your Traditionalist spiritual temperament score is probably somewhat high.

After reading the description of the Traditionalist, check your spiritual temperament score on page 27. Do you agree with your Traditionalist score? If not, review the spiritual temperament questions

on pages 21 to 26 (particularly questions 9, 18, 27, 36, 45, and 54), and
see how you might revise your answers. Even though your exact score
is not as important as the insight you've gained about yourself and your
relationship with God, record your revised score here: _____ .

ON YOUR OWN
Consider the following:

Do other people come to mind who may be Traditionalists? If so,
list them in your journal.

Is there someone you might want to talk with this week about
what you have learned about this spiritual temperament?

What have you learned about yourself from reading about this
spiritual temperament?

If you have a Traditionalist spiritual temperament, thank God now
for the gift of grace He has given you to embrace ceremony and
hold tightly to the community of faith that is grounded in centuries
of well-established practices. Thank the Lord, too, for the part you
play in displaying the ageless One to a world that values the new
and novel, and for the gift you are to the Lord and to others. Write
out your prayer in your journal.

FOR FURTHER REFLECTION AND DISCUSSION

1. After reading about each of the nine spiritual temperaments, circle
   any of the following outcomes you hope to gain from learning
   more about your spiritual preferences:

a. I aspire to enhance my spiritual growth as I understand more completely how my spiritual preferences affect my sense of closeness to God.

b. I desire to redeem feelings of guilt, inadequacy, or shame that have arisen in the past from comparing myself with others and their walks with God.

c. I look forward to moving past feelings of being stuck, dry, bored, or frustrated in my relationship with God.

d. I want to comprehend and appreciate the unique wiring of those around me whom I love.

e. I hope to gain balance in my spiritual life from spiritual temperaments that are unlike my own, giving me a fresh glimpse of God.

f. Other:

2. What surprises, if any, did you experience while reading this chapter?

3. What aspects of your relationship with God were confirmed in reading about the nine spiritual temperaments?

4. What did you learn from this chapter about those close to you and their spiritual temperaments?

4

HOW DOES MY SPIRITUAL TEMPERAMENT HELP ME LOVE GOD?

"Now what?" Kim asked after discovering that she has a Sensate spiritual temperament. "Do I simply keep worshipping God like I always have? Or since learning how I best connect with the Lord, is there more for me to do?" I was thrilled with her question!

I told Kim that knowing our spiritual temperaments is only a starting place. It is a bit like learning about our spiritual gifts; the information brings new insight, but once we have that insight, we must learn to use our gifts, develop our gifts, and mature as Christians with our gifts. First Corinthians 13 tells us that a spiritual gift does not a mature Christian make. In fact, the apostle Paul says it is possible to speak with the tongues of men and of angels, have all knowledge, possess the faith to move mountains, and give all our possessions to the poor, yet still miss the point of loving God and others. In the same way, it is possible to have an Ascetic spiritual temperament—to fast, pray, and spend long periods in silence with God—yet not grow to maturity because in our quietness, we are not responding to Jesus when He tells us to leave our sanctuary and give our neighbor a ride to work. Or we can have a Traditionalist spiritual temperament and know and cherish all the creeds of the faith, but if we aren't willing to obey God when that hurting person next to us who seems to be getting it all wrong is in need, how will the Lord and His body be benefited?

Yes, while loving God and walking with Him according to how we are wired is important, spiritual growth also requires that we keep on maturing in the grace and knowledge of our Lord Jesus Christ (see

2 Peter 3:18)—going from little children spiritually who realize our sins are forgiven, to spiritual young adults who have overcome the evil one, to fathers and mothers of the faith who know God intimately and fully (see 1 John 2:12-13). Our lives progress day by day until Jesus' prayer is answered and the oneness He shared with the Father becomes our oneness, enabling us to reflect the Lord to a world that desperately needs Him (see John 17:20-23).

As you develop the kind of partnership with God that brings a greater and more full-orbed life with Him, you will move past simply knowing your spiritual temperament. That connection is your starting point with God—your "soil preference," as it were—but then you must plant the seeds of faith and tend the seedlings as the fruit of God's life is produced in you. There really is more for us to do.

Gary Thomas tells a story about two women who planted vegetable gardens. Both prepared the soil and planted the seeds, but only one tended her garden, watering and weeding it, putting little cages around her tomato plants to protect them as they grew. She delighted in her garden, and when her food was ready to be harvested, she gathered a basketful of vegetables every day, enough for herself and her family, with extra veggies to share with her neighbors.

The other woman in his story left her garden untended as she waited for her vegetables to grow. When the time came for the food to be harvested, she found that all her tomatoes were rotten and the other plants were already picked over by birds and squirrels. While she did manage to harvest a few edible vegetables, she barely had enough for her own family, much less anything to share with others. After that, the woman decided she didn't really want a garden, opting instead to use the grocery store, which was a much easier way for her to eat.[1]

I like this story because classical spirituality encourages Christians to think of their souls as gardens where they commune with the Lord. The way to nurture that garden will be unique according to each spiritual temperament, but the nurturing itself is crucial for all. Understanding your spiritual temperament or God language provides a pathway for you to care for your soul-garden; then, once you understand your preference, you can choose to cultivate your soul—in both familiar and unfamiliar ways—as you enlarge your capacity to know and love God.

Knowing and appreciating how we best and most naturally connect with God frees us to move unhindered toward the Lord in that way. Jesus said we please the Father when we love Him with all our hearts, souls, minds, and strength, as well as love our neighbors as ourselves. With that in mind, we can be assured that God Himself will do His part in maintaining our relationship of loving intimacy. For the Lord not only longs for that relationship with us, He also promises to help it grow forever (see Philippians 1:6).

GOD'S PART AND OUR PART

One summer while I was in college, I needed a place to stay for a few months. As a fairly new Christian, I asked a friend who had known the Lord a lot longer, "How do I go about finding an apartment? I mean, do I just pray and wait, or do I get out there and pound the pavement looking for rentals?" My friend said something I will never forget: "The Lord can't move a parked car, so just start looking *and* praying for a place at the same time; then see what He provides." After that he added, "Remember, the Christian life is 100 percent God's business and 100 percent our business; in other words, God will do *everything* for us we cannot do for ourselves, but He won't do *anything* for us we can do for ourselves—or He would ultimately be spoiling and disempowering us, and we would never grow up." This perspective has remained with me all these years.

So it is in all of our lives with God; He does His part and we do ours. However, I think we sometimes get our part and God's part mixed up, trying to do things we cannot do (such as making ourselves more like Jesus) while neglecting to do the things we can do (such as talking to God openly and honestly about every detail of our lives). We have a part to play in the equation, but God is the One who causes the internal spiritual change to take place. Just as we must till the earth, plant the seeds, and water them—that's our part—we also depend on God to change the seed in the hiddenness of the earth and create a living plant—that's His part. As the Bible says,

> Just as you trusted Christ to save you, trust him, too, for each
> day's problems; live in vital union with him. Let your roots

grow down into him and draw up nourishment from him. See
that you go on growing in the Lord, and become strong and
vigorous in the truth you were taught. Let your lives overflow
with joy and thanksgiving for all he has done.

Colossians 2:6-7 (TLB)

THE PLACE OF DESIRE AND DISCIPLINE IN LOVING GOD

I've heard that in order for soil to remain healthy, the farmer must
rotate the crops. One farmer I know said that planting different crops
each year is vital because different plants require different minerals
from the soil and they also give back to the soil different types of nutri-
ents. Therefore, the quality of the crops—year after year—depends
upon rotating and alternating them.

When it comes to our soul-gardens, two essential ingredients also
need to be rotated: *spiritual desire* and *spiritual discipline.* Spiritual desire
draws us to Jesus, and spiritual discipline keeps us engaged. Spiritual
desire and spiritual discipline actually feed each other: Discipline
protects and nurtures desire, while desire grows more healthy when
disciplined. In other words, desire brings me to the table so I can eat,
and discipline helps me decide what to eat, when to eat, and how much
to eat.

Jesus often utilized both desire and discipline to draw followers
to Himself. Remember the rich young ruler who came to Jesus seeking
eternal life? Jesus affirmed the man's *desire* to have eternal life, then
added a *discipline* to it—something for the young man to do. Jesus
told him to sell all his possessions and make space in his life to live
with Him. Once the young man made being with Jesus his priority,
he would find what he'd been looking for—eternal life with God (see
Matthew 19:16-22).[2]

Today the Lord offers us the same deal. We come to Him with
our desires and He shows us how those desires will be met through
the discipline of walking with Him and trusting Him. As we develop
well-formed habits of the heart, our desires for Him are safeguarded,
strengthened, and protected. Thus, our spiritual temperaments are
starting points that direct our desires toward God, while discipline
provides the tools we need for that love to broaden and deepen.

HOW SPIRITUAL DESIRE AND DISCIPLINE WORK TOGETHER

Where is it that your passion for Christ is most often stirred? Where do you find your sacred space? That is the place to begin, the place where your spiritual temperament is operating. As Thomas states:

> God wants to know the real you, not a caricature of what somebody else wants you to be. He created you with a certain personality and a certain spiritual temperament. God wants your worship, according to the way he made you. That may differ somewhat from the worship of the person who brought you to Christ or the person who leads your Bible study or church.[3]

Your God-given desires serve as your basic starting point and can continue to function as a compass along the way. James Houston, author, professor, and spiritual director, says that when we come to God, we must begin where He is creating desire for Himself within us. The spiritual disciplines are only helpful as they nurture, give shape to, strengthen, and protect that desire.[4]

Thus, it is good to begin—and return often—to your God-given desires when you are growing in your relationship with Jesus. Then the spiritual disciplines become space holders, practices that allow your love to grow. They act as friends that help you get from where you are to where you want to be spiritually. The disciplines provide accountable routines that water and nurture the outcomes you desire—and these outcomes *will* follow, because the Lord, in His goodness, has built the law of sowing and reaping into His universe.

> Don't be misled—you cannot mock the justice of God. You will always harvest what you plant.   *Galatians 6:7 (NLT)*

In other words, when you sow love-disciplines, you reap more love. As you use the spiritual disciplines to train and strengthen your desire, the result is more desire, which requires more discipline to integrate that desire, and so on. Like crop rotation, it becomes a circular process that keeps going: desire, discipline, more desire, more discipline. As James Houston writes, we must be careful that we don't let ourselves off the hook because of our temperaments, since growth often lies in the opposite direction of what feels most natural,[5] and we will shrink our souls if we feed them only what they want.[6]

MORE ABOUT THE PLACE OF SPIRITUAL DISCIPLINES

Although I have been writing and speaking about the place of spiritual desire and discipline for years, I recently found a book that confirms what I believe. Adele Ahlberg Calhoun's book *Spiritual Disciplines Handbook: Practices That Transform Us* describes the interplay between desire and discipline quite nicely. She says that our desires come from our innate need to open our lives to God in worship, and the spiritual disciplines fuel those desires.[7] For example, when you desire to know how God's mind and heart intersect with your life, you employ the spiritual discipline of Bible study; when you desire to gaze more deeply upon God in His works and words, you use the spiritual discipline of meditation; and when you desire to be a safe person who offers others the grace, shelter, and presence of Jesus, you utilize the spiritual discipline of hospitality. In this way, spiritual hunger (desire) and spiritual habits (discipline) go hand in hand.

So what disciplines do you need? Much has been written about the spiritual disciplines (in the Greek, *askein*, meaning "to practice"), but let me highlight a few definitions that might be helpful. Richard Foster says that the spiritual disciplines are God's way of getting us into the ground (as a farmer sows a seed) and that they become "the means by which we place ourselves where [God] can bless us."[8] To this, Dallas Willard adds that spiritual disciplines are activities we do that are within our power in order to bring about changes that only God can do, which are outside our power.[9] According to Henri Nouwen, spiritual disciplines create space in our souls for us to hear the voice of the One who calls us His beloved. Marjorie Thompson says that spiritual disciplines provide structure and direction, patterns in life—attitudes, behaviors, and elements that are routine, repeated, and regular—and these structures act like trellises that help us as we grow spiritually.[10] And finally, Eugene Peterson likens spiritual disciplines to gardening tools that we use as needed from our spiritual toolsheds.[11] Thus, the spiritual disciplines become space holders, tools, and avenues of grace that can deepen our relationship with God.

I like to think of the spiritual disciplines as "love aids." They require effort on our part, but they must be practiced in grace rather than as a means of pleasing or gaining favor from God. The disciplines are not ends in themselves, but rather vehicles that propel us to where we want to go in our lives with the God who already completely loves us.

Let me give an illustration of how these love aids work in my life. Before I was married, I used to do certain household tasks only when I wanted to, such as doing the laundry or going to the grocery store. As a single person, I could sometimes go weeks without doing the laundry or going grocery shopping, yet once I was married, I learned rather quickly that my husband did not enjoy opening the fridge and finding it empty. Nor did he hold the same fascination with seeing what clothing combinations he could come up with when only a few clean items remained in his closet. I realized that because I loved him, I needed to add some disciplines to our lives together—some "love aids." These disciplines helped nurture the commitment we already shared by placing the routines and structures around our love that would protect it as it grew. Therefore, I inserted the discipline of weekly grocery shopping and laundry into my schedule.

In the same way, as we grow in our love for Jesus, the spiritual disciplines can be tools—love aids—that help us address our particular and specific areas of need. For example, if I find myself negative and complaining about the routine, mundane tasks I do for my children every day, I may choose to employ the discipline of service—doing big and little deeds for others that press me beyond myself as if I am doing them for Jesus. Thus, the discipline redirects me to the Lord in love. If I find myself constantly tempted to make poor choices, I can use the discipline of accountability within community to help me guard my heart and make wise decisions. From our toolshed of spiritual disciplines, we select the tools that speak to our particular needs at any given time. And because God created us for an eternal love relationship with Himself—a relationship that will always be our highest calling and joy (see John 15:9, 11)—we can trust that all the "gardening tools" we need to cultivate that relationship will forever be available to us.

Spiritually Healthy Disciplines

Spiritual disciplines are designed to promote spiritual health. Circle a few of the disciplines that might be helpful to you now. In your notebook or journal, consider how you can incorporate each of these into your daily routine.

Personal Spiritual Disciplines: Between You and the Lord

Bodily exercise—caring for your physical body in recognition that it is connected to your soul

Fasting—abstaining from food to increase your spiritual hunger

Journaling—recording your prayers, reflections, and devotions as offerings to God

Keeping the Sabbath—dedicating one day a week to God as a time to rest and remember Him

Praying the psalms—using Scripture to shape and inform your conversations with God

Silence—quieting yourself inwardly and outwardly so you can hear God more clearly

Solitude—spending dedicated time alone with God

Spiritual reading and meditation—allowing God's Word to speak into your life

Study—applying your mind and heart to God's Word

Relational Spiritual Disciplines: Between You, the Lord, and Others

Accountability—inviting someone to regularly ask you the hard questions about your life with God

Chastity—respecting your body and the bodies of others with purity in thought and action

Godly speech—committing to only enter into conversation that speaks truth and encouragement to others

Hospitality—welcoming others into your home and presence as you would receive Jesus

Justice—seeking in fairness the good, protection, and gain of others

Secrecy—ceasing to make your good deeds known

Service—doing big and little deeds for others that press you beyond yourself, just as you would do them for Jesus

Simplicity—ridding your life of the unnecessary so that God's Kingdom can be central

Witnessing—telling others your story about the life-changing power and love of God in your life

Corporate Spiritual Disciplines: Between You, the Lord, and the Community of Faith

Common worship—joining with your faith community as you praise God together

Communion—remembering Christ's sacrifice as you partake of the symbols of His body and blood with others

Confession—telling another person how you are missing the mark with God and praying together (see James 5:16)

Fellowship—practicing the "one anothers"—loving one another, praying for one another, encouraging one another, bearing one another's burdens, confessing sins to one another—in faithful, connected community (see John 13:34)

MORE ABOUT OUR GARDEN

The garden analogy is so fitting because the spiritual journey is about cultivating the beauty of our lives with God. The disciplines help us in the cultivation process as we prepare the soil and remove the rocks in our soul-gardens—those false notions about who we are or places in our hearts that have hardened around idols, becoming resistant to God's ways. Only in God's toolshed of grace can we find the implements needed to tend our gardens well.

My husband and I both love roses. In fact, we've planted nearly thirty rosebushes in our yard. But every time we place a new rosebush in the ground, we have to go through the same process of digging a hole, discovering a large rock just inches below the surface of the soil, removing the rock, mulching and fertilizing the soil, then planting the rosebush. You see, we live in Upland, California (which my husband has affectionately renamed *Rockland* for its endless supply of rocks). Upland—though a lovely city—was apparently built on a riverbed. Therefore, every time it rains, new rocks (I'm talking about one-foot by one-foot boulders!) seem to rise to the surface of the soil miraculously, out of nowhere.

My husband and I usually do the planting together: I decide what kind of rosebush should go where, he digs the hole and discovers the rocks, and I hand him a trowel or a shovel—but if neither of those works (one shovel actually broke while trying to remove a large rock), I bring him the pickax. Once the rocks are removed, we then mulch the soil and put the new bush into earth that is deep and rich enough for its roots to survive. Truthfully, if we didn't love roses so much, we certainly wouldn't go to this much trouble. But because we enjoy the beauty of a yard full of lovely, fragrant flowers year-round, we just keep working at it!

So it is with our soul-gardens. It takes a lot of desire to see the good stuff of God planted in our hearts—His beauty, grace, calmness, compassion, goodness, mercy, generosity of heart, patience, forgiveness, gentleness, self-restraint, others-centered love, peace, kindness, courage, faithfulness, strength, wisdom, goodness, and joy. And preparing the soil and planting the seeds is not something we can do alone. Just as I need the strength of another to remove the rocks in my yard, so we need God's Holy Spirit to remove the obstacles in our souls. Just as I use different implements in my rose garden, so the spiritual disciplines become tools that help create space for God's beauty and life to grow in me as you and I partner together in this endeavor. Attending to my

---

ON YOUR OWN

Draw a picture of your soul-garden in your notebook or journal. Include the flowers God has planted in you, those places of beauty that show others He lives in you.

What fruit of the Spirit do you see in your soul-garden?

What rocks remain that you need to trust God to partner with you to remove?

What tools (spiritual disciplines) might help you in this process of tending to your soul-garden?

"soul rocks"—those undeveloped places in my character that can choke the life of God right out of me—is indeed essential. Otherwise my faith may become shipwrecked or I may resort to wearing a spiritual facade (which would be equivalent to planting artificial flowers in my yard).

SPIRITUAL TEMPERAMENTS AND THE SPIRITUAL DISCIPLINES

To love God with all our hearts, souls, minds, and strength, we will eventually need to stretch beyond what feels like "home" spiritually. Once we've learned about our spiritual temperaments, we will always find those preferences helpful. But eventually we must choose to employ practices outside those preferences, some that may even feel awkward, not so that we can change our spiritual temperaments or master others, but because we know that certain spiritual practices will create the balance and maturity we need. As we stretch ourselves by deliberately exposing our souls to those unfamiliar practices we might otherwise resist, we *do* change and grow and deepen and broaden. As Kenneth Boa affirms,

> It is wise and spiritually healthy to identify your opposite preference, type, and temperament and to engage in the discipline of stretching yourself by trying an approach you would normally not pursue. Deliberate participation in a style or facet of spirituality that you are ordinarily inclined to avoid can be a significant source of spiritual growth and greater balance.[12]

We'll address this in much detail in part 2 of this book, where we look at several weeks of spiritual practice exercises for each of the nine spiritual temperaments. Remember that exposure to a breadth of spiritual practices can increase our hunger for God.

A SUMMARY

Knowing and capitalizing upon your spiritual desires and preferences while also attending to those practices outside your comfort zone can bring about the sturdiness needed to sustain a lifetime of faith. Eventually you may even grow to a place where your preferences no

longer direct you all that much, because your whole life is given over
to God; thus, every aspect and every situation becomes an opportunity
to love the Lord and His people. As your spiritual life becomes one of
greater, ever-deepening transformation through your surrender to
God's nature in you, you may find that you even develop an appetite for
dimensions of God that you did not have before. M. Robert Mulholland
Jr. describes it this way:

> The way to spiritual wholeness is through an increasingly faithful
> response to the One whose purpose shapes our path, whose grace
> redeems our detours, whose power liberates us from crippling
> bondages . . . and whose transforming Presence meets us at
> each turn on the road. In other words, holistic spirituality is a
> pilgrimage of deepening responsiveness to God's control of our
> lives and being.[13]

This is the journey; this is the spiritual life. But there is still more
to come, because as we partner with God together, our differing spiritual temperaments not only show forth various aspects of our Creator,
they also bring very real challenges as we live with others in the body
of Christ. Let's look now at how we can deal with our differences
creatively.

FOR FURTHER REFLECTION AND DISCUSSION

1. As you look at your spiritual temperament scores, what have you
   learned about yourself thus far? What spiritual longings do your
   temperaments reveal?

2. Since spiritual desire and spiritual discipline feed one another, how
   do desire and discipline play themselves out in your life? Is your
   desire for God calling out for more intentional use of the spiritual
   disciplines? How is your use of the spiritual disciplines creating
   more desire for God in you?

3. The Bible speaks about having a life with ever-deepening roots:
   "Blessed are those who trust in the LORD and have made the LORD
   their hope and confidence. They are like trees planted along a
   riverbank, with roots that reach deep into the water. Such trees are
   not bothered by the heat or worried by long months of drought.

Their leaves stay green, and they never stop producing fruit" (Jeremiah 17:7-8, NLT). Think about your life. If you are settling for a soul that lacks God's fruit, beauty, and strength, list several people who might be able to help you identify the obstacles that are preventing your roots from going deeper into the Lord. Ask God to help you have an authentic dialogue with one or more of these people about your soul-garden this week.

4. In Dallas Willard's book *Renovation of the Heart*, he says, "We usually know very little about the things that move in our own soul, the deepest level of our lives, or what is driving it. Our 'within' is astonishingly complex and subtle."[14] So it is with our soul-gardens. While God's desire is to nurture His life in us—His beauty, grace, calmness, compassion, mercy, generosity of heart, patience, forgiveness, self-restraint, others-centered love, peace, courage, and joy—we sometimes do not take the time to let the Lord do His unseen spiritual work in us. Reflect upon God's desire to nurture you, asking Him to reveal more to you about your own inward journey. Write your prayer here:

5

DENOMINATIONS AND DIFFERENCES IN THE CHURCH TODAY

Bruce really enjoys the small group that meets in his home every week. It is a lively bunch of individuals, and Bruce is especially delighted with the assortment of people. Leah is the facilitator of the group from Community Christian Church that has been together for two years. But lately a few people have not been showing up. One is Barry, a quiet man with an Ascetic spiritual temperament, who finds the times of silence in the group too infrequent and longs for the stillness that allows him to focus more completely on God. Then there is Olivia, an outgoing Enthusiast whose spiritual temperament brings gusto to the group. She likes to sing, stand, and clap during worship, but she has been hesitant to come, wondering if the group has enough zeal and faith for her liking.

Neil has also been missing the group, sometimes exasperated by Barry's admonitions about the spiritual disciplines, Olivia's tendency to say "Amen!" at the most inopportune times, and the group's general lack of interest in the poor. Neil has been slipping out to spend that evening helping at a nearby soup kitchen instead, or volunteering at a community tutoring program. He actually wonders if he should find some folks to gather with who express their faith by caring more for the needs of others.

Leah, the leader, has also been discouraged. While she works hard to give direction to the group and craft thought-provoking questions, people do not share her interest in deep theological truths, nor has anyone taken her up on her offer to borrow her books or commentaries. Leah has been considering finding another group to lead that is more motivated to study the Scriptures in depth.

Bruce is unaware of the unspoken struggles happening beneath the surface in the group. He misses Barry, Olivia, and Neil, and he is always glad for the chance to gather with Leah and those who love God, folks whose differences keep his warm, Contemplative heart filled with new expressions of affection for Jesus.

So . . . does this scenario sound even vaguely familiar? Can you relate to the struggles that surface when people meet together over an extended period of time, even those who genuinely love Jesus? Do you identify with Barry, Olivia, Neil, or Leah, and have you found some of the same types of behaviors irritating? Or are you like Bruce, appreciating others and oblivious to those who struggle with differences? And what's a good Christian to do in a situation like this? Are we to verbalize to one another our often unspoken inner dialogues, or do we simply ask the Lord to give us more love for those who get under our skin? It's easy to understand why some in this group might prefer to slip away quietly to find people whose style is more similar to their own.

I have seen situations like this many times—in missionary circles and in families, among small groups, on ministry teams and elder boards, with pastors and church staffs, within Christian organizations and at seminaries and Bible schools. People who spend prolonged periods of time together eventually see spiritual differences surface. But most of these differences need not be indicators of unity or disunity, maturity or immaturity, spiritual passion or spiritual indifference; they simply signal the presence of differing spiritual temperaments. For when it comes to how we most naturally love and serve God, we were not all created the same, and our differences become bold statements of how God has legitimately, though diversely, wired us!

As preferences emerge, what are we to do? Even among people who try not to label others as right or wrong, aren't the disparities important to notice, probably even talk about? Isn't it important to figure out why people see the same faith journey so differently? And doesn't it make sense to affiliate with those whose spiritual values line up with our own? The answers to these questions are not simple, but if we were to give a straightforward response, it would be an emphatic *yes* . . . and an emphatic *no*!

ON YOUR OWN

Read Luke 24. Then record examples of each of the spiritual temperaments found in the passage:

Activist:

Ascetic:

Caregiver:

Contemplative:

Enthusiast:

Intellectual:

Naturalist:

Sensate:

Traditionalist:

(Possible answers: Activist: *Luke 24:21*; Ascetic: *Luke 24:16-17*; Caregiver: *Luke 24:1, 22, 42-44*; Contemplative: *Luke 24:6, 15, 35-36*; Enthusiast: *Luke 24:23, 52*; Intellectual: *Luke 24:11, 14, 18-20, 27, 32-34, 45-48*; Naturalist: *Luke 24:1, 13, 28-29*; Sensate: *Luke 24:1, 4, 12, 30, 42-44*; Traditionalist: *Luke 24:5, 30, 53*)

FINDING COMMON GROUND

Yes, there are advantages to worshipping and serving God with people whose spiritual preferences match our own, just as there are advantages to having dinner with people who like the same food or going on vacation with those who enjoy the same rhythms when they travel. Similarities are always nice, and we usually get more done when we work alongside those who are like-minded.

For example, where spiritual temperaments are concerned, some find it peaceful to walk into a church where the atmosphere is solemnly reverent during the serving of the Eucharist. Here the setting allows all present to silently wait upon God as they receive the body and blood of Christ in prayerful adoration. Others find it equally pleasant to enter a gathering where the music and movement flow freely among those who love Jesus with vigor. They like the sense of connection that comes during more exuberant worship times. Both environments—one quiet and respectful, the other demonstrative and exhilarating—give those involved permission to unself-consciously attend to God alone. No effort needs to be made to explain one's behavior. Instead, each community of like-minded individuals finds a sense of strength in numbers, harmony in consensus, and spiritual authority in agreement.

On the other hand, when all in the group are similar, growth may not be happening as much as when its membership comes bringing differing points of view. Change most often occurs when we are with others who think divergently, giving us an opportunity to consider our own perspectives. As someone once said, "If two people see things just alike, one of them isn't necessary." But when we see the world through parallel, though not conflicting, lenses—allowing differing values to emerge—then we have the best chance of operating like the body of Christ in an authentic way, united yet with our many members. New possibilities become exposed, new options unleashed, and more choices possible.

In the language of the spiritual temperaments, when we experience all manner of diversity in loving God under one roof, it is more than okay—it is necessary! A greater glimpse of God's nature can be revealed as each of us brings our small piece of His likeness to the table.

Denominations and the Temperaments

This having been said, as long as we have choices, we will most likely be drawn to those who are on the whole like us. People tend to cluster around similarities—in interests *and* spiritual temperaments. And truthfully, there is nothing wrong with that; worshipping and serving God with those who are similar to us—providing the worship is God centered and Spirit inspired—is great. In fact, it makes good sense to affiliate with people whose preferences align with our own. This results in churches and denominations that are filled with like-minded individuals, whole denominations of Activists or Caregivers or Intellectuals all moving together with similar goals and initiatives. Thus, it makes sense when an Enthusiast who finds himself in a Ascetic church thinks about looking for a congregation that's more lively, just as it is reasonable when a Contemplative who finds herself in a denomination with an Intellectual emphasis considers seeking out a warmer setting. Once we understand that our spiritual preferences are choices we make rather than indicators of right or wrong, we can view differences with respect and select accordingly.

Unfortunately, differences are not always seen as okay. Recently I was teaching a seminar on spiritual temperaments in a church, and the pastor was present, vigorously interacting with the content and asking some very good questions. After the seminar, he walked up to me and said, "This has been one of the most insightful conversations I've ever had, because I now realize that most of the people who have left our church have gone away more because of their spiritual temperaments than because of doctrinal differences."

This was an important discovery for the pastor to make. And how true it is—our spiritual temperaments often determine how and where we worship and serve the Lord. In fact, a person's theology may even flow along spiritual temperament lines. For example, some prefer the emphasis of Martin Luther, who stressed *sola scriptura*, making the Bible and the pulpit the focus of worship, while others prefer to value the altar as the center of corporate worship, with the cross and the Eucharist as the hub. These differing spiritual preferences— one focusing on understanding God with the mind while the other emphasizes experiencing God through mystery and symbol—point to differing spiritual temperaments. We even notice that some denominations have synthesized around spiritual preferences—such as the caregiving nature of the Salvation Army or the Traditionalist value of ritual and continuity in the Anglican church. However, recent studies have shown that it is not essential for healthy churches to be formed around similar spiritual preferences. Let's look at what these studies reveal in more detail.

Differences in Healthy Churches

Obviously, there is more to choosing a church or denomination than one's spiritual temperament. Yet within the last few decades, it has been interesting to see the results as many people have begun to study church growth and the dynamics of healthy, vibrant congregations. Christian Schwarz and Christoph Schalk, who founded the Institute of Natural Church Development in Germany, have done a great deal of research in more than a thousand churches in thirty-two countries. Their extensive study concluded that every congregation has a unique, God-given nature that, when discovered and developed organically, causes the church to grow.

Two of the essential elements they found in healthy churches are "inspiring worship" and "passionate spirituality." But Schwarz and Schalk concluded that these two fundamentals need not look the same in every church. To the contrary, the secret of a strong church is its *level* of passion and faith, not its form.[1] In other words, when faith is lived out with commitment, fire, and fervor, its style is found to be unimportant. Moreover, differing expressions of faith all seem to work just as well. It was discovered that the techniques of one church need not be projected onto another; instead, the more important consideration is that a church is worshipping in ways that are significant and meaningful to the people who attend—whether free flowing or liturgical.[2]

Thus, it was found that passionate spirituality looks different from church to church—depending upon the preference of its people. Typically, we think we are seeing *passionate spirituality* when we enter a church of Enthusiasts (who are overt in their worship) or Contemplatives (who are talking about hearing God and experiencing intimacy with Him) or Ascetics (whose focus is on prayer and the spiritual disciplines). But Schwarz and Schalk found that healthy churches can all look different in the way their people organically and naturally worship and serve God!

Seeing the Full Person of the Godhead

Not only can healthy churches look different in their styles of worship, growing churches can also be seen in congregations that are made up of differing spiritual temperaments. The world will never see the full expression of the Person of God without each part of the body of Christ expressing itself differently. Just as my spiritual temperament is God's gift to me, so it is also my gift back to God and you. In the same way, your spiritual temperament is God's gift to you, your gift back to God, and your gift to me. When an Enthusiast is in the room, I'm not likely to forget that in God's presence is fullness of joy (see Psalm 16:11), yet with a Traditionalist around, I may be informed that Jesus is the same yesterday, today, and forever (see Hebrews 13:8). When a Contemplative enters, I will likely be reminded of God's love and nearness (see John 14:3), yet an Activist may exhort me not to compromise God's heart and standards (see Psalm 15). My thinking will be sharpened when I spend time with an Intellectual (see Proverbs 27:17), but I might learn to value silence with the Lord when an Ascetic is present (see Habakkuk 2:20). If I hang out with a Sensate, I'll be prone to notice the beauty and splendor of God's sanctuary (see Psalm 96:6), though with a Naturalist, I might end up praising God as we walk together in His creation (see Isaiah 61:11). As Mother Teresa said, "I am a little pencil in the hand of a writing God who is sending a love letter to the world." God writes His message for all to read through each one of us—both individually and corporately—according to our own unique wiring.

Yes, we need each other more than we realize; we truly are God's gift to one another and the world. But the challenge is to learn to get along as we love the Lord according to how we were designed, to confess the truth that Jesus values everyone equally, and to commit to celebrating the differences within our faith communities. We will not grow into the people God designed us to be otherwise.

WHEN WE DISCOUNT THE SPIRITUAL TEMPERAMENTS

At times getting along can be easier said than done. Differences often bring out our insecurities, resulting in comparisons and judgments rather than appreciation and strength. Accepting and being grateful for differences requires true humility and the grace of God to regard one another as more important than ourselves (see Philippians 2:3). Harmful consequences occur when we forget that the Lord has wired us differently and that those differences are very much needed in the body of Christ. Here are just a few of the traps we can fall into when we fail to appreciate and honor one another's spiritual temperaments as indispensable gifts from God:

1. *Judgmentalism*—"Look how she's worshipping! She is so showy!" When we begin to evaluate others through our own spiritual styles—believing that all expressions of faith must look like mine or they are wrong—we begin to set ourselves up as judges, becoming critical and negative. Others feel marginalized in these environments, and God's love is not experienced. Therefore, when we gather, it is vital for us to remember that the Lord made each of us with spiritual differences. Someone else's worship will never look the same as mine, and not only is that okay, it is a very good thing! Each person brings joy to the Lord in his or her own way, and those who worship differently undoubtedly bring something to God and His world that I can never bring.

2. *Prescriptionism*—"Just do what I do if you want to know God better." This attitude is the result of believing that there is only one right way to know and love Jesus, and therefore what works for me should also work for you. Not only is this approach untrue, it can also be harmful and oppressive. Instead, we must remain humble, remembering that each person has a specific spiritual temperament and cluster of spiritual preferences. Instead of forcing people to fit into our mold, we can offer them ideas that will be more aligned with their own wiring.

3. *Elitism*—"My group is more spiritual than your group!" When we begin to think that our spiritual temperaments are more

special and godly than those of others, we elevate ourselves above others with an "If you're not like me, you're less than" mentality. It's important to remember that each preference demonstrates a vital yet distinct aspect of God—such as His justice, holiness, beauty, transcendence, or immanence. Recalling that God created each one for a different purpose will help us realize that we are not better; we are only one part of making God visible to a watching world.

4. *Isolationalism*— "Let's start our own group where we can *really* pray!" Although it is okay to prefer one style of worship to another, we get into trouble when we react disapprovingly to other styles, equating simple differences with lukewarmness or spiritual error. Sometimes this attitude causes people to break away—thinking they must become God's "true remnant"—in order to worship in a way that appears more devoted as they disassociate with others. Regrettably, this attitude of superiority brings isolationism, and this isolationism feeds false superiority. If this occurs, who can speak into the lives of those who have separated themselves from the larger body of Christ, since they already feel that everyone is wrong except those in their own little group (see Galatians 5:20, TLB)? Only God's Spirit can bring the humility necessary for us to realize that Jesus put us in the body for a reason, and therefore we need one another. Isolation is not the answer.

5. *Denominationalism*—"Those Bapticostals certainly don't take Communion like they should." Because we want to affiliate with spiritually like-minded people, we often choose a church—Baptist, Presbyterian, Anglican, or Foursquare—based on our spiritual preferences, which can be fine initially. But choosing to partner with others who hold similar spiritual distinctives is not the same as deriving worth, value, or importance from being a part of a denomination rather than being a child of God. The "us versus them" or "we are us because we aren't them" attitude does not please the Lord, who wants all His children to experience unity within His body.

God's solution to each of these *isms* is rather simple; He says we should live a humble life of loving unity by the power of His Spirit:

You have been called to live in freedom, my brothers and sisters. But don't use your freedom to satisfy your sinful nature. Instead, use your freedom to serve one another in love. For the whole law can be summed up in this one command: "Love your neighbor as yourself." But if you are always biting and devouring one another, watch out! Beware of destroying one another. So I say, let the Holy Spirit guide your lives. Then you won't be doing what your sinful nature craves. The sinful nature wants to do evil, which is just the opposite of what the Spirit wants. And the Spirit gives us desires that are the opposite of what the sinful nature desires. These two forces are constantly fighting each other, so you are not free to carry out your good intentions. But when you are directed by the Spirit, you are not under obligation to the law of Moses. When you follow the desires of your sinful nature, the results are very clear: sexual immorality, impurity, lustful pleasures, idolatry, sorcery, hostility, quarreling, jealousy, outbursts of anger, selfish ambition, dissension, division, envy, drunkenness, wild parties, and other sins like these. Let me tell you again, as I have before, that anyone living that sort of life will not inherit the Kingdom of God. But the Holy Spirit produces this kind of fruit in our lives: love, joy, peace, patience, kindness, goodness, faithfulness, gentleness, and self-control. There is no law against these things! Those who belong to Christ Jesus have nailed the passions and desires of their sinful nature to his cross and crucified them there. Since we are living by the Spirit, let us follow the Spirit's leading in every part of our lives. Let us not become conceited, or provoke one another, or be jealous of one another. *Galatians 5:13-26 (NLT)*

FINDING VALUE IN EVERY SPIRITUAL TEMPERAMENT

Within the body of Christ, certain groups have long been overlooked, while others are overvalued because of their spiritual temperaments. For example, in some circles the Intellectual spiritual temperament is most highly lauded, and anything else is thought to be second rate.

Temperament Types

Active	Active & Receptive	Receptive
(Those who primarily act)	(Those who act and respond to God and His people)	(Those who primarily respond to God and His people)
Activist	Enthusiast	Ascetic
Caregiver	Sensate	Contemplative
Intellectual	Traditionalist	Naturalist

Elsewhere the Traditionalist is thought to be the ultimate standard of faith, and other expressions are considered to be sloppy or too changeable. Some groups extol the quiet dignity and disciplined life of the Ascetic or the tendency of the Caregiver to reach out and attend to others, or . . . well, we could go on and on. Our preferences show when we treat others as "more than" or "less than," granting favoritism to some spiritual temperaments over others. It may be helpful to consider the nine spiritual temperaments in the following way:

Some churches value the more *active* spiritual temperaments, while others prefer spiritual temperaments with more *receptive* postures. Actually, the active-receptive difference has become a modern-day discussion between *doing* and *being* that can be traced back as early as the story of Mary and Martha. Here we see the tension building between the actively busy Martha (a Caregiver, perhaps?) and the receptively poised Mary (a Contemplative?), in which the strain seemed heightened as the Lord declared that Mary had chosen the one thing necessary, "the good part," while her sister, Martha, received a mild correction (see Luke 10:41-42, NASB).

Hence this juxtaposition between doing and being has evolved, pitting engagement in ministry against spending time at Jesus' feet. However, this comparison is unnecessary, as God obviously loved and included both Mary and Martha in the Gospels, and we find both types in our churches today as well. Besides, *doing* and *being* are interrelated disciplines: what we do is often a reflection of who we are, just as who we are is often demonstrated by what we do. God created us to be both *rulers*—influencers who exert authority over our domains—as well as *worshippers*—lovers who are devoted to our Creator. Consequently, all our doing must be based upon being with Jesus, abiding in Him in a posture of trust and rest.

All this to say, comparing the spiritual temperaments for the purpose of establishing one above another is pointless—whether we do it because of a doing versus being contest or because of our own groups' DNA. Because we were all created in the image of God—the *imago Dei*—a human soul is the fingerprint of God, and we do violence to one another when we marginalize and censure each other. Besides, when Activists are esteemed above Ascetics, aren't we forgetting that God commands us to both watch *and* pray? Since each temperament makes a significant contribution to the Kingdom of God, applauding one spiritual temperament above another not only damages Christ's body, it harms the cause of the gospel as well. When we were ignorant about spiritual temperaments and their practices, we might have felt justified elevating one pathway above another. But now that we understand how we are different by design, we can no longer promote or demote any of the spiritual temperaments. As a body, we truly do need one another!

FINDING COMPATIBILITY

After all is said and done, we need to find a way to live compatibly with one another's differences. For that reason, it may be helpful to pay attention to how each spiritual temperament tends to relate to the others. It appears that there may be actual couplets of temperaments that—because of their common ground—get along with one another more readily. We can pair the Intellectuals with Activists, Enthusiasts with Contemplatives, Traditionalists with Ascetics, and Naturalists with Sensates—with the Caregivers getting along with pretty much everyone.

Consider the illustration on page 123. Many people find that they are most comfortable with those whose spiritual temperaments are nearest their own on the wheel. They also find that the spiritual temperaments directly across from their own can be the most different and thus difficult to celebrate, providing the greatest "rub" for them. Of course, this is not an absolute, but it may be a helpful concept upon which to reflect.

ON YOUR OWN

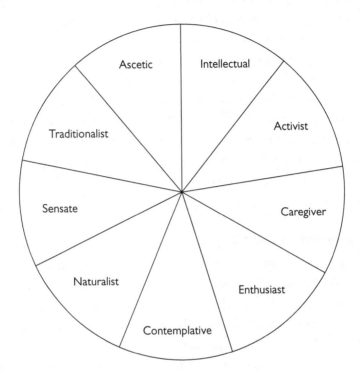

What are your most passionate spiritual temperaments? Which temperaments seem to be the most difficult for you to celebrate? How does this wheel help explain that?

Interestingly, it is often the spiritual practices of those temperaments that are most unlike our own that offer us what we lack and truly need. For example, an Enthusiast is often helped by learning to employ the solitude and silence of the Ascetic, while the Ascetic soul is often in need of the joy and celebration of the Enthusiast. The Intellectual is often aided by a Contemplative's spiritual warmth and closeness to God, while the Contemplative is generally assisted by the well-reasoned mind of the Intellectual. Isn't it just like the Lord to fashion within the hearts of those who irritate us most the very blessing we require? When we can see those who are least like us as offering us our greatest gift, then we are blessed indeed!

Thankfully, as we mature spiritually, we begin to actually transcend our spiritual temperaments and their differences, learning to receive from everyone—including those who are most unlike us—in our love for Jesus and desire to serve Him. Because the church of Jesus Christ is to function as His body in the world and carry out His Kingdom mandate, we need each other and the differing strengths each temperament brings. Isn't it reassuring to know that we don't have to be everything to everyone, nor do we need to be able to do everything? Each of us has a distinct part to play. We don't need to be all things to all people; we only have to love God according to how He has wired us. Whew! That is certainly good news!

Compatibility in the Church

While similar spiritual temperaments may get along more easily—just as churches that attract people of like temperaments may accomplish great things for the Lord (with their like-mindedness propelling them forward to further God's cause in the world)—in most gatherings, we will find the majority of the spiritual temperaments represented. Therefore, we will need to learn to become comfortable with those who are not like us. But take heart! Though it may not be easy, great rewards come from interacting with those of differing spiritual temperaments. For instance, we may grow to care more practically for others when we are around Caregivers or learn to attend to the plight of the poor and oppressed as we rub shoulders with Activists. Growing from those who are not like us—seeing their strengths and our weaknesses—only happens when we work side by side.

For that reason, it's important to interrelate with Christians with different spiritual temperaments, even though there is bound to be more tension. But in the midst of the effort, our unevenness is exposed as we see God and His world through fresh eyes. When we remember this, we are able to appreciate those we might otherwise find annoying. We eventually learn to relax into who we are because we know that God designed us this way—just as He designed others another way. While rubbing is bound to occur, the friction can be God's method of polishing and smoothing off our rough edges—the way a diamond is polished, for instance. The result is greater maturity, even gratitude for those who are different from us, and oneness with Jesus is experienced more fully.

Compatibility at Home

Differing spiritual temperaments not only turn up in the church, they are also found in our homes. I have a friend who attends an inner-city church of Enthusiasts, but her little girl does not enjoy her parents' worship style at all. In fact, she feels so overwhelmed by the noise and outward expression of praise that this young Ascetic child often covers her ears, seeking out a quiet corner where she can sit quietly with Jesus. Another friend has chosen to forgo her own worship preferences to settle into a church that primarily suits her teenage son's spiritual temperament. She reminds herself often that she and her son worship God differently, and she has chosen to sacrifice some of her own preferences for his sake. Both friends are mindful of the spiritual temperaments of their children, yet each takes a differing approach in dealing with the spiritual temperaments of those closest to them.

So what should a family do if everyone in the home has a different spiritual temperament? Obviously, when this is the case, every preference won't be met, and some needs may even be conflicting. But while each household must decide how to meet the spiritual needs of their family, here are some practical ideas that might be of assistance.

The most important step in unifying your family is to know and understand the spiritual temperament of each family member; then when spiritual differences arise, viewing these differences through the lens of spiritual temperaments can help put things into perspective.

In addition, it is also crucial to honor these differences through many conversations about how God created each of us differently, thus acknowledging that differences are more than okay—they are God's idea! Whether parents help their child appreciate loud praise music or the family decides to look for a calmer church setting, it is imperative that each person in the family be taught to understand and wholeheartedly value every other member. Parents need to know and respect the spiritual temperaments of their children, and young people must also be taught to honor and respect the spiritual temperaments of their parents.

When it comes to selecting one place for the family to worship, compromises will be called for, and those compromises will look different from home to home. But knowing, understanding, honoring, and respecting every person spiritually is essential.

So how might this honor be fleshed out? Certainly, when your children are at sensitive ages in their faith development—such as in their junior high or high school years—it's important to pay attention to the things that capture their interest in serving and worshipping the Lord. As parents, we want to bless our children spiritually, which may even require selecting a solid biblical church that appeals to their preferences, while supplementing our own worship through books, tapes, or small groups outside the church. Adults have more options than children; therefore, it is important to find a gathering that does not bore or antagonize our children, if possible.

Certainly there are multiple factors that go into these family decisions, but even when our children are in college or out on their own, it's imperative to support their worship preferences, in spite of whether or not they may suit our own tastes.

A colleague recently told me that her college-age daughter was attending a congregation that was as far as possible from the traditional church in which she'd been raised. When this friend heard about her daughter's choice, she responded on the phone with, "Oh, no!" But after we talked, she realized that her daughter had long been unhappy with the highly Intellectual, conventional faith environment in which she had been raised. Suddenly it was not a shock that her daughter chose a church more in line with her own spiritual temperament.

Surely it is essential that we teach our children the difference between having a life-giving relationship with God and simply attending a Bible-believing church—no matter what worship style that church embraces. Though they are both crucial, they are not the same. Therefore, as long as our children are fostering their relationship with Jesus, where they choose to attend church needs to be more about *their* spiritual temperament preferences than our own.

In marriage, if you and your spouse have differing preferences, compromise is vital for you as well. It's probable that no church will meet all the needs of both partners, but prayerfully trust that you will find a congregation that adequately meets enough of those needs. I have friends who have even chosen to attend separate churches for a season, and that worked when it was done for only a short period of time. But when possible, finding a church where you can worship the Lord together seems like a better long-term solution.

Spiritual preferences are an important factor to consider when we live in close proximity with others, whether with family members or dear friends. Judgments and comparisons, misunderstandings and bewilderment are bound to occur from time to time. Personally, I find the lesson Jesus teaches in John 21 helpful in this regard. Here Jesus gave Peter some firm instructions about his life, but Peter did not receive the directives wholeheartedly. Instead, he directed Jesus' comments to John, saying, "Lord, and what about this man?" (verse 21, NASB). It seems clear that Peter was asking not because of his concern for John but because Peter wanted to deflect Jesus' comments from himself. To this Jesus answered, "If I want him to remain until I come, what is that to you? You follow Me!" (verse 23). So it needs to be in our homes and close relationships. We grow enormously when we concentrate on what Jesus is saying to us rather than trying to control others or feed them the same spiritual diet we enjoy.

Creating Greater Compatibility

Whether in the church, the home, the school, or on the mission field, compatibility is something we must nurture among differing spiritual temperaments. When we find that our needs are colliding, here are a few ideas about how to adjust in our homes, small groups, or churches:

- Understand your own wiring. When you know yourself, you can see more clearly what your challenges might be stemming from. Knowing yourself allows you to resist the temptation to compare yourself with others and become critical. Because you are not wired exactly like anyone else—nor are they wired like you—we each can choose to love God according to our own preferences, just as we can also choose to expand our repertoire to experience new and unfamiliar spiritual practices, which will be discussed more fully in part 2.

- Help others know and better understand themselves. Awareness is often half the battle and can actually transform irritations into opportunities. Rather than allowing differences to become gnawing aggravations that eventually drive people apart, it's imperative to help others identify and appreciate their own spiritual temperaments as well.
- Talk openly and honestly about the differing spiritual temperaments you see in your home, church, and small groups. As you listen carefully and respectfully to others, preferences can be seen as invitations to new and different ways of participating with God's Spirit, not as spiritual mandates, absolutes, or battlefields where right and wrong must be established. Acknowledging differences openly can be the beginning of greater mutual understanding, respect, and trust.
- Always try to be sensitive to those whose spiritual temperaments are unlike your own—especially in worshipful gatherings. While the Ascetic may prefer to worship God in stillness, the Traditionalist may enjoy a dignified, reverent approach. The Sensate might be moved by classical hymns played melodically, while the Activist may not want to sing at all—given the condition of the world. The Intellectual may need some time to think about models of truth, while the Contemplative prefers to simply sit and soak in the Lord's presence. Because of the inherent differences in the way the spiritual temperaments come to God, awareness and deference are always necessary. While you may be ready to dance around the room, you also need to consider how others will be affected by your actions. Because each spiritual temperament worships God in a unique way, great care and thoughtfulness are required for all the styles to find expression when they come together.
- Give yourself permission to congregate with those whose spiritual temperaments affirm and strengthen your own. Do so with an attitude of respect and deference for those who are different, yet just as you gather at times in homogeneous groups with those of like gender, age, life stage, or interest, so it is a good thing to enjoy the support of those who connect with God like

What does it mean to worship the living God?

Does it mean coming with a spirit of humble reverence . . .
or does it mean coming with a spirit of joyful celebration?
Yes!

Does it mean standing as though we are citizens before a royal Sovereign . . .
or lifting our hands as though we are children before a loving Parent?
Yes!

Does worship mean sitting before God in attentive receptivity . . .
or dancing before God in reckless affection?
Yes!

Does it mean singing those stately hymns, poetically exact, theologically deep . . .
or does it mean singing those simple choruses, which, because of their repetition,
allow the heart to simply bask in the presence of God?
Yes!

Is the God we have gathered to worship the transcendent One,
high and exalted above all the heavens . . .
or is the God we worship the Immanent One, dwelling among us and with us and in us?
Yes!

Is the Bible the work of human beings like you and me, the prayerful memory of the
words and deeds of Jesus . . .
or is it the work of the Spirit, God's inspired Word?
Yes!

Is Jesus the holy One, whose purity is like fire that melts us
into brokenhearted confession . . .
or is Jesus the gracious One, who throws His arms around us even while we're still
dressed in the filthy rags of our sin?
Yes!

Is Jesus the Lion whose roar brought into being the universe with all its galaxies . . .
or is He the gentle Lamb whose shed blood takes away the sin of the world?
Yes!

Is He coming again to one day redeem the created order...
or is He already here, redeeming even now?
Yes!*

*Darrell W. Johnson, Associate Professor of Pastoral Theology, Regent College.

you do. These groups become rich storehouses where deeply meaningful worship can happen.

- Walk and live among those who are different. Remember that God's world was set up heterogeneously and that we grow most profoundly when we are forced to stretch and learn from one another's differences. Listen to one another, cherishing each story—which is itself the work of Jesus in each life.

- Begin to intentionally celebrate spiritual differences whole-heartedly—even if initially you must do it simply by faith. Work on developing lenses that allow you to see the world through the eyes of those who are not like yourself. Be purposefully thankful for the spiritual temperaments of others and the work God is doing as you interface with them. Pray for the very person who is hardest for you to love, asking God to give you a picture of how He sees that person—fully redeemed—and hold that picture in your mind's eye, envisioning that individual (and yourself!) as you both will look once God's work is complete. Those who invite God's grace to meet and transform them in the differences deeply honor God's heart of unity within diversity.

- Find or create eclectic environments where all the spiritual temperaments can find expression. My husband and I attend a church where this happens, and it is a blessing indeed. But even when others do not foster that welcoming environment, you can become a person of safety, calling out those whose spiritual temperaments are different so they can be seen and honored.

MATURING INTO THE IMAGE OF CHRIST

When the apostle Paul wrote that the goal of the spiritual life is to "attain to the unity of the faith, and of the knowledge of the Son of God, to a *mature* man, to the measure of the stature which belongs to the fullness of Christ" (Ephesians 4:13, NASB, emphasis added), he was talking about *imago Christi*: being formed into the image of Christ (see 2 Corinthians 3:18). This is God's plan for His children; this is God's desire for humankind.

The Greek term Paul uses for maturity in Ephesians is the same word Jesus used when He said, "You are to be perfect [mature], as your heavenly Father is perfect [mature]" (Matthew 5:48, NASB). This is the word *teleios*, meaning, "to bring to its finished end, to become fully mature." It is the same word used when the Bible says that Jesus Himself was made perfect (*teleios*) through the things He suffered (see Hebrews 2:10).

God is not saying here that we are expected to become flawless in this life, though holiness is actually about living out the full humanity of Jesus free from the power of sin, and to that end we are constantly moving. Though the apostle Paul said at the finale of his life that he was not yet perfect (*teleios*), he also talked of pressing on to apprehend that for which he had been apprehended by Christ (see Philippians 3:12-14). God is, in essence, asking us to enter into a process that is quite similar to the one we ask our children to undertake: to grow up and become fully developed adults who take on aspects of the character and likeness of the family. Yes, God the Father intends for us to grow up and become fully developed spiritual adults who take on aspects of the character and likeness of His family. It was for *teleios* that God planned (see Romans 8:29-30; Philippians 1:6), and it was for *teleios* that Jesus prayed:

> [My prayer is] that they may all be one, even as You, Father, are in Me and I in You, that they also may be in Us, so that the world may believe that You sent Me. The glory which You have given Me I have given to them, that they may be one, just as We are one; I in them and You in Me, that they may be perfected [teleios] in unity, so that the world may know that You sent Me, and loved them, even as You have loved Me. *John 17:21-23 (NASB)*

For the first two decades of my Christian life, I thought this verse was about getting along with other Christians. I believed Jesus was saying, "I wish you guys would get it together and live in harmony with one another. Can't you quit fighting and just get along? Sheesh!" Then one day a deeper truth hit me: I realized that Jesus wasn't just talking about unity with other believers. In this prayer to His Father, He was inviting us to come into oneness with *Him*, the same oneness He has with His Abba. He is saying that He wants and is praying for us to have the same capacity for intimate interaction that He shares within the Godhead—that same quality of knowing and being known, that exact experience of close companionship and love that exists between Father, Son, and Holy Spirit.

Jesus is inviting us into the same relationship, connection, bond, rapport, closeness, warmth, harmony, and agreement that He experiences within the Trinity. He is inviting us into union with Himself, a merger that goes far beyond mere service or what we do for Him; it is an intimate connection that is exactly like the one the Godhead shares.

Wow! This is rather mind blowing. And yes, Jesus is also praying that we will become mature (*teleios*) in our oneness with each other. What does that oneness look like? Well, when I am one with others, I don't deliberately hurt or dishonor them, because in hurting another with whom I am one, I am also hurting and dishonoring myself. As unity and maturity (teleios) develop, I will value others as I value myself. That is why we need each other so badly. Others in the body of Christ become instruments that aid our own maturity. Therefore, when we see ourselves unable to love and accept someone else, we see our own lack of *teleios*—places in our hearts and characters that God still needs to work on so that we will treat all people with the dignity and respect with which we would like to be treated.

We obviously hinder each other when we stifle our God-given differences and refuse to learn from one another's spiritual temperaments. When we fail to accept those who are different, we actually obstruct our own growth and union with God. Without others, we cannot mature. Yes, differences bring obstacles, but when we grow in *teleios*, we realize that even those obstacles are invitations from God to taste more oneness with Him.

The Lifelong Process of Maturing

Growing in *teleios* is a day-in and day-out process, and this *teleios* requires a lifetime. But because we have sin natures and live in a fallen world, the word *perfect* (even though it means "mature") can be a dangerous word to get wrong. When we misunderstand *teleios*, our own flesh begins to beat a drum that calls us to try harder and harder. Our old natures love to set an impossible standard for us, trapping us in perfectionism, getting our eyes off Jesus and onto ourselves, imprisoning us in some form of legalism. It's easy to lose perspective and cease to be able to relax in God's grace and mercy—a mercy that is warm and broad and full of surprises. We subtly shift from seeking God to seeking to revamp one another and ourselves, even despising our own messy souls. Mike Yaconelli says it well in *Messy Spirituality*:

> Spirituality is not a formula. It's not a test. It is a relationship—one not about competency, but about intimacy. It is not about perfection, but connection. . . . Spirituality is anything but a straight line; it is a mixed-up, topsy-turvy, helter-skelter godliness that turns our lives into an upside-down toboggan ride full of unexpected turns, surprise bumps, and bone-shattering crashes. In other words, messy spirituality is the delirious consequence of a life ruined by a Jesus who will love us right into His arms.[3]

Amen and amen! *Teleios* is about a life that, in the end, brings freedom and joy as we mature in the Lord Jesus Christ. He is the One who is present in the "tangledness of our lives, not to simply fix us but to be present with us in the mess of our unfixedness."[4] He invites us to come to Him, to be loved and touched and healed by Him, to know Him, and in that knowing to feel the security of His heart. There is freedom in His love; there is grace.

Therefore, *teleios* is not primarily about constructing a five-year plan to acquire spiritual growth, nor is it about attaining personal holiness, becoming more useful to God, or achieving psychological and spiritual wholeness. *Teleios* is about union with God; it's about entering more deeply into the eternal love relationship with Jesus for which we were created. While personal holiness, usefulness to God, and psychological and spiritual wholeness are worthy by-products of that union, they are not worthy objectives. Only as we enter into a deep, abiding love relationship with a living Person—a relationship that will endure forever—will *teleios* even make sense. God clearly created us for Himself, and it is into this union that we enter at salvation and grow for the rest of our lives, treasuring as our model the union the Son enjoys with the Father and the Spirit (see John 17:11, 20-23).

Our Ongoing Transformation

As a result of this lifelong journey with God, transformation and *teleios* occur—we mature in our desire to know God, we develop in our capacity to love Him, and we grow in our ability to trust Him. As spiritual formation happens, the way we look and act will progressively change. This is a formation that affirms both the earlier stages of discipleship and the later stages of spiritual growth, affecting our total lives, characters, and responses to the triune God.[5]

In order for ongoing transformation to take place, it is not only indispensable to know and understand our spiritual temperaments, it is also essential to place ourselves in communities of faith where *teleios* is valued. It is there that we can learn to stretch and grow beyond our comfort zones, knowing and understanding our spiritual temperaments and practices, but also choosing to utilize the spiritual disciplines to help us grow as we value and listen to one another. More fully living out the Good News of the Kingdom, we realize how much we need one another if God's Kingdom is to come to earth.

Now we must continue on in the lifelong journey of knowing a loving God, and as we do, there are lots more surprises ahead!

FOR FURTHER REFLECTION AND DISCUSSION

1. In your church or small group, what spiritual temperaments can you identify in the people you know well? How do the differences you see affect the interpersonal dynamics between you and others? What improvements might result from your new awareness?

2. In your home, what spiritual temperaments can you identify in each person? How do these differences affect the interpersonal dynamics in your family? What can you share with your family members that might help everyone appreciate, value, and celebrate one another more fully?

3. At work, at school, or in your ministry, what spiritual temperaments can you identify in each person? How do these differences affect the interpersonal dynamics in your environment? What can you share that might help others appreciate, value, and celebrate differences more?

4. What spiritual temperaments do you need to more actively appreciate? How will you do this?

6

THE LIFELONG JOURNEY OF
KNOWING A LOVING GOD

I can still remember it as if it were yesterday. It had been impossible to sleep the night before as my seven-year-old brain was going bonkers with all the visual images dancing in my head. The anticipation was enormous. So many possibilities. As I tried to hold on until morning, I kept picturing what I had seen on our ten-inch black-and-white TV—streets lined with gift shops, restaurants, and dozens of thunderous rides. My mom told me it would be bigger and more fun than I could imagine—better than the circus and brighter than the county fair. I could hardly wait: Tomorrow my family was going to a new theme park called *Disneyland*!

Morning finally dawned, and Mom dressed me in my new full skirt and matching blouse. I sat quietly in the backseat, not wanting to wrinkle my firmly starched petticoat as we drove for what seemed like hours. We finally arrived, and there were so many cars, so many people; I was overwhelmed. As my dad bought our tickets, I walked over to peer through the gates at the most massive flower bed of brightly colored flora I'd ever seen. The word *Disneyland* spoke through the voice of yellow marigolds. As I looked more closely, a gigantic face of Mickey Mouse appeared in black and white seeds beneath the plants. Oh, how my little heart soared! I couldn't talk; I could hardly breathe! I had literally entered a fairy tale.

As I looked around, I saw horse-drawn carriages, a woman dressed just like Cinderella, and lines of people waiting to board mind-blowing rides. Little shops and kiosks were everywhere, with food and memorabilia beckoning to be procured. *Nothing* I had pictured in my mind could even compare with what I was experiencing! My mom's description had not begun to prepare me for a place so big, so beautiful, so full of fun and exciting things to explore. This was a day I knew I'd never forget, and now—some fifty years later—I still remember it vividly.

How wonderful it is to remember days like that. (Do you remember the first time you went to Disneyland . . . or saw the movie *Star Wars* . . . or watched fireworks?) What a great gift God has given us in our cameralike eyes and record-keeping minds: our ability to capture snapshots of life all around us—not only scenes from our past, but also pictures of a possible future as we look ahead with anticipation. The imagination, God's great gift to us, is not just a device for children to use but a priceless apparatus for us all. With it, we create visions of our future, forming pictures and ideas of real people, places, and events still waiting to be experienced. I anticipate seeing Paris someday—the Eiffel Tower and the Arc de Triomphe—but until then, I can only imagine them.

Interestingly, faith requires the use of our imagination, because faith is the assurance of things hoped for, the reality of things not yet seen (see Hebrews 11:1). I daresay few of us have ever seen Jesus standing in our living room, but with our eyes closed, we may have pictured Him many times—or envisioned the throne of God or watched with our mind's eye the Dead Sea parting, or imagined what it will be like one day to dance on streets of gold. As Christians we have the added privilege of using our God-redeemed, God-surrendered, God-enlivened imaginations—not to make things up that don't exist, but to visualize more clearly what is there as recorded in biblical history. Our imaginations help us to picture Jesus walking on a liquid sea of black at night, to feel the texture of the food as He fed the five thousand, or to hear His ear-shattering cry on the cross when His collapsed lungs heaved, *"Eli, Eli, lama sabachthani?"* (Matthew 27:46, NASB). Can you picture it? Because of our imaginations, we can envision what it must have been like, and we are left feeling wonder, amazement, and profound gratitude.

To see the unseen—not clearly but through a glass dimly—is one of the greatest gifts God has given us. For Naturalists, the unseen is experienced when a look at the nighttime sky allows us to imagine what it might have been like as the Lord was fashioning the heavens while the morning stars sang and the sons of God looked on with shouts of joy (see Job 38:6-7). For Contemplatives, the invisible is witnessed in Zephaniah 3:17, when suddenly a knock at the door is perceived, and as it opens, there stands the Lord Himself dressed as a warrior, informing us that He's moving in. And as He does, we notice His singing . . . not a song we know, but a calming chorus of love, with words spoken directly to us that soothe our hearts. Or as Sensates, we recognize the invisible when our minds capture the great Artist as He is revealing to Michelangelo the first instant He reached out to humankind, and with that revelation, the beginning strokes of the Sistine Chapel come into existence.

Our redeemed imaginations help us—whatever our spiritual temperaments might be—to see the unseen, because they are places we meet our risen Lord, experiencing His love, His beauty, His timeless truths. Like a prized scrapbook lined with memories of Jesus—moments when He has met us and answered our prayers, bringing us comfort, guiding us, and speaking to us—our imaginations are lined with snapshots, freeze-frames of every treasured experience we've ever had with God!

Yes, one day we'll see the Lord just as clearly as He now sees us; we'll know Him directly and fully, just as He now knows us (see 1 Corinthians 13:12). But for a while, we still need to use our eyes of faith to enjoy what is undoubtedly true about the unseen realities. Like this song says about heaven:

> *I can only imagine what it will be like, when I walk by Your side*
> *I can only imagine what my eyes will see, when Your face is before me!*
> *Surrounded by Your glory, what will my heart feel?*
> *Will I dance for you, Jesus, or in awe of You be still?*
> *Will I stand in Your presence or to my knees will I fall?*
> *Will I sing hallelujah? Will I be able to speak at all?*
> *I can only imagine! I can only imagine!*[1]

Thankfully, the day will finally come when we will see what is now withheld from our physical eyes, and undoubtedly those realities will be better than we could have imagined. My husband works for

---

ON YOUR OWN
Consider the following:

Think back over your life. If you were to make a photo album of all
your memories with Jesus—times when He met you and answered
prayers, bringing you comfort, guiding you, speaking to you—
which pictures would you include? Which snapshots with Jesus
taken in your everyday life, freeze-frames of treasured moments
with Him, are most significant? Draw or list some in your journal.

---

a humanitarian organization that provides assistance to the poor in
East Africa. Often we hear stories about orphans from Kenya who are
adopted into loving homes. When these children first come to their new
homes, they are uncertain and unsure of what to expect. As they see
their new beds for the first time—arriving as virtual "unbelievers"—
they don't quite know what to do; most of them have never slept in a
bed before (or if they have, it was a small mattress on the floor shared
with four other people). When they initially see their beds, they often
exclaim, "You mean I get to sleep here all by myself? I don't have to
share this bed with anyone?" Even after they are told that the bed is
indeed theirs alone, it sometimes takes quite a while for them to own
the reality. Days later, some still ask their new parents, "Do you think
I could sleep in that bed again tonight?" When they finally come to
believe that the bed is truly theirs—that it belongs wholly to them—
their little hearts are filled with wonder, amazement, and profound
gratitude. For children who have lived all their lives in poverty—never
owning a single possession of their own—receiving a bed is a mind-
altering reality indeed!

So it is for us when we begin to grasp the love of God. His love is
a mind-altering reality, one that we can hardly wrap our heads around.
But with our imaginations, we get a glimpse of what is definitely true.
We don't get to have a bed all to ourselves because we are smart or
clean or well behaved. We get the bed because we belong to Someone

who knows our needs—Someone who is infinitely good, Someone who cares about every detail of our lives. That kind of unearned, undeserved love shakes us to the core.

Won't it be wonderful when we are finally able to settle down, like these orphans, into our little beds and really feel assured that God's love and goodness and presence (and presents!) are here to stay? One of the good gifts God has given us is our spiritual temperaments—our love languages with Him—and this gift is ours forever. God comes to us humbly because of His love, and in that coming we are met, known, understood. Yes, God is a very good God. And in His mercy, He speaks our language and wires us to speak His, too.

Still, in spite of His goodness, we come to the Lord most days like orphans: so uncertain, virtual unbelievers. We need to be reassured again and again that we are loved, known, and safe in a relationship that will never be taken away. We, too, have been adopted, though it will take us a lifetime to fully understand all that became ours the day He brought us into His family. As Anders Nygren, bishop of Lund, said, "God's love defies reason. It is 'irrational.'"[2] That is why in France on Easter morning you will see written on the sides of buildings and the backs of buses—in block print, script, or graffiti—"*L'amour de Dieu est folie . . . L'amour de Dieu est folie!*" The love of God is folly! The love of God is folly! I am told the French sometimes sing this phrase in their Christian churches; they recite it, they chant it, they even speak it out as a phrase of greeting as they pass on the streets Easter morning, because they know that the extravagant, unearned love of God is crazy, ridiculous, preposterous![3] A holy, perfect, all-sufficient God loves *us*? Doesn't that sound absurd?

And to us it is! For God's love has no corresponding likeness—no known corollary on this planet except in the pure, selfless life of Jesus of Nazareth. Thus, for us to own this love for ourselves can take quite a while. We come to realize slowly in an up-and-down, back-and-forth motion who this God really is, this Abba who has adopted us, this One who loves us because it is His nature to love. Eventually we will see that we never motivated God's love—we didn't earn it because we were smart or clean or well behaved—thus, we can't unmotivate Him. As A. W. Tozer said in *Knowledge of the Holy*, "Thou hast declared Thine unchanging love for us in Christ Jesus. If nothing in us can win Thy love, nothing in the universe can prevent Thee from loving us. Thy love is uncaused and undeserved. Our troubled hearts will be at peace when we come to trust not in what we are but in what Thou hast declared Thyself to be." In Christ this divine love is revealed to be so amazing, so astounding, that it breaks all bounds, refusing to be controlled by the value of its object, determined only by its own intrinsic nature.[4]

In the midst of this generous love, we get more than good things—we get God Himself. His holy affection draws us in until finally we are moved beyond a life that is centered on ourselves and our preoccupation with *getting*. We are invited to progress beyond looking for more and better ways to be satisfied, to a life that is God centered, one that allows our whole beings to revolve around the triune God, through whom and for whom we were created. We were born to experience the glorious liberty of being children of God. This is a position, a stature, and a privilege that elevates us beyond human love—an affection that can actually war with God's love because the two loves belong to entirely separate spiritual worlds. While human love wants to get and possess, God's love wants to give and empower. Human love can be fickle, conditional, and reliant upon the quality, beauty, and worth of its object, while God's love is permanent, unconditional, sacrificial, and determined only by the quality, beauty, and worth of God Himself. Human love was never meant to be our substance and sustenance, for we were created to live in a love that does not respond to value at all but rather creates it. As Saint John of the Cross says, "When God looks, He loves, and by this look of love, He makes the Beloved gracious and pleasing to Himself."[5] Here is how Brennan Manning articulates it:

> The God and Father of Jesus loves men and women, not for what He finds in them, but for what He finds in Himself. It is not because men and women are good that He loves them, nor only good men and women that He loves. It's because He's so unspeakably, unutterably, unimaginably good that the God and Father of Jesus loves all men and women—even sinners! He does not detect what is congenial, attractive, and appealing and respond to it with His favor; He doesn't respond at all! For the God of Jesus is the Source; He acts, He does not react. He initiates love, a love

ON YOUR OWN

Look at the following quotes about God's love.
Underline the words that move your soul toward Him.

"The love of God is not a mild benevolence but a consuming fire."

Bede Griffiths

"One of the keys to a real religious experience is the shattering realization that no matter how hateful we are to ourselves, we are not hateful to God. This realization helps us to understand the difference between our love and His. Our love is a need, His a gift." *Thomas Merton*

"Again and again, God is seen afresh by Jesus as a God of surpassing goodness and of boundless, infinite mercy. My friends, I believe that Christianity happens when men and women experience the reckless, raging confidence that comes from knowing and experiencing the God of Jesus Christ. With this God, there's no need to be wary, no need to be scrupulous, and no need to be afraid." *Brennan Manning*

"We know from revelation that we exist because God desires us into being and keeps us in being. God, it would seem, is madly in love with us, and is always attracted to us. The problem is that most of us do not really believe it." *William Barry*

"The greatest gift I've ever received in my life in Jesus has been the Abba experience. He said, 'No one knows the Son except Abba, and no one knows Abba except the Son and those to whom the Son chooses to reveal Him.' I can only stutter and stammer about the life-changing power of the Abba encounter. . . . I mean freedom: freedom from the fear of life, freedom from the fear that I'm going to betray Jesus by my own malice, and freedom from the fear of death. . . . That is not sloppy sentimentality; that is daring to pray with the simplicity, childlike candor, boundless trust, easy familiarity and deep reverence of Jesus. Because of the central revelation of Jesus—and by the way, that great Lutheran scholar, Erimaeus, says the four letter word 'Abba' is the primary, most important revelation of Christ in the entire New Testament—we have opened to us (by Jesus) the possibility of undreamed of, unheard of intimacy with God in prayer, that the Abba of Jesus loves us unconditionally, as we are, and not as we should be." *Brennan Manning*

"While they were still a long way off, his father saw him and was deeply moved with compassion. He ran to him, he clasped him in his arms, and he couldn't stop kissing him. He simply could not stop kissing him."

Luke 15:20 (translated by Frank Montalbano)

without motive, and because His love is creative, it originates good rather than rewarding it. That's why Saint Augustine could write those lyrical lines: *"Qui amas di me . . . amabile"*—"In loving me, you made me lovable."[6]

Our chief end is to know this God and enjoy Him forever. And as we do, we will then allow ourselves to be led by One whose ever-guiding, ever-guarding love is judicious; it knows when to give and when to hold back. It is assertive; it knows when to press in and when to ask for more from us. It is a love built on both desire and discipline, for though it is a continual flow of unmerited kindness that is gracious, merciful, and slow to anger, it is also a wise, bold, all-knowing covenant love (*hesedh*) that always works on our behalf and never quits or walks away. It is exasperatingly persistent, gallingly relentless, this *hesedh* love.

Hesedh is the Hebrew word for covenant that describes the promised relationship God offers us, one that is deep, lasting, and full of affection, with an undeterred attitude of goodwill.

"Though the mountains be shaken and the hills be removed, yet my unfailing love for you will not be shaken nor my covenant of peace be removed," says the LORD, who has compassion on you.

Isaiah 54:10

Incline your ear and come to Me. Listen, that you may live; and I will make an everlasting covenant with you, according to the faithful mercies shown to David.   *Isaiah 55:3 (NASB)*

Know therefore that the LORD your God is God; he is the faithful God, keeping his covenant of love to a thousand generations of those who love him and keep his commands.   *Deuteronomy 7:9*

God's *hesedh* love lasts forever because it is the essential nature of God Himself.[7]

This covenant love relationship is demonstrated partly through our distinct spiritual temperaments. In this way, we respond differently to our outrageous Lover, who comes personally to each of us, beckoning us to respond in love as well. And He is pleased with our responses—

whether they originate in our minds because we are Intellectuals, or come from our hands and feet because we are Caregivers, or are forged through encounters with this evil age because we are Activists—since God longs for our reply, as any lover would. And how we express that love to Him is as individual as His invitation is to us.

Knowing and experiencing God's love ultimately frees us to surrender our hearts to Him. When we are able to grasp how freely and fully our God gives of His love, there remains nothing for us to do to gain more. And once we understand that, we no longer love God as a means of getting our own needs met. Instead, we are able to love Him with a pure and unfeigned affection that flows from grateful, responsive hearts that know who we are and whose we are. When we gaze at Him, we are captivated by what we see, and as love replies with love, a dual encounter takes place. In time we grow to love God merely for Himself—compelled only by His tender beauty, unlimited goodness, enduring faithfulness, and all-encompassing strength—and we come to love Him because every aspect of life culminates in the One for whom we were created.

WE CAN RESIST THIS INVITATION

While God is always extending His covenant invitation to us, His love is not necessarily easy to receive. We have to first acknowledge our need for Him and secondly acknowledge that His love is completely and thoroughly undeserved. Our bent toward pride doesn't yield easily. Just as the Pharisees opposed Jesus' declaration of God's unmerited love, so we, too, often resist this freely given love. Instead of receiving it humbly, we contend that we must work and strive to obtain it, yet as we do, questions arise in our souls that form deposits of unwanted residue on our hearts. *Have I done enough? Is there more to do? Did I pray sufficiently? Is God truly pleased with my efforts?*

It's as if we're orphans who—after undeservedly being welcomed into our new homes wearing only our old, tattered rags—now begin to think we must *earn* our new families, homes, and beds by keeping our clothes clean, tidying our rooms, and completing our chores. Love's initiation and invitation are lost, and suddenly it feels like it's all up to us.

Once we slip into this mind-set, no matter how hard we try to silence the questions, they return, requiring more and more work from us, taunting us with doubts about God's love for us, God's goodness, God's motives. Sometimes we even begin to unconsciously transfer the unloveliness we see in ourselves onto God Himself. As Bill Thrall, Bruce McNicol, and John Lynch illustrate in their book *TrueFaced*, there are two very different places from which we can live this journey with God. The first is from the "Room of Good Intentions," a life of constantly trying to get it right, striving to be better, working hard to please God and be loved. The second is from the "Room of Grace," a life lived out of the truth of being loved as much now as we ever will be. Here is their explanation:

> We discover in The Room of Grace that the almost unthinkable has happened. God has shown all of His cards. He reveals a breathtaking protection that brings us out of hiding. In essence, God says, "What if I tell them who they are? What if I take away any element of fear in condemnation, judgment, or rejection? What if I tell them I love them, will always love them? That I love them right now, no matter what they've done, as much as I love my only Son? That there's nothing they can do to make My love go away?
>
> "What if I tell them there are no lists? What if I tell them I don't keep a log of past offenses, of how little they pray, how often they've let me down, made promises that they don't keep? What if I tell them they are righteous, with my righteousness, right now? What if I tell them they can stop beating themselves up? That they can stop being so formal, stiff, and jumpy around me? What if I tell them I'm *crazy* about them? What if I tell them, even if they run to the ends of the earth and do the most horrible, unthinkable things, that when they come back, I'd receive them with tears and a party?
>
> "What if I tell them that if I am their Savior, they're going to heaven no matter what—it's a done deal? What if I tell them they have a new nature—saints, not saved sinners who should now 'buck-up and be better if they were any kind of Christians, after all he's done for you'? What if I tell them that I actually live in them

now? That I've put my love, power, and nature inside of them, at their disposal? What if I tell them that they don't have to put on a mask? That it is ok to be who they are at this moment, with all their junk. That they don't need to pretend about how close we are, how much they pray or don't, how much Bible they read or don't. What if they knew they don't have to look over their shoulder for fear if things get too good, the other shoe's gonna drop?

"What if they knew I will never, ever use the word *punish* in relation to them? What if they knew that when they mess up, I will never 'get back at them'? What if they were convinced that bad circumstances aren't my way of evening the score for taking advantage of me? What if they knew the basis of our friendship isn't how little they sin, but how much they let me love them? What if I tell them they can hurt my heart, but that I never hurt theirs? What if I tell them I like Eric Clapton's music too? What if I tell them I never really liked the Christmas handbell deal with the white gloves? What if I tell them they can open their eyes when they pray and still go to heaven? What if I tell them there is no secret agenda, no trapdoor? What if I tell them it isn't about their self-effort, but about allowing me to live my life through them?"

When you stand at the crossroad, you decide which road to choose largely upon how you see God's "gamble." *Do I really believe this stuff will hold up—for me?* This is the way of life in The Room of Grace. It is the way home to healing, joy, peace, fulfillment, contentment, and release into God's dreams for us. It almost feels like we're stealing silverware from the king's house, doesn't it? Truth is, the king paid a lot so that you wouldn't have to try to steal any silverware. He gets to give it to you, and other stuff so big and good and beautiful that we couldn't even begin to stuff it into our bag of loot. Wow! It takes the eyes some adjustment to look into such light, huh?[8]

I had to read that quote twice to be sure I'd read it correctly. The first time I saw those words was after a "disagreement" with my husband over his personal list—the one I'd just verbalized for him to work on. After reading this passage, I was reminded about how I am loved—without a list—and I realized I had slipped back into the Room of Good Intentions (which, by the way, is where those who live there want us to make our homes). I read these words to my husband and asked his forgiveness. Together we did some apologizing. Yes, it is easy to fall back into the Room of Good Intentions, thinking that this is the place God wants us to be.

I still reread those words every once in a while. Interestingly, Jesus said similar ones in a parable. In the story Jesus tells, we realize that God has already shown us all His cards and removed all elements of our fear, condemnation, judgment, and rejection. He made it clear that we are in a relationship with One who will always love us—right now, no matter what we've done—as much as the Father loves the Son. And there's nothing we can do to cause His love to grow stronger or make it go away. Before the foundation of the world, the Father loved the Son, and now He declares He loves us with a love that is exactly the same in quality and quantity:

> In the same way and to the same extent that the Father loves
> Me, in that same way and to that same exact extent I love you.
> Continually remember and drink in the full dimension of My depth
> of committed love for you.   *John 15:9 (my paraphrase)*

This is a love that calls us to rest because we are assured that we are eternally safe.

Here's the story Jesus tells:

> There was once a man who had two sons. The younger said to
> his father, "Father, I want right now what's coming to me." So the
> father divided the property between them. It wasn't long before
> the younger son packed his bags and left for a distant country.
> There, undisciplined and dissipated, he wasted everything he had.
> After he had gone through all his money, there was a bad famine
> all through that country and he began to hurt. He signed on with
> a citizen there who assigned him to his fields to slop the pigs. He
> was so hungry he would have eaten the corncobs in the pig slop,
> but no one would give him any.

That brought him to his senses. He said, "All those farmhands working for my father sit down to three meals a day, and here I am starving to death. I'm going back to my father. I'll say to him, Father, I've sinned against God, I've sinned before you; I don't deserve to be called your son. Take me on as a hired hand." He got right up and went home to his father.

When he was still a long way off, his father saw him. His heart pounding, he ran out, embraced him, and kissed him. The son started his speech: "Father, I've sinned against God, I've sinned before you; I don't deserve to be called your son ever again."

But the father wasn't listening. He was calling to the servants, "Quick. Bring a clean set of clothes and dress him. Put the family ring on his finger and sandals on his feet. Then get a grain-fed heifer and roast it. We're going to feast! We're going to have a wonderful time! My son is here—given up for dead and now alive! Given up for lost and now found!" And they began to have a wonderful time.

All this time his older son was out in the field. When the day's work was done he came in. As he approached the house, he heard the music and dancing. Calling over one of the houseboys, he asked what was going on. He told him, "Your brother came home. Your father has ordered a feast—barbecued beef!—because he has him home safe and sound."

The older brother stalked off in an angry sulk and refused to join in. His father came out and tried to talk to him, but he wouldn't listen. The son said, "Look how many years I've stayed here serving you, never giving you one moment of grief, but have you ever thrown a party for me and my friends? Then this son of yours who has thrown away your money on whores shows up and you go all out with a feast!"

His father said, "Son, you don't understand. You're with me all the time, and everything that is mine is yours—but this is a wonderful time, and we had to celebrate. This brother of yours was dead, and he's alive! He was lost, and he's found!"

Luke 15:11-32 (THE MESSAGE)

The generosity, grace, and expansive mercy of God the Father are unlike anything we've ever experienced! As Brennan Manning says, "The prophets of Israel had revealed the God of Abraham, Isaac, and Jacob in a warmer, more passionate manner, but only Jesus revealed—to an astonished Jewish community—that God is truly our Father, offering the love of all the best mothers and fathers who ever lived in the course of human history. Think about that for a moment. If you take all the goodness, kindness, patience, fidelity, wisdom, tenderness, strength and love, and unite all those qualities into a single person, that person would only be a faint shadow of the love and the mercy in the heart of God the Father, addressed to you and to me this moment."[9] When we live our lives from this place of total acceptance *now*—knowing the truth that we are already loved as much as we will ever be in the spacious Room of Grace—then we will not constantly be trying to get it right, striving to do it better, working hard to please God and secure His love in the Room of Good Intentions. We will be at peace knowing we are fully known, fully wanted, and fully enjoyed. As the apostle Paul said to the Galatian church:

> Answer this question: Does the God who lavishly provides you with his own presence, his Holy Spirit, working things in your lives you could never do for yourselves, does he do these things because of your strenuous moral striving or because you trust him to do them in you? . . . The obvious impossibility of carrying out such a moral program should make it plain that no one can sustain a relationship with God that way. The person who lives in right relationship with God does it by embracing what God arranges for him. Doing things for God is the opposite of entering into what God does for you. Habakkuk had it right: "The person who believes God, is set right by God—and that's the real life."
>
> *Galatians 3:5, 11 (THE MESSAGE)*

This is a truth we must own, because it really does set us free!

COMMUNICATING LOVE

As we come to understand our spiritual temperaments—the unique spiritual languages God has given us to communicate with Him—we begin to realize that this is just one more way that our Creator, the majestic One, has come near to meet us, listen to us, and let His glory shine through us. The eternal God, *Jehovah Elohim*, has invited us to be His, to use our "God languages" to speak to Him—our Lover and Lord—in a way that brings Him joy. Whether we are Sensates or Caregivers, we know we can snuggle down into His heart—the place for which we were created—and find it safe to be with the One who is seeking us as we follow the longing in our souls that He deposited there Himself.

Isaiah had it right when he said that our names are tattooed on the palms of God's hands (see Isaiah 49:16). Can you imagine what that must look like? Do you see with the eyes of your imagination the Father as a biker dude with names tattooed all over Him? Or does another image come to mind? When I think of this metaphor, I picture my friend who has the name of his baby daughter tattooed across his chest in one-inch Gaelic letters. With my God-redeemed, God-surrendered, God-enlivened imagination, I see the holy One of Israel seated on His throne, looking down at His hand. And as He turns it over and gazes at His palm, He reads my name—and yours—words that are permanently etched there. Can you see His face with your mind's eye? Is He smiling? Is He thinking about you *right now* because He loves you as a mother loves the child at her breast? His heart is moving toward you in affection, wanting your best, having died to secure it. Daily He empowers you by judiciously saying yes, no, or wait, helping you grow to full maturity, causing every situation in your life to ultimately be used for your good as He delights in each step you take. Do you see yourself through God's eyes and feel the wonder of His loving presence, His burning heart, which—though you are flawed—envisions you as you truly are in Christ Jesus? Can you imagine it?

Whether you are a Naturalist who senses God's invitation as you wade into a mountain stream or an Activist who discerns God's pleasure as you right a wrong in His name, do try to picture this God of love coming to meet you as you consider the following messages about how He feels toward His children:

I, the Lord, will love you and bless you and multiply you; I will bless the fruit of your womb and the fruit of your ground, your grain and your new wine and your oil, the increase of your herd and the young of your flock, in the land which I, the Lord, swore to give your forefathers. *Deuteronomy 7:13 (my paraphrase)*

Do you think anyone is going to be able to drive a wedge between us and Christ's love for us? There is no way! Not trouble, not hard times, not hatred, not hunger, not homelessness, not bullying threats, not backstabbing, not even the worst sins listed in Scripture. . . . I'm absolutely convinced that nothing—nothing living or dead, angelic or demonic, today or tomorrow, high or low, thinkable or unthinkable—absolutely nothing can get between us and God's love because of the way that Jesus our Master has embraced us. *Romans 8:35, 38-39 (THE MESSAGE)*

We know how much God loves us, and we have put our trust in his love. God is love, and all who live in love live in God, and God lives in them. And as we live in God, our love grows more perfect. So we will not be afraid on the day of judgment, but we can face him with confidence because we live like Jesus here in this world. Such love has no fear, because perfect love expels all fear. If we are afraid, it is for fear of punishment, and this shows that we have not fully experienced his perfect love. *1 John 4:16-18 (NLT)*

You are precious in My sight . . . you are honored and I love you. *Isaiah 43:4 (NASB)*

"Even if the mountains walk away and the hills fall to pieces, my love won't walk away from you, my covenant commitment of peace won't fall apart." The God who has compassion on you says so. *Isaiah 54:10 (THE MESSAGE)*

The LORD your God is living among you. He is a mighty savior. He will take delight in you with gladness. With his love, he will calm all your fears. He will rejoice over you with joyful songs. *Zephaniah 3:17 (NLT)*

Take me away with you! Let's run off together! An elopement with my King-Lover! We'll celebrate, we'll sing, we'll make great music. Yes! For your love is better than vintage wine. Everyone loves you—of course! And why not? . . . My lover has arrived and he's speaking to me! Get up, my dear friend, fair and beautiful lover—come to me! Look around you: Winter is over; the winter rains are over, gone! Spring flowers are in blossom all over. The whole world's a choir—and singing! Spring warblers are filling the forest with sweet arpeggios. Lilacs are exuberantly purple and perfumed, and cherry trees fragrant with blossoms. Oh, get up, dear friend, my fair and beautiful lover—come to me! . . . You're so beautiful, my darling, so beautiful.

Song of Solomon 1:4; 2:10-13; 4:1 (The Message)

There is so much love to be internalized. What are we waiting for? There's an eternity of God Himself to be explored! How awesome! How wonderful! How exciting!

Christ will make his home in your hearts as you trust in him. Your roots will grow down into God's love and keep you strong. And may you have the power to understand, as all God's people should, how wide, how long, how high, and how deep his love is. May you experience the love of Christ, though it is too great to understand fully. Then you will be made complete with all the fullness of life and power that comes from God. *Ephesians 3:17-19 (NLT)*

Perhaps you are wondering if you really know this Jesus we've been talking about and if you have officially begun your journey with Him. Scripture makes it clear that eternal life is available to every person (see Romans 10:13). Pain, sickness, disease, and death are all part of this fallen world; however, we have already overcome the worst this world has to offer—even death—when we have Christ (see 1 John 5:4-5). Do you want this unending life with Him? Do you desire to be in a relationship with God forever?

God makes a promise to us: "This is what God has testified: He has given us eternal life, and this life is in his Son. Whoever has the Son has life; whoever does not have God's Son does not have life. I have written this to you who believe in the name of the Son of God, so that you may know you have eternal life" (1 John 5:11-13, NLT). Today you can *know* that you have eternal life. You can say yes to God's invitation. "*Yes, I* believe You. *Yes*, I want You to be the center of my life. *Yes*, I know I can't earn Your love, don't deserve it, and never will. But *yes*, I receive Your mercy and forgiveness for my revolt against Your love, and I ask for Your ongoing decontamination of my soul, Your release from all that has bound me, Your healing power. *Yes*, I will follow Your lead as You guide me every day. *Yes*, teach me how to walk with You, and *yes*, by Your grace, allow me to live more fully in Your love, for as I do, I know I will never be the same. Thank You, Lord Jesus."

Seal this with God right now as you say *yes*. Pause, won't you, and pray . . . whether for the first time or not . . . responding to the One who loves you and made you to be His sheep for the rest of your life.

ON YOUR OWN

Today I say *yes* to Jesus!
Write the date and your own words in your journal as you say *yes*.

After you have said *yes*, perhaps others are coming to mind who need to hear this amazing truth too. Maybe there are people you know who want to say *yes* to Jesus as well, to know that they are eternally God's children. For "how great is the love the Father has lavished on us, that we should be called children of God! And that is what we are!" (1 John 3:1). If people are coming to mind, why not stop and pray for them right now. Just lay them in the loving arms of Jesus and ask Him to bring them to a place where they will say *yes* to Jesus too. Can you imagine it?

Now remember that it will take you a lifetime to learn all the ins and outs, the intricacies and specifics of this life God has given you. There are more privileges ahead than you could ever count. But as we continue this journey of knowing Jesus—for when we put our trust in Him, the journey truly begins—we are assured we are in a covenant journey with a fully committed, loving God, and He will be with us every day in a journey that will never end! May we grow in our ability to both give love and receive love more and more each day . . . until the kingdoms of this world become the Kingdom of our God.

For Further Reflection and Discussion

1. Reflect upon your own spiritual temperament, or love language with God. How has knowing that about yourself helped you receive God's love at a deeper level?

2. Reread this passage and then write it in your own words, filling in your name where appropriate: "In the same way and to the same extent that the Father loves Me [Jesus], in that same way and to that exact same extent I [Jesus] love you, _____ [your name]. Continually remember and drink in the full dimension of My depth of committed love for you, _____ [your name]" (John 15:9, my paraphrase).

3. In the Gospel of Mark, we read about a time when Jesus took Peter, James, and John up a mountain. The Bible tells us that suddenly they saw the God-Man clothed in brilliant light, surrounded by such glory and overwhelming beauty that all Peter could say was something like, "Oh, Jesus, let me build a shelter for us and then we can stay here together—forever!" (see Mark 9:5). Peter, overcome with love, saw God, and the only thing he wanted to do in that moment was be with His Lord forever. Jesus made Peter's longing come true when He said, "I am going there to prepare a place for you . . . that you also may be where I am" (John 14:2-3). Try to imagine it now. See the glorious mountain through Peter's eyes, and then see Jesus in all His magnificence. Join them on the mountain as you are welcomed in. Sit with this picture awhile. Then record your thoughts in your journal.

4. Since we left Eden, we have been longing for the magnificence and closeness we had with God in the beginning—total access, walking and talking face-to-face in the cool of the day, being instructed in safety, undisturbed in perfect love and trust. Though we must live outside Eden for now, the book of Revelation says that someday we will once again experience that complete face-to-face communion God intended for us. And once again God will live among us forever; there will be no sadness or tears or death or pain. In that day there will be a wedding, and we will be the bride, sharing the extravagant brilliance of our Groom. There will not be any sun or moon, for the brightness of the glory of God will be our illumination. And all the nations will be there. A river with crystal clear, life-giving water will flow right down the middle of the street from the very throne of God and of the Lamb, and the tree of life

will be available with its healing leaves. We will see God's face forever, worshipping Him in the fullness of truth, and His name will be written on our foreheads. Forever and ever we will endlessly reign with Him (see Revelation 22:1-5). Close your eyes now and sit in God's presence. Ask Him to allow you to picture a bit of His beauty in this moment . . . enough to hold you for the rest of the day.

PART TWO

THE SPIRITUAL PRACTICE EXERCISES

7

RENEWING SPIRITUAL PASSION, PLEASURE, AND POTENTIAL

God has given each of us a spiritual temperament—a unique love language or way of knowing and loving Him. Your spiritual temperament shows your spiritual *preferences* or desires—how you most naturally and intrinsically tend to come to God. But you are also helped as you incorporate spiritual *practices* or habits—how you intentionally and deliberately choose to come to God. This section of the book is designed to help you align your spiritual preferences with your spiritual practices, encouraging greater spiritual passion for the Lord.

In this section, the spiritual temperaments are divided into subsets, depending upon the strength of each spiritual temperament:

- your *passionate* temperaments—those that are strongest and stir your passion for God most readily (where you scored *high*)
- your *pleasurable* temperaments—those that you enjoy and that nurture your relationship with God (where you scored *moderate*)
- your *potential* temperaments—those that are relatively unused and undeveloped, almost foreign to you (where you scored *low*)

Look at your scores for the Spiritual Temperament Inventory on page 27 and the Spiritual Practices Inventory on page 34, and record your scores on page 158. A score of 18 to 24 on the Spiritual Temperament Inventory shows a *high* preference for that spiritual temperament, and on the Spiritual Practices Inventory, a score of 18 to 24 indicates *high* activity in that spiritual practice. A score of 12 to 17 shows a *moderate* preference for that spiritual temperament or *moderate* activity in that spiritual practice. A score of 11 or under shows a *low* preference for that spiritual temperament or *low* activity in that spiritual practice.

Your Spiritual Temperament and Practices Scores

	Temperament Scores (page 27)	HML		Practices Scores (page 34)	HML
Activist	_____	_____	Activist	_____	_____
Ascetic	_____	_____	Ascetic	_____	_____
Caregiver	_____	_____	Caregiver	_____	_____
Contemplative	_____	_____	Contemplative	_____	_____
Enthusiast	_____	_____	Enthusiast	_____	_____
Intellectual	_____	_____	Intellectual	_____	_____
Naturalist	_____	_____	Naturalist	_____	_____
Sensate	_____	_____	Sensate	_____	_____
Traditionalist	_____	_____	Traditionalist	_____	_____

High Preferences	Moderate Preferences	Low Preferences

In this section, you will find several weeks of exercises designed to help you develop your spiritual practices in one or more of the spiritual temperaments. Though you will be encouraged to begin with those spiritual temperaments in which you scored the highest—your most passionate spiritual temperaments—you will also be given an opportunity to explore practices in those spiritual temperaments in which you scored moderate or low—your pleasurable or potential spiritual temperaments. You will not only get to focus on the joy that comes from knowing God in the way you were uniquely made—through your spiritual temperaments—but you will also have a chance to experience the growth that comes when you try new and unfamiliar practices outside your preferences.

These exercises are not exhaustive by any means; they are only a sampling to get you started. Just as people can't rely on only a few exercises at the gym to permanently strengthen all their muscles, so these exercises are simply starting places to raise awareness and give initial direction.

On the following pages, the exercises are listed alphabetically from Activist to Traditionalist. Each section is broken down into weeklong spiritual practices for those who consider themselves to be beginners (those who score within the low range of a particular spiritual temperament).

For those who scored within the moderate or high range of the spiritual temperament, intermediate and advanced exercises are available at www.ChristianBookGuides.com.

THE ESSENCE OF THE SPIRITUAL EXERCISES

A spiritual exercise utilizes certain practices to help you focus more completely on God. Just as physical exercise addresses specific physical muscles, so these practice exercises address specific spiritual muscles.

My husband and I recently joined a gym, and I received several sessions with Ellen, a personal trainer. I have to admit that there were days when I met with Ellen simply because the sessions were a part of the package we'd already purchased. Most days it was not easy to carve out time from my already busy schedule to go to the gym. Some days I canceled my appointments with Ellen. But she was there every time I showed up; I just had to look for her. Ellen was a good exercise coach, companion, and cheerleader, and I'm happy to say that within several months, my body began to change; I felt much better too—in every way. The pain in my right knee that had been there for a over decade no longer bothered me, and my clothes fit better as well. Though I didn't see the payoffs of my time with Ellen immediately, eventually they came, and I was very glad I'd made the effort.

While it may take months for you to feel the benefits of your spiritual growth and progress as you move through these exercises, be assured that spiritual growth *will* come. Remember, the goal is not to simply complete the exercises but to know and love God more fully and deeply. Let His Spirit lead you as you meet Him faithfully through the exercises. He will be your spiritual Coach, your Companion, and your Cheerleader, and He will be there each time you show up; just look for Him.

Remember, these are exercises, and who among us gets ecstatic about the prospect of a strenuous workout, especially when we are addressing muscles that are undeveloped or unused? Begin to work your new spiritual muscles slowly. If the exercises feel awkward, try them anyway. Do what you can, asking God to make the experiences real to you. If your heart is surrendered to Jesus, He will meet you. In a month or a year, you may return to these same exercises and find that what once felt awkward has become easier, maybe even enjoyable.

Getting Started

Because the goal of this section is to help you both expand your spiritual practices as well as match them with your spiritual preferences, begin by looking at "Your Spiritual Temperament and Practices Scores" on page 158. Find your highest spiritual preferences (those temperaments in which you scored highest)—areas where you are most passionate in expressing love for God. Now look at your corresponding spiritual practice scores. If high practice scores match high temperament scores, chances are you are currently doing well and feeling quite fulfilled with the Lord in that area.

However, all your high temperament scores may not have corresponding high practice scores. Find where your highest spiritual temperament scores and practice scores do *not* match—where your practice score is lower than your preference score. When any of your high spiritual temperament scores are not matched by high spiritual practice scores, that is the place to begin using the spiritual exercises for that temperament.

Next, find the exercises located for that spiritual temperament in this section. In other words, if you scored high as a Sensate but your spiritual practice scores were low, start with the Sensate spiritual practice exercises. If you find the exercises for the beginning Sensate too simplistic, move on to the intermediate, and then to the advanced exercises at www.ChristianBookGuides.com. Stay with the Sensate temperament until all the exercises are completed. Then move to the next highest spiritual temperament scores where your spiritual practice scores were lower than your preference scores. Continue with the exercises for that spiritual temperament. Keep working through the spiritual practice exercises for each of your passionate spiritual preferences—those spiritual temperaments in which you scored in the high range—wherever you find your spiritual practice scores less than their corresponding preference scores.

Continuing On

You can't rush spiritual growth. Just as physical exercise is easier when you move along at a reasonable pace, so spiritual growth also requires patience and pacing. Therefore, after you have given yourself several weeks to work through the spiritual practice exercises for your high or passionate spiritual preferences, move on to the temperaments in which you scored in the moderate or pleasurable range. Find the spiritual practice exercises for each of those spiritual temperaments. If you are having difficulty selecting one temperament from your moderate range, begin with the temperament in which your spiritual practices score is lowest. Start with the exercises for beginners, then go to www.ChristianBookGuides.com for the intermediate and advanced exercises for that temperament.

Settling into a Rhythm

After you have worked on exercises in your passionate (high) and pleasurable (moderate) spiritual temperament ranges, you will have likely begun to establish a good rhythm. As in all exercise, you will probably be seeing the consistency in your life with God bear fruit. Remember to give yourself a lot of grace, because it is only by God's grace that we are transformed, and it is within God's grace and unalterable love that we live—even when we fall short of our own standards. Just keep your eyes on Jesus, for He is your goal!

Finally, find a spiritual temperament in which you scored low. This is an area that is least developed in your spiritual life and has the greatest potential for growth. When you are ready to begin exploring new practices in this area, you might find it to be the most profound—albeit challenging—work the Lord does in your life. Start with the spiritual practice exercises found in that spiritual temperament for the beginner. If you are having difficulty selecting one temperament from your low range, begin with the temperament in which you scored the highest in the spiritual practices. Then continue until you have worked through all the spiritual practice exercises for your lowest spiritual preferences.

A WORD OF CAUTION

Remember that life with God is about having an ongoing love relationship with Him; it's a process, a lifelong journey. Don't be surprised if in developing that relationship, you encounter the enemy, who comes to steal, kill, and destroy your life with Jesus (see John 10:10). He often uses the traps of performance and perfectionism to ensnare his victims. This happens when we take our eyes off the Lord and focus increasingly on ourselves, becoming either proud or discouraged. Then the relational aspect of the journey gradually slips away and legalism takes over.

Unfortunately, the enemy is not the only one who will try to ambush us. We also have fallen natures, which are bent toward trying to achieve perfection on their own. Be attentive to your own human tendency to care more about the process of how perfectly you are doing the spiritual practice exercise than about how your heart is being moved toward God and His truth. At every turn, your flesh will try to take center stage and push the relationship to the side. When your flesh is active, you will know it because you'll begin to put more emphasis on how much you are accomplishing rather than how your love for Jesus is growing. Just remember that the goal of these exercises is to create a genuine connection with Jesus as you come to Him in His righteousness alone.

GOD WILL DO HIS PART

It is wonderful to realize that when all is said and done, only God can change us. No amount of spiritual exercise offers any benefit apart from the transforming work of God's Holy Spirit. You can only change by God's grace, and only God can give you the desire to know and love Him more. In this process, your part will be fivefold: (1) seeing and acknowledging the areas of your life that are in need of God's development, (2) opening yourself to God's Spirit to make the changes, (3) telling Jesus that you need Him, (4) asking Him to do His deep work within you, and (5) responding to His already present Spirit as the work begins and continues. It is a partnership and a cooperative effort. Just as two people on a dance floor move together, God is the leader in your spiritual life, and responding to His lead is essential.

This being said, we all have a choice: We can resist His influence, or we can receive it. As Philippians 2:12-13 says:

> My beloved, just as you have always obeyed, not as in my presence only, but now much more in my absence, work out your salvation with fear and trembling; for it is God who is at work in you, both to will and to work for His good pleasure. *(NASB)*

As you put yourself into places that expose you to God's transforming Spirit, He will consistently meet you there. Over time, you will begin to grow and change. This is a law God has built into His universe, the law of reaping and sowing (see Galatians 6:7-8). What you sow, you will surely reap; thus, your part is to sow to the Spirit as you depend upon God to graciously work in you. Sowing to the Spirit simply means giving God access to the soil of your heart, trusting Him as you plant His Word inside. It means letting God's truth dwell in you through obedience so the Spirit of God can do His supernatural work inside you . . . knowing the results will eventually follow.

As you begin these exercises, use a journal to record your answers. Ask Jesus to do the work of transforming you as you put yourself in the place of willing reception, inviting His grace to do its divine job. Remember, just as we began by grace, it is grace that leads us home. As Richard Foster says:

God will not enter many areas of our lives uninvited.

So we invite God to enter every experience of life:

We invite God to set our spirit free for worship and adoration.

We invite God to animate our preaching and praying and singing.

We invite God to heal our bodies.

We invite God to inform our minds with creative ideas for our business enterprises.

We invite God to touch broken relationships and resolve conflicts at work or home.

We invite God to make our homes holy places of worship and study and work and play and lovemaking.

We invite . . . we invite.

Perhaps we could speak of this as "invited grace."[1]

May God's invited grace usher you more deeply into His heart—day by day—as you move by His Spirit through these exercises.

8

THE ACTIVIST

Loving God through Confrontation with Evil

Record your temperament score for the Activist from page 158. _____
Is it high, medium, or low? _____

Record your practice score for the Activist. _____
Is it high, medium, or low? _____

In spiritual development, repetition is one way the Lord brings growth and transformation. Through repetition, God's Spirit can deal with us at ever-deepening levels and in more detail, which is why we will be focusing on one exercise for an entire week. It will be helpful for you to read and review the weekly activity each day, asking God to increase your capacity to know and love Him each time you revisit the exercise.

SPIRITUAL PRACTICES FOR THE BEGINNING ACTIVIST

Week 1

Read: The dictionary defines *activism* as the practice of direct and vigorous action in support of or in opposition to an issue.[1] The Activist spiritual temperament is in contrast to others because the Activist doesn't simply speculate, think about, or ponder a situation; he or she takes action in a wise, judicious manner.

Sometimes God invites His people to take action primarily through prayer. James 5:16-20 says:

Confess your sins to each other and pray for each other so that
you may be healed. The prayer of a righteous man is powerful and
effective. Elijah was a man just like us. He prayed earnestly that it
would not rain, and it did not rain on the land for three and a half
years. Again he prayed, and the heavens gave rain, and the earth
produced its crops. My brothers, if one of you should wander from
the truth and someone should bring him back, remember this:
Whoever turns a sinner from the error of his way will save him
from death and cover over a multitude of sins.

Reflect: Think of someone in your life who appears to be compromising
with evil, someone moving toward darkness and away from God's light.
How may the Lord be inviting you to pray for that person?

Respond: If you had the opportunity to talk with that person, what
would you say? Write down some ways you might begin that conversation in a spirit of humility and compassion.

Now spend time praying for this person, asking God to have mercy
on her or him and to give you the compassion to listen as well as the
courage to speak His truth in love.

Record: How did you take action this week?

What follow-up needs to be done in the future? Share your progress
with a friend you can trust, asking this person to check in with you next
month about the situation and the action you took.

Now write a prayer in your journal, committing your steps to the Lord
(see Psalm 37:5).

Week 2

Read: After God created humanity in His likeness and image, He gave
this mandate: "Be fruitful and increase in number; fill the earth and
subdue it. Rule over the fish of the sea and the birds of the air and over
every living creature that moves on the ground" (Genesis 1:28). On that
day, God made us responsible for life on earth.[2] He intended that we

carry out this assignment by working in a "conscious, personal relation-ship of interactive responsibility with Him. We are meant to exercise our 'rule' only in union with God, as He acts with us."[3]

Jesus gives us a picture of how He intends for us to "subdue and rule" in partnership with Him when He says, "Our Father in heaven, hallowed be your name, your kingdom come, your will be done on earth as it is in heaven" (Matthew 6:9-10). When you wonder if something is right or wrong on earth—if it pleases or displeases God, if it gladdens or saddens His heart—you have only to ask yourself this question: Is this sanctioned by God in heaven, and if not, why is it being done on earth?

Reflect: Obviously, you cannot right every wrong or fight every battle. Jesus didn't. He did, however, obey His Father and confront the evil the Father gave Him to meet head-on (see John 5:19). Ask the Lord now if there are wrongs within your sphere of influence that He wants to give you the courage and wisdom to confront—not for confrontation's sake, but so that your piece of earth will look a little more like heaven.

Respond: What is God showing you?

What action will you take this week?

Perhaps there is another person God is calling to take action in this same area. Invite the Lord to lead you to that person so that, together, the two of you can see more of God's Kingdom come on earth.

Record: How did you take action this week?

What follow-up do you need to do in the future? Share your progress with a friend you can trust, asking him or her to check in with you next month about this situation and the action you took.

Now write a prayer, committing your steps to the Lord (see Psalm 37:5).

Week 3

Read: In Mark 6:34, we see in Jesus one of the greatest motivations behind activism: "When Jesus went ashore, He saw a large crowd, and

He felt compassion for them because they were like sheep without a shepherd" (NASB).

Reflect: The most mature, effective Activist of all time was One who was moved with compassion. Ponder now how Jesus' compassion must be the underlying motivation for all you do as an Activist.

Respond: How much are you moved by compassion in the causes you champion?

If not compassion, what *does* move you? Talk honestly with the Lord now about how you would like your heart to become more like His.

Record: How did you take action this week?

What follow-up do you need to do in the future? Share your progress with a friend you can trust, asking him or her to check in with you next month about this situation and the action you took.

Week 4

Integration: Review the last few weeks. What has God taught you?

How will you integrate what you've learned into your life?

If there are ways you need to take action in the future, write them in your journal.

Go to www.ChristianBookGuides.com for intermediate and advanced-level exercises.

9

THE ASCETIC

Loving God through Solitude and Simplicity

Record your temperament score for the Ascetic from page 158. _____
Is it high, medium, or low? _____

Record your practice score for the Ascetic. _____
Is it high, medium, or low? _____

In spiritual development, repetition is one way the Lord brings growth
and transformation. Through repetition, God's Spirit can deal with us
at ever-deepening levels and in more detail, which is why we will be
focusing on one exercise for an entire week. It will be helpful for you
to read and review the weekly activity each day, asking God to increase
your capacity to know and love Him each time you revisit the exercise.

SPIRITUAL PRACTICES FOR THE BEGINNING ASCETIC

Week 1

Read: Thomas Kelly speaks of our need to return often to the quiet
place within us where God dwells. He writes:

> Deep within us, there is an amazing inner sanctuary of the soul,
> a holy place, a Divine Center, a speaking Voice, to which we may
> continuously return. Eternity is at our hearts, pressing upon our
> time-torn lives, warming us with intimations of an astounding
> destiny, calling us home unto Itself. . . . In this humanistic age we

suppose man is the initiator and God is the responder. But the Living Christ within us is the initiator and we are the responders. God the Lover, the accuser, the revealer of light . . . God the initiator, God the aggressor, God the seeker, God the stirrer into life, God the ground of our obedience, God the giver of the power to become children of God.[1]

Reflect: It has been said that when we are centered, our bodies flow with ease, and our minds are more present and aware.[2] Think about times when you feel most centered. What is happening for you at these times?

Consider what Kelly calls the "Divine Center." Do you think it is realistic for you to live from that place?

Why or why not?

What most distracts you from living peacefully from this inner sanctuary of the soul?

Respond: God is the Initiator, and we are the responders. The Lord is always working on our behalf, caring for us, watching over us, and loving us. It is good to pause and remember that Jesus ever lives to make intercession for us (see Hebrews 7:25) and that when we pray, it is the Holy Spirit who is present to pray and intercede for and through us (see Romans 8:26-27). The result is that we can rest and be quiet inside because the all-powerful, sovereign God is always at work.

The fathers and mothers of the faith used a discipline called "breath prayer" to experience the deep, abiding truth that God is always watching over us. This week, begin using breath prayer—exhaling and breathing out anything that needs to be released, and giving all that you have carried to God (such as fear, worry, guilt, resentment, anger, grief, sadness, hatred, and unforgiveness); then inhale and breathe in God's truth (His sovereign, all-seeing, all-knowing wisdom and His goodness and grace), receiving God's provision of peace and freedom.

Begin now by relaxing your body. Notice any points of tension, and consciously give each one to God. Imagine Him touching your neck, for example, absorbing the tension and weight of responsibility you carry. Then begin to breathe, starting with your physical body, saying:

(Exhale): I release to You, Lord, the tightness in _____ [my back, for example].

(Inhale): I receive now Your grace to wear Your yoke, which is easy and light [see Matthew 11:30]. Help me, Lord.

Continue this process until your body is fully relaxed. Next exhale anything emotional that is spinning in your mind or heart, always ending each breath with the words, "Help me, Lord."

(Exhale): I release to You _____ [my fear of the future, for example].

(Inhale): I receive now Your watchful care that has written every day of my life in Your book before there was even one [see Psalm 139]. Help me, Lord.

(Exhale): I release to You _____ [the foolish comment I made to my boss yesterday, for example].

(Inhale): I receive now Your grace and forgiveness for all the less-than-perfect comments I've made, and I breathe in the truth that You know every word I'm going to say even before I say it and that You accept me, Lord, knowing that I am but dust [see Psalm 139:4; 103:13-14]. Help me, Lord.

(Exhale): I release to You _____ [my loneliness and need for friends, for example].

(Inhale): I receive now Your promise to never leave me or forsake me and to provide for my emotional needs [see Hebrews 13:5; Philippians 2:19-29]. Help me, Lord.

Continue this process until your heart and mind are quieted.

Next exhale anything spiritual that is standing between you and the Lord, or you and another person, ending each breath with the words, "Help me, Lord."

(Exhale): I release to You _____ [my fear about my son and his choices, and my doubts that You are big enough to take care of him as he wanders, for example].

(Inhale): I receive now Your promise that You love my son more than I do, and the darkness does not hide his way from You [see Psalm 139]. Help me, Lord.

(Exhale): I release to You _____ [my jealousy and envy that one of my friends has a new car and went on another vacation to Europe, while my car is worse than hers, and I've never been to Europe, for example].

(Inhale): I receive now Your promise that day by day, You will always supply all that I need as I seek You first [see Matthew 6:33]. Help me, Lord.

Finish your time by praying this paraphrased version of the Shield of Saint Patrick:

This day I bind to myself the strong name of the Trinity, eternal Father, Spirit, Word;

Praise to the God of my salvation, salvation is of Christ the Lord!

I bind to myself by Christ's incarnation the power of God to hold and lead,

His eye to watch, His might to stay, His ear to harken to my need,

The wisdom of my God to teach, His gentle hand, His shield to ward,

The Word of God to give me speech, His heavenly host to be my guard:

Christ to the right of me, Christ to the left of me, Christ in my lying, Christ in my sitting, Christ in my rising; Christ in the heart of all who think of me, Christ on the tongue of all who speak to me, Christ in the eye of all who see me, Christ in the ear of all who hear me.

This day I bind to myself the strong name of the Trinity, eternal
Father, Spirit, Word;

Praise to the God of my salvation, salvation is of Christ the Lord!

Record: How would you describe your times of breath prayer this week?

What did you learn during these times?

Share your progress with a friend you can trust, asking him or her to
check in with you next month about your use of breath prayers.

Write a prayer, committing your steps to the Lord (see Psalm 37:5).

Week 2

Read: It sometimes seems impossible that we could ever reach a place in
life where inner peace and quiet are common in our soul. Annie Dillard
said this of trying to maintain quietness within:

> All I can do is try to gag the commentator, to hush the noise
> of useless interior babble. . . . The effort is really a discipline
> requiring a lifetime of dedicated struggle. . . . The world's spiritual
> geniuses seem to discover universally that the mind's muddy river,
> this ceaseless flow of trivia and trash, cannot be dammed, and that
> trying to dam it is a waste of effort that might lead to madness.
> Instead you must allow the muddy river to flow unheeded in the
> dim channels of consciousness; you raise your sights; you look
> [beyond it] . . . without utterance.[3]

We raise our sights to God. Henri Nouwen said it this way:

> Oh Lord Jesus, your words to your Father were born out of your
> silence. Lead me into this silence, so that my words may be spoken
> in your name and thus be fruitful. It is so hard to be silent, silent
> with my mouth, but even more, silent with my heart. There is
> so much talking going on within me. It seems that I am always
> involved with inner debates with myself, my friends, my enemies,
> my supporters, my opponents, my colleagues, and my rivals. But
> this inner debate reveals how far my heart is from you.[4]

Reflect: How difficult is it for you to quiet the inner "commentator," the interior babble and debates that keep you captive to the mind's muddy river?

As you reflect on the inner noise, what "mind mud" seems to bog you down the most?

Is there a time of day that seems to bring more of a natural stillness within?

When is it that the inner noise is the loudest? the most silent?

Respond: The Hebrews thought of God's Spirit as *ruach*—the breath or wind of God. Sit now, and every day this week, for five or ten minutes, allowing God's *ruach* to fill and calm you. Set a timer so you are not tempted to watch the clock. During this time, make it your sole purpose to allow yourself to be centered and quieted by God. I call it "combing the tangles out of my soul," for only the Holy Spirit can manage what is unmanageable within.

The first few days you attempt this, keep a notepad nearby in case something comes to mind that becomes a distraction. If this happens, jot it down for later. By the end of the week, you should be able to release those distractions to God without giving them attention—as if you are sitting on your front porch and all your worries, fears, tasks, and thoughts are merely cats strolling by. Do not call the cats over to you or allow them to sit on your lap. Just let them walk by and out of sight.

As you begin, it is good to remind yourself that to be present to God is to arrive just as you are and then to open up to the Other. The instant you begin, remember that God is already present and He has been waiting for you. He always arrives before you do, desiring to connect with you even more than any of your most intimate friends. Take a moment now to greet your loving God.

During this quieting activity, you may want to pray the "Jesus Prayer": "Lord Jesus Christ, Son of the Living God, have mercy on me." Then allow God's internal metronome—your breathing—to take you down into a still place in your soul. As you exhale, allow all the noise to exit, and as you inhale, take in God's pure, peaceful presence. Remind yourself that as you sit here now, God is gazing on you with love and tenderness. Pause for a moment and think of this.

Permit yourself to be with the Lord without words. Don't forget that when you are with someone whose love you trust, you often do not need to talk. (The Curé of Ars described prayer in the words of an old peasant who used to sit for hours in the church, saying, "I look at the good God, and the good God looks at me." He called this the "Prayer of Simple Regard": no words and no distractions, just a silent presence.) If concerns and anxieties bubble up in your mind, let them gently burst on the surface and dissipate.[5]

As the days go by, let five to ten minutes become fifteen to twenty, when possible. The Contemplatives of old believed it took at least thirty to sixty minutes daily to reach a state of quiet union with God.

Record: How would you describe your time of quieting and centering this week?

If the exercise is a struggle, is there someone you can talk with who might be able to help you?

Share your progress with a friend you can trust, asking him or her to check in with you next month about this situation and the action you took.

Write a prayer, committing your steps to the Lord (see Psalm 37:5).

Week 3

Read: Quiet places or centers of prayer are becoming increasingly important in our fast-paced concrete jungle. "In a 'restless' society, where even 'free time' is filled up with sports, touring, or 'social' obligations, monasteries are the refuge of authentic leisure."[6]

Interestingly, we often think of monasteries as places where the highly religious live so they can get away from worldly distractions. But though the first monastics went to the desert to be away from all that would keep them from purely seeking God, our monastic brothers and sisters have always had a "tremendous influence on the world they sought to escape."[7]

The earliest Christian monastics were known as the desert fathers and mothers, and they most often lived solitary lives in the deserts of Egypt. The word *monk* is derived from the Greek *monachos*, which means "solitary," and these silent disciples have given the church great gifts that help us in our single-minded devotion to God.

Reflect: How well are you able to be alone for extended periods of time?

Though some of us don't enjoy being alone much, it's important that we make friends with our aloneness and ourselves. How would you feel about spending a day in a monastery to pray and be with the Lord?

As you consider that option, what are your hesitations?

What are your anticipated delights?

Respond: Find a monastery close to you. Call this week and schedule a day to spend time on the grounds, including an overnight stay, if possible. Take only some personal items, your Bible, your journal, and your calendar with you. Do not take your cell phone (perhaps leave it turned off in your car) or any outside reading or work. This is not a time to accomplish, produce, or complete something; it is a relational time designed for you to bring yourself to a living Person . . . to be with the Trinity as the Godhead comes to you. It is a time to rest, listen, rest, read your Bible, rest, pray, rest, and be quiet with the Lord. We often find it so difficult to allow ourselves to rest. Consider using the following eight-hour guide, though you may wish to vary this to better meet your needs:

> *Hour 1*: Arrive, settle in, find the dining room and bookstore, and explore the grounds.

> *Hour 2*: Go into your room and begin to center your thoughts on the Lord. Read Psalm 103 as you begin, and dialogue with the Lord through the passage.

- Verses 1-2: Recount God's blessings in your life. If you prefer to use your journal, write your prayers.
- Verse 3: Confess your sins to God, and as past confessed sins come to mind, thank Him for His forgiveness. Perhaps there are ways you have really been trying to change. Surrender those areas completely, acknowledging that you can't change yourself and asking Him to do His work of grace in you.
- Verse 3: Pray for the healing of your body in any way it needs to be healed, and thank Him for your health or times of prior healing. Pray for the healing of those you love.
- Verse 4: Thank the Lord for the ways you have seen Him redeem your life in the past. Be as specific as possible. Draw a before-and-after picture of yourself, including all that God has already healed and redeemed in you.

Continue praying through Psalm 103. Then pray through Psalm 139 in the same way.

Hour 3: Take a walk with God. In John 10, we read that Jesus is our Good Shepherd and His sheep hear His voice as He calls them by name. Begin to listen to the Lord. What might He be saying to you?

What impressions seem to be coming as you anticipate a dialogue with Him?

Once back in your room, use your journal to record your experience.

Hour 4: Eat and take a nap. Set your alarm, if necessary. If you do not choose to sleep, at least use this time to be "off duty." Reflect on how good it feels to let go and remember that God is in charge of the universe and you are not. Bask in the truth that you can take a nap or go off duty when you need to, and that your sovereign God oversees all things and never slumbers. Rest deeply in this truth.

Hour 5: Open your calendar and begin to pray through the events of the coming weeks and months. Since the Lord goes before you and behind you and lays His hand of blessing on your head (see Psalm 139:5, TLB), ask Him to give you a sense of how to pray specifically for each event. Pray as He directs, allowing the Holy Spirit to give you a sense of the need so you can agree with Him. Linger when you have no direction as to how to pray. You may want to simply sit the whole time in God's presence. As you picture each event, lift it to God's throne, asking Him to accomplish all that's on His heart for that day. This is a silent praying, a "wordless trust" in the Holy Spirit to pray through you (see Romans 8:26-27).

Hour 6: Make this a time of intercession for your family, your friends, your job, your church, your nation, and the events in the world that come to mind.

Hour 7: Spend this hour in holy leisure. "Waste" it on the Lord. If this monastery has offices of prayer—services where you can speak and sing Scripture with the monks or nuns—feel free to join them. If they have a theological library, you may want to look at their books. But because this is *holy* leisure—time you are "wasting" on God, not just leisure for leisure's sake—practice the presence of God, reminding yourself often that you are not alone in this adventure. Avoid conversations with others when possible, focusing mainly on God's accompanying Spirit.

Hour 8: Wrap up your day with the Lord. If you need to, set an empty chair in front of you and speak to Jesus as if He were sitting in that chair. Talk with Him about anything He said today that you want to remember.

Record: How would you describe your retreat at the monastery?

What were your high and low points?

Be sure to journal anything that you want to take with you from this day.

Will there be a next time? If so, what will you do differently?

Many people who are especially busy try to take one day every month or two in silence and solitude. Some prefer to take four to seven days each year for more extended time away.

Share your progress with a friend you can trust, asking him or her to check in with you next month to see how your extended times alone with God are going.

Write a prayer, committing your steps to the Lord (see Psalm 37:5).

Week 4

Integration: Review the last few weeks. What has God taught you?

How will you integrate what you have learned into your life?

If there are ways you need to take action in the future, write them in your journal.

Go to www.ChristianBookGuides.com for intermediate and advanced-level exercises.

---

autonomous and self-governing   harmonious and accommodating

Place an "N" on the continuum where you are now.
Then place an "L" on the continuum to represent where you would like to be.

10

THE CAREGIVER

Loving God through Serving Others

Record your temperament score for Caregiver from page 158. _____

Is it high, medium, or low? _____

Record your practice score for Caregiver. _____

Is it high, medium, or low? _____

In spiritual development, repetition is one way the Lord brings growth and transformation. Through repetition, God's Spirit can deal with us at ever-deepening levels and in more detail, which is why we will be focusing on one exercise for an entire week. It will be helpful for you to read and review the weekly activity each day, asking God to increase your capacity to know and love Him each time you revisit the exercise.

SPIRITUAL PRACTICES FOR THE BEGINNING CAREGIVER

Week 1

Read: Jesus makes quite a statement in John 15 when He calls us His friends:

> I no longer call you servants, because a servant does not know his master's business. Instead, I have called you friends, for everything that I learned from my Father I have made known to you.
>
> *John 15:15*

The Bible sets a high standard for friendship, saying that a friend loves at all times (see Proverbs 17:17) and even lays down one's life for another (see John 15:13). We also see what real friendship looks like in the life of David and Jonathan:

> After David had finished talking with Saul, he met Jonathan, the king's son. There was an immediate bond of love between them, and they became the best of friends. From that day on Saul kept David with him and wouldn't let him return home. And Jonathan made a solemn pact with David, because he loved him as he loved himself. Jonathan sealed the pact by taking off his robe and giving it to David, together with his tunic, sword, bow, and belt.
>
> *1 Samuel 18:1-4 (NLT)*

Reflect: What qualities particularly impress you about the kind of friend the Bible describes?

What kind of caregiving friend do you tend to be?

Respond: Ask the Lord to show you this week which one of your friends needs some practical, hands-on TLC. It may be that you write a note of encouragement or send flowers, or maybe you clean someone's home or invite a person to have coffee so you can listen attentively to that person's heart.

Record: How did you demonstrate tangible caregiving to your friend this week?

What was his or her response?

How did you feel while reaching out to this friend?

What will you do in the future?

Share your progress with a friend you can trust, asking him or her to check in with you next month about your tangible caregiving to your friends.

Write a prayer, committing your steps to the Lord (see Psalm 37:5).

Week 2

Read: God's Word makes caregiving a priority, especially caring for widows and children without parents:

> Religion that God our Father accepts as pure and faultless is this: to look after orphans and widows in their distress and to keep oneself from being polluted by the world. *James 1:27*

Reflect: Who in your sphere of influence represents children without parents or women without husbands?

Often widows, widowers, and single parents need practical help—someone to run an errand for them, fix something around the house, or take them out to eat or to see a play or a movie. Children need very practical help as well: someone to take them to the park, share an ice cream with them, or help them with their schoolwork. All in all, it's about giving them your time and attention.

Ask God how He might lead you to show hands-on, face-to-face care this week to a widow or orphan in distress. (If no children without parents or widows come to mind, ask one of the pastors in your church whom they would recommend.)

Respond: How did God lead you to care for an orphan or a widow this week?

Check your schedule. When can you spend a chunk of time with that person again, talking and listening to her, finding out what she needs, and showing her hands-on care as you are able?

Record: What was it like to give care to an orphan or widow this week?

How will you show care to that person in the future?

What follow-up needs to be done next?

Share your progress with a friend you can trust, asking him or her to check in with you next month about this situation and the action you took.

Write a prayer, committing your steps to the Lord (see Psalm 37:5).

Week 3

Read: Caregivers welcome others into their lives and homes, offering warmth and support with hospitality. Saint Benedict's rule instructs that all guests who present themselves are to be welcomed as Christ. Esther deWaal comments on this rule: "Hospitality means more than simply the open door, and the place at table; it means warmth, acceptance, enjoyment in welcoming whoever has arrived."[1]

Because hospitality extends beyond the provision of lodging and meals and involves "making room inside yourself for another person,"[2] DeWaal observes, "I cannot become a good host until I am at home in my own house, so rooted in my centre (as stability has taught) that I no longer need to impose my terms on others but can instead afford to offer them a welcome that gives them the chance to be completely themselves."[3] Harald Schützeichel adds, "If Christ is present in others, including people who are a nuisance for the community and for myself, then I am not permitted to write anybody off."[4] So the people in one's community—whether they are familiar friends, nuisances, or traveling strangers—are always welcomed as Jesus.[5]

Reflect: Evaluate your heart of hospitality:

How well do you welcome all guests as Christ—with warmth, acceptance, and enjoyment? What makes that difficult or easy for you?

How well do you make room inside yourself for others? What is challenging about that for you?

How comfortable are you in your own house (both literally and figuratively)? Are you so rooted in your center that you no longer need to impose your terms on others, but instead offer them a welcome that gives them the chance to be completely themselves? What do you find most difficult about that?

Whom are you least likely to welcome with an open heart—family, friends, or strangers? Why do you think that is true?

Respond: Spend time talking with God about your answers. Invite Him to give you His generosity of heart.

If Christ is present in others, then we are not permitted to write anyone off. In your journal, list the names of people who are seen as nuisances by your community (and by you) because their lifestyles, needs, personalities, or habits rub you the wrong way and demand more of you than you can easily give.

Talk with God now about your attitude—be it selfish, unloving, or judgmental—and ask the Lord to enlarge your heart toward each person on your list.

Now pray a blessing over each one, thanking God for this person's presence in your life.

Ask the Lord to give you an opportunity this week to love and serve someone on your list as you would love and serve Christ Himself.

Ask the Lord for the grace to make room inside yourself for these people and to extend warmth, acceptance, and enjoyment in welcoming them into your life this week.

Record: How would you describe your ability to care and show hospitality this week?

As an act of service and love for God, were you able to show care to someone on your list? If so, how would you describe the experience?

What was the most difficult part of being hospitable? What was the most rewarding part?

Talk with God now about why you struggle with this aspect of God's heart, and invite Him, by faith, to enlarge your capacity.

What follow-up do you need to do in the future?

Share your progress with a friend you can trust, asking him or her to check in with you next month about your heart of hospitality and the action you took.

Write a prayer, committing your steps to the Lord (see Psalm 37:5).

Week 4

Integration: Review the last few weeks. What has God taught you?

How will you integrate what you have learned into your life?

If there are ways you need to take action in the future, write them in your journal.

Go to www.ChristianBookGuides.com for intermediate and advanced-level exercises.

11

THE CONTEMPLATIVE

Loving God through Adoration

Record your temperament score for the Contemplative from page 158. _____
Is it high, medium, or low? _____

Record your practice score for the Contemplative. _____
Is it high, medium, or low? _____

In spiritual development, repetition is one way the Lord brings growth and transformation. Through repetition, God's Spirit can deal with us at ever-deepening levels and in more detail, which is why we will be focusing on one exercise for an entire week. It will be helpful for you to read and review the weekly activity each day, asking God to increase your capacity to know and love Him each time you revisit the exercise.

SPIRITUAL PRACTICES FOR THE BEGINNING CONTEMPLATIVE

Week 1

Read: The psalms are filled with prayers written directly to God, words that express deep feelings poured out from the heart:

> O God, you are my God, earnestly I seek you; my soul thirsts for you, my body longs for you, in a dry and weary land where there is no water.
> *Psalm 63:1*

How long, O LORD? Will you forget me forever? How long will you hide your face from me? How long must I wrestle with my thoughts and every day have sorrow in my heart? How long will my enemy triumph over me?   *Psalm 13:1-2*

God's Word tells us we can share our hearts with Him: "O my people, trust in him at all times. Pour out your heart to him, for God is our refuge" (Psalm 62:8, NLT). It also invites us to share what is on our minds: "Come now, let us reason together" (Isaiah 1:18). Thankfully God wants us to bring our authentic, honest selves to Him, no matter what we are thinking or feeling.

Reflect: When God invites you to pour out your heart to Him or tell Him what's on your mind, what thoughts and feelings emerge?

Is there anything that keeps you from pouring out your heart and mind to the One who invites you to come?

Respond: Ask God now to give you the courage and clarity to pour out your heart and mind to Him. Perhaps you want to do that in the form of your own psalm, poem, or song. If so, write your psalm, poem, or song in your journal. Remember, God wants you to come authentically.

Record: How did it feel as you began to more intentionally pour out your heart to the Lord?

What was the greatest joy about sharing yourself so openly with the Lord?

What was most difficult?

What did you learn about yourself?

What did you learn about the Lord?

What needs to be done in the future?

Share your progress with a friend you can trust, asking him or her to check in with you next month about your growing intimacy with God.

Write a prayer, committing your steps to the Lord (see Psalm 37:5).

Week 2

Read: In Old Testament times, King David seemed to know how to prioritize his life. Of all the things he had to do as king of Israel, he understood his number one priority:

> One thing have I desired of the LORD, that will I seek after; that
> I may dwell in the house of the LORD all the days of my life, to
> behold the beauty of the LORD, and to enquire in his temple. . . .
> When thou saidst, Seek ye my face; my heart said unto thee, Thy
> face, LORD, will I seek.   *Psalm 27:4, 8 (KJV)*

Reflect: Think for a moment about David's life. Notice that he was neither a priest nor a prophet; he was the leader of Israel—the king. He must have been very important, very powerful, very wealthy, and very busy. No doubt he had deadlines and scheduling pressures. Yet his life was grounded in his *one* thing—a relationship with the living God.

If you were to model your spiritual life and priorities after David's, what would it mean for you in the twenty-first century?

Look again at Psalm 27:

> One thing have I desired of the LORD, that will I seek after; that
> I may dwell in the house of the LORD all the days of my life, to
> behold the beauty of the LORD, and to enquire in his temple. . . .
> When thou saidst, Seek ye my face; my heart said unto thee, Thy
> face, LORD, will I seek.

Supposing there is an application of this verse other than attending church every day, what would it look like for you to dwell in the house of the Lord all the days of your life?

What would it mean for you to behold the beauty of the Lord?

What does it mean when God invites us to inquire of Him?

Why do you think God said, "Seek ye my face" (Psalm 27:8)?

What do you think it means to seek the face of God?

Respond: Look up the following words in your dictionary, jotting down ways you can apply them in your relationship with God:

- *dwell* (in the house of the Lord)
- *behold* (the beauty)
- *inquire* (in His temple)

Now spend some time with God, *dwelling, beholding,* and *inquiring.*

Record: How would you describe your experience with the Lord this week as you were dwelling, beholding, and inquiring of Him?

What did you learn about yourself?

What did you learn about the Lord?

Share your progress with a friend you can trust, asking him or her to check in with you next month about how your intimacy with God is growing.

Write a prayer, committing your steps to the Lord (see Psalm 37:5).

Week 3

Read: Throughout the ages, a marvelous way of loving God has been to spend time with Him in what the ancients called *otium sanctum,* or "holy leisure." Because union with God was their ultimate goal, Contemplatives sought to spend their whole lives in the presence of God, simply adoring Him and being together in unhurried, relaxed time. It is said that "holy living is not abrupt living. No one who hurries into the presence of God is content to remain for long. Those who hurry in, hurry out. Holy leisure prepares us to receive the gift of inwardness."[1]

The saints who practiced holy leisure believed that the sin nature would surface in four major areas: inappropriate sexual desire, gluttony, the drive for power and advancement, and hurriedness.[2] They saw that human effort would not win out against these subtle, hard-to-detect internal vices, so discipline was a matter of the inner reign of Christ. "He will be victorious when He is allowed full sovereignty. Thus the best way to deal with sin is not to attempt reform but to adore the Savior. Winning over our lower nature is made possible by *adoration.*"[3]

Only by worshipping Christ, who is enthroned in hearts, can continued growth and transformation occur.

As you learn to be with God and in holy leisure, you will begin to relax in God's presence and grace. There will come a time when you welcome His call to leave the drivenness and frantic pace of life, because your attachment to those things that produce an "intolerable scramble of panting feverishness" will be broken.[4] Like Jesus, you will hunger to get away to a lonely place because you ultimately know that all work is the Father's work; you need only carry the pieces He gives you.

Reflect: How would you like to enjoy holy leisure with the Lord today?

Write the words that come to mind when you consider taking time for God in the midst of your busy life.

Respond: Take as much time as possible this week—ideally, at least twenty minutes a day and one two-hour block—to enjoy the discipline of holy leisure with Jesus. Of course, holy leisure is not the same thing as playing golf or sleeping in. It is a love choice to "waste time with God"— being with Him in a relaxed, nothing-pressing-to-do-or-say atmosphere.

If you cannot find a two-hour block of time to just "hang out with God," consider spending a Sunday morning with the Lord in a genuine, relaxed dialogue, without people around or distractions of any kind. If need be, go alone to a local park, to the beach, or to the mountains to find leisure with the Lord.

Record: How would you describe your times of holy leisure this week?

What were the most enjoyable aspects of these times?

Did you encounter any surprises?

What did you learn from your time with God that you would like to remember?

Share your progress with a friend you can trust, asking him or her to check in with you next month about how your intimacy with God is progressing.

Write a prayer, committing your steps to the Lord (see Psalm 37:5).

Week 4

Integration: Review the last few weeks. What has God taught you?

How will you integrate what you have learned into your life?

If there are ways you need to take action in the future, write them in your journal.

Go to www.ChristianBookGuides.com for intermediate and advanced-level exercises.

12

THE ENTHUSIAST

Loving God through Mystery and Celebration

Record your temperament score for the Enthusiast from page 158. _____
Is it high, medium, or low? _____

Record your practice score for the Enthusiast. _____
Is it high, medium, or low? _____

In spiritual development, repetition is one way the Lord brings growth and transformation. Through repetition, God's Spirit can deal with us at ever-deepening levels and in more detail, which is why we will be focusing on one exercise for an entire week. It will be helpful for you to read and review the weekly activity each day, asking God to increase your capacity to know and love Him and His truth each time you revisit the exercise.

SPIRITUAL PRACTICES FOR THE BEGINNING ENTHUSIAST

Week 1

Read: The Enthusiast knows how to focus on a God who is always worthy of worship. In fact, the Enthusiast is a person who, in spirit, joins the four living creatures at the throne of God who, day and night, do not cease to say, "Holy, holy, holy is the Lord God Almighty, who was, and is, and is to come" (Revelation 4:8). All God's people are instructed to "continually offer up a *sacrifice of praise* to God, that is, the fruit of lips that give thanks to His name" (Hebrews 13:15, NASB, emphasis added).

Reflect: Sacrifice is defined as giving up something valuable or important for somebody or something considered to be of more value or importance. How consistently do you offer a sacrifice of praise to God, even when you don't feel like it?

Think about God and who He is. Ponder His attributes and all the reasons He deserves your praise. Considering what He has done for you, what are you most thankful for in your life?

As you consider the above, would it be a sacrifice to thank and praise God? Why or why not?

Respond: Spend some time now thanking and praising the Lord. If you have a hymnal, find some of your favorite hymns and sing them to Jesus. Only He is listening, and you can make a joyful noise, no matter how well you sing (see Psalm 98:4). If it feels awkward or uncomfortable to you, do it as a *sacrifice of praise* to God.

As you praise the Lord, picture Him in the room with you, enjoying you as you enjoy Him. Repeat this exercise as often as possible this week.

Record: How did it feel to offer up a sacrifice of praise to God this week?

When you attend church next time, sing and worship God with all your heart, no matter how you feel. Remember, worship is about God and who He is, not about us or our feelings.

Describe your experience in your journal.

Share your progress with a friend you can trust, asking him or her to check in with you next month about how your worship of God is progressing.

Write a prayer, committing your steps to the Lord (see Psalm 37:5).

Week 2

Read: Of course, worshipping God is not just something we do on Sunday mornings when we sing. Everything we say and do ought to be done in an attitude of worship, whatever form it takes—whether we are singing or serving the poor, telling someone about Jesus or cleaning the bathroom. Worship happens when what we do is done unto the Lord, with the eyes of our hearts turned toward Him. The Bible says,

> As the eyes of servants look to the hand of their master, as the eyes of a maid to the hand of her mistress, so our eyes look to the LORD our God, until He is gracious to us.   *Psalm 123:2 (NASB)*

As we look to the Lord, we fix our eyes upon Jesus, certain that His eyes are fixed on us too (see 2 Chronicles 16:9; Proverbs 15:3; 1 Peter 3:12). Consider this old hymn that helps us turn our eyes heavenward:

> *O Soul, are you weary and troubled? No light in the darkness you see?*
> *There's light for a look at the Savior, and life more abundant and free!*
>
> *Turn your eyes upon Jesus; look full in His wonderful face,*
> *And the things of earth will grow strangely dim,*
> *In the light of His glory and grace.*[1]

Reflect: When you worship during a church service, what is usually your focus?

Why do you think that is true about you?

How easy or difficult is it for you to look away from those around you during worship and focus the "eyes of your heart" upon the Lord Jesus *only*, giving Him all your attention?

Respond: This week, practice worshipping by fixing the eyes of your heart upon the Lord. Begin at home with some worship music. Close your eyes and intentionally turn your heart toward Jesus, allowing Him to fill your soul with a vision of Himself. See Him there with you, receiving your affection and praise.

Then the next time you are in a church service singing worship songs with the congregation, remember to fix the eyes of your heart upon the Lord by closing your eyes, allowing Him to fill your mind with Himself.

Record: How would your describe your time of worship this week?

How was your time of worship at home?

How was your worship at church with the congregation?

What do you need to do, or with whom do you need to pray, so that the eyes of your heart will become fixed upon Jesus?

Share your experience with a friend you can trust, asking him or her to check in with you next month about how you are growing in worshipping Jesus.

Write a prayer, committing your steps to the Lord (see Psalm 37:5).

Week 3

Read: More than fifty of the psalms in the Old Testament are said to have been written by David. They are songs he wrote to the Lord when he was fleeing from his enemies, being rescued from Saul, dedicating the Temple, or repenting from his sin. Whether David was happy or sad, scared or confident, vengeful or penitent, he often wrote songs to God as a way of sharing his life with Him. Here is an example of one of David's songs:

> *My soul waits in silence for God only;*
> *From Him is my salvation.*
> *He only is my rock and my salvation,*
> *My stronghold; I shall not be greatly shaken.*
> *How long will you assail a man,*
> *That you may murder him, all of you,*
> *Like a leaning wall, like a tottering fence?*
> *They have counseled only to thrust him down from his high position;*
> *They delight in falsehood;*
> *They bless with their mouth,*
> *But inwardly they curse.*
> *My soul, wait in silence for God only,*
> *For my hope is from Him.*
> *He only is my rock and my salvation,*
> *My stronghold; I shall not be shaken.*
> *On God my salvation and my glory rest;*

The rock of my strength, my refuge is in God.
Trust in Him at all times, O people;
Pour out your heart before Him;
God is a refuge for us.
Men of low degree are only vanity and men of rank are a lie;
In the balances they go up;
They are together lighter than breath.
Do not trust in oppression
And do not vainly hope in robbery;
If riches increase, do not set your heart upon them.
Once God has spoken;
Twice I have heard this:
That power belongs to God;
And lovingkindness is Yours, O Lord,
For You recompense a man according to his work.   Psalm 62 (NASB)

Reflect: In which verses in the psalm above does David use the following:

- Talking to his own soul?
- Reminding himself of who God is?
- Recounting his problems?
- Proclaiming God's character to others?
- Repeating the most important things?

If you were to write a psalm about your life right now, what would it be about?

What would you say to your own soul?

What about God would you need to remind yourself?

What problems in your life would you recount?

What of God's character would you proclaim to others?

What might be worth repeating?

Respond: Write your psalm to God. Don't worry about making it rhyme or sound perfect. Simply express your heart to God.

Record: How did it feel to express your heart to the Lord in a psalm?

Did you simply speak your psalm to God, or did you try putting the words to a melody and singing it?

Share your experience with someone who would benefit from hearing your psalm or knowing what you gained from writing it.

Write a prayer, committing your steps to the Lord (see Psalm 37:5).

Week 4

Integration: Review the last few weeks. What has God taught you?

How will you integrate what you have learned into your life?

If there are ways you need to take action in the future, write them in your journal.

Go to www.ChristianBookGuides.com for intermediate and advanced-level exercises.

13

THE INTELLECTUAL

Loving God through the Mind

Record your temperament score for the Intellectual from page 158. _____
Is it high, medium, or low? _____

Record your practice score for the Intellectual. _____
Is it high, medium, or low? _____

In spiritual development, repetition is one way the Lord brings growth and transformation. Through repetition, God's Spirit can deal with us at ever-deepening levels and in more detail, which is why we will be focusing on one exercise for an entire week. It will be helpful for you to read and review the weekly activity each day, asking God to increase your capacity to know and love Him each time you revisit the exercise.

SPIRITUAL PRACTICES FOR THE BEGINNING INTELLECTUAL

Week 1

Read: Many people find that using a journal is useful for spiritual reflection; it is a tool that can help you reflect and record your thoughts and musings. Harry Cargas, author of *Exploring Your Inner Space*, says, "A journal is not a diary. A diary is a record of things you have experienced. The journal is more concerned about the meaning of these experiences. Some overlapping is necessary, but to keep a historical record is far different than interpreting it."[1] You can use a journal as you read your Bible each day. You may want to consider the day's events, how they affected you, and if anything in particular occurred that you need to think through and process with the Lord.

A journal can also be helpful for writing down your prayers. This helps you focus and be specific, as well as providing a record for you to refer to later in order to see how God has answered.

Reflect: Whether or not you now use a journal, how do you feel about writing down your thoughts, prayers, and feelings about what is happening in your life?

What about that, if anything, seems helpful or makes you feel excited?

What about that, if anything, seems like a hindrance or makes you feel uneasy?

Respond: If you do not already use a journal, purchase a notebook and begin to record your daily thoughts, prayers, and reflections. If you find that you are simply recording the events of the day, ask the Lord to help you reflect upon your experiences and the lessons you are learning.

Now write a journal entry to reflect upon this day thus far. Spend fifteen to twenty minutes reviewing the day and recording your reactions and reflections. Think back to when you first woke up this morning, and consider how the day began. How were your first encounters? Write a paragraph or more that captures the essence of the day. Once you have begun to journal, add to your practice the discipline of writing your prayers. Continue this practice all week long.

Record: How did journaling help you this week?

Was it helpful to write your prayers? If so, in what ways?

At the end of the week, reread what you wrote in your journal. How does it make you feel to see this record of your life on paper? Share your thoughts regarding journaling with the Lord.

What follow-up do you need to do in the future?

Is there someone in your life who could benefit from what you have learned? Share your experiences with that person.

Write a prayer, committing your steps to the Lord (see Psalm 37:5).

Week 2

Read: Karl Barth, who is recognized as one of the most influential theologians of the twentieth century, suggested that Christians should encounter life with the Bible in one hand and the daily newspaper in the other. He believed that a meaningful, vibrant faith must always be lived in conjunction with the reality of what is happening in the world around us. In other words, a "salt and light" Christian must learn to interpret current events through the lens of the Bible, and our Bible reading must be seen through what is happening historically every day.

Reflect: How often do you read the newspaper?

Do you prefer to get the news from the radio, television, Internet, or newspaper—or do you avoid the news altogether?

How is your faith relevant to world events that are happening now?

Consider why your faith seems relevant or irrelevant.

How do you think Jesus viewed the historical events of His time?

Respond: Incorporate spiritual reflection into your reading of the daily news. Begin by finding today's newspaper and reading through the world and local news.

As you read, reflect upon each story in light of your faith. Try to develop a mental dialogue between your faith perspective and the life events presented in the newspaper. As you read each story, consider the following questions:

- What faith themes does this story suggest (hope, reconciliation, justice, truth, betrayal, mercy, evil, death, power, temptation, healing, love)?

- Is some aspect of your faith challenged by this story? What and how?
- Is some aspect of your faith confirmed by this story? What and how?
- Are God's values being challenged by this story? Which ones and in what way?
- Does the gospel help you to make sense of this story? If so, in what way?

Pray for an awareness of God's presence in the lives of the individuals, families, communities, and nations you are reading about.[2]

Record: How are you looking at the world differently this week because of your reflections on the news through biblical eyes?

Will you do this again in the future? If so, how will you do it differently? the same?

Share your progress with a friend you can trust, asking him or her to check in with you next month about this experience and the action you took.

Write a prayer, committing your steps to the Lord (see Psalm 37:5).

Week 3

Read: After God led the apostle Paul to the city of Philippi, Paul developed a strong friendship with the people there. Paul, who had helped establish the Philippian church, was later sent financial help from that congregation in a time of need. Paul wrote a letter to the church while he was in prison, assuring them of his thankfulness and affection for them. At the end of his letter, we read,

> My dear brothers and sisters, stay true to the Lord. I love you and long to see you, dear friends, for you are my joy and the crown I receive for my work. *Philippians 4:1 (NLT)*

Reflect: When you think about your life, what person or group of people come to mind whom you long to see, people whom you consider to be your joy and the reward for your work?

Why is this person or group of people special to you?

How have some of those people helped you during your times of need?

How might these people or others be encouraged by a letter from you?

Respond: In the spirit of Paul, write a letter of encouragement. You may want to include some of the following:

- your love and appreciation for them
- acknowledgment of the ways in which they've touched your life
- your desire to see them
- ways in which they've brought you joy
- your appreciation for any help they've given
- encouragement in their current journey
- expressions of confidence about their future with the Lord
- your commitment to keep them in prayer

Record: How did you feel about writing this letter of encouragement?

Even though we do not give encouragement to receive a response, if the person or group of people responded to your letter, how did their response affect you?

Is there someone else who has been important in your life that might need a letter of encouragement from you as well?

What will you do in the future regarding this person?

Share your experience with a friend you can trust, asking him or her to check in with you next month about this situation and the action you took.

Write a prayer, committing your steps to the Lord (see Psalm 37:5).

Week 4

Integration: Review the last few weeks. What has God taught you?

How will you integrate what you have learned into your life?

If there are ways you need to take action in the future, write them in your journal.

Go to www.ChristianBookGuides.com for intermediate and advanced-level exercises.

14

THE NATURALIST

Loving God through Experiencing Him Outdoors

Record your temperament score for the Naturalist from page 158. _____
Is it high, medium, or low? _____

Record your practice score for the Naturalist. _____
Is it high, medium, or low? _____

In spiritual development, repetition is one way the Lord brings growth and transformation. Through repetition, God's Spirit can deal with us at ever-deepening levels and in more detail, which is why we will be focusing on one exercise for an entire week. It will be helpful for you to read and review the weekly activity each day, asking God to increase your capacity to know and love Him each time you revisit the exercise.

SPIRITUAL PRACTICES FOR THE BEGINNING NATURALIST

Week 1

Read: The creation speaks loudly of a Creator God. The psalmist said,

> The heavens declare the glory of God; the skies proclaim the work
> of his hands. . . . The heavens proclaim his righteousness, and all
> the peoples see his glory. *Psalm 19:1; 97:6*

The universe testifies to all people everywhere of God's existence, just as Minucius Felix noted:

If upon entering some home you saw that everything there was well-tended, neat, and decorative, you would believe that some master was in charge of it, and that he himself was superior to those good things. So too in the home of this world, when you see providence, order, and law in the heavens and on earth, believe there is a Lord and Author of the universe, more beautiful than the stars themselves and the various parts of the whole world.[1]

Reflect: What does nature say to you about God?

In what ways do you feel closer to God when you are in the midst of His creation?

Think back to how the creation spoke to you of God before you knew Jesus. What do you remember?

How did God use His created universe to bring you to Himself?

Respond: Today, spend time with the Lord outdoors. Go for a walk or sit outside and observe the beauty of nature. If it is too hot or cold to go outside, sit where you can observe nature from a window. Consider the beauty of God and what you realize about His glory as you observe the world outdoors. Practice this exercise as many times as possible this week.

Record: How was your interaction with the creation—and the Creator—this week ?

What did you learn about yourself as you pondered His handiwork?

What did you learn about the Lord?

Is there someone who would benefit from what you have learned? Share your findings with that person.

Write a prayer, committing your steps to the Lord (see Psalm 37:5).

Week 2

Read: The Bible says,

The LORD God had planted a garden in the east, in Eden; and there he put the man he had formed. . . . Then the man and his wife

heard the sound of the LORD God as he was walking in the garden
in the cool of the day. *Genesis 2:8; 3:8*

Reflect: Have you ever wondered what it would have been like to walk
with God in the Garden in the cool of the day?

Why do you think God literally planted a garden and brought
humankind—His most valued and treasured creation, made in His
likeness and image—to the Garden to be with Him? Why not a
mountaintop, where His vastness could be seen, or an ocean, where His
immense power could be felt? Why a garden?

What does that say to you about God's desire for an intimate
relationship with us?

Think about your "garden" experience with God, that place of
connection where you meet Him. Where is your garden place?

Respond: Find a garden or a quiet place of beauty and solitude outside.
As you go to that place, consider that God wants to meet you there and
that He is the One who prepared the garden and awaits your coming.
He is there before you arrive. Go with expectancy, ready to meet Him in
face-to-face, heart-to-heart dialogue.

In your garden setting, begin by reading the words to this song called
"In the Garden":

> *I come to the garden alone,*
> *While the dew is still on the roses,*
> *And the voice I hear falling on my ear,*
> *The Son of God discloses.*
>
> *And He walks with me and He talks with me,*
> *And He tells me I am His own.*
> *And the joy we share, as we tarry there,*
> *None other has ever known.*
>
> *He speaks, and the sound of His voice*
> *Is so sweet, the birds hush their singing,*
> *And the melody that He gave to me*
> *Within my heart is ringing.*[2]

Now spend time with God sharing, talking, listening, and communing with Him. Practice this exercise as many times as possible this week.

Record: How was your time in that quiet garden with God this week?

What did you learn about yourself and the Lord?

How will you take your garden experience with you wherever you go, knowing that now the garden—your meeting place with God—is *within*?

Share your garden experience with a friend you can trust, asking him or her to talk with you next month about how you are continuing to meet God in the garden.

Write a prayer, committing your steps to the Lord (see Psalm 37:5).

Week 3

Read: At times when we are outdoors, we see aspects of God's beauty, and they become like little love notes to us from our great Romancer, God. This happened one morning to my friend Diane as she was walking to a meeting. She rounded a corner and saw everything covered in spiderwebs—delicate, spun-to-perfection webs covering limbs, ground, ivy—everywhere. The early morning mist was blowing in and highlighting each graceful strand against the sunlight. Diane was torn, wanting to get her camera so she could capture this elegance with a photograph, yet not wanting to be late to the meeting. Just then she heard the Lord speak: "Diane, you will never be able to capture all My beauty with your camera. What you are amazed by is simply the stroke of My finger; I can do this and so much more anytime I please. I delight in giving you this pleasure—this day, this moment—but don't be distracted or discouraged. Keep on your way; I can provide this or something even greater and more beautiful for you tomorrow. Don't struggle; receive and enjoy My gift today. Take in what I have created for you, something no one else has even seen, for many have walked past and not noticed . . . as this was just for you."

Reflect: How aware are you of God's beauty in creation—His little love notes to you—when you spend time outdoors in nature?

How do you interpret these pieces of God's beauty? Do you walk right past without noticing, or do you stop and allow your soul to be awakened by these little love notes from your Beloved?

Consider what might happen if you asked God to make you aware of His love for you through His creation. How might that change the way you interact with the world today as you go about your usual business?

Respond: As you walk in and out of your home today—or your office or school—ask God to make you aware of His beautiful, tender love notes just for you. Even in a crowded city, ask Him for little glimpses of His heart. Dialogue with Him about what you see and what that seeing inspires in you. Let your soul take in God's handiwork all around you, and let it be a form of dialogue with your Creator.

Try to find one scene from the outdoors to hold in your memory as a reminder this day of your relationship with God. Practice this exercise as many times as possible this week.

Record: How was your awareness of God's beauty in the outdoors heightened for you this week?

Were you able to slow down enough to see and receive God's love letters?

What did you learn about yourself and about the Lord?

Share your experience with a friend you can trust, asking him or her to check in with you next month about the way you are watching for love letters from God.

Write a prayer, committing your steps to the Lord (see Psalm 37:5).

Week 4

Integration: Review the last few weeks. What has God taught you?

How will you integrate what you have learned into your life?

If there are ways you need to take action in the future, write them in your journal.

Go to www.ChristianBookGuides.com for intermediate and advanced-level exercises.

15

THE SENSATE

Loving God through the Senses

Record your temperament score for the Sensate from page 158. _____
Is it high, medium, or low? _____

Record your practice score for the Sensate. _____
Is it high, medium, or low? _____

In spiritual development, repetition is one way the Lord brings growth and transformation. Through repetition, God's Spirit can deal with us at ever-deepening levels and in more detail, which is why we will be focusing on one exercise for an entire week. It will be helpful for you to read and review the weekly activity each day, asking God to increase your capacity to know and love Him each time you revisit the exercise.

SPIRITUAL PRACTICES FOR THE BEGINNING SENSATE

Week 1

Read: Jesus called Himself the light of the world. For centuries since that time, God's people have been using light to signify His presence. A candle can be used not only to symbolize God's presence and light but also to symbolize His warmth and the fire of His Holy Spirit.

Reflect: In your times with God, do you ever use a symbol to remind you of His presence, warmth, and light? If so, what is it?

Respond: Lighting a candle at the beginning of your time with God can symbolize your invitation to Him, as you explicitly welcome and acknowledge His presence with you.

Enter your time with God by finding a quiet place to sit, and use a candle as a symbol of God's light, warmth, and Holy Spirit. Light the candle as you begin, saying words such as, "Come now, Light of the World, and illumine my mind. Come now, Fire of God, and warm my heart."

Spiritual light itself is a gift from God; it shows us the way. Consider now the dark places in your life that you have walked in this week and this month.

Where do you want the light of Christ to shine in your life? in your surroundings?

Thank God now that He is aware of those dark places, and invite His light to shine there more brightly.

Now think of Jesus' crucifixion, and imagine yourself watching as darkness descended over the land (see Mark 15:33-39). Blow out the candle and sit in the darkness for a while. How would it feel if you did not know Jesus and had no spiritual light by which to see?[1]

Contemplate the Cross, a time when the light of Christ went out momentarily. Think of Jesus in the dark tomb without life or light. Picture the women coming on Easter morning to anoint the body and hearing the words, "He is not here; he has risen!"

Focus on the truth that God is never extinguished. Jesus, who was dead and buried, is now alive forevermore.

Relight the candle. Speak these words as you light it: "The light shines in the darkness, and the darkness can never extinguish it" (John 1:5, NLT). Think of dark areas in your life and the lives of those you love, and rejoice with God because His light can permeate every dark corner. Commit each dark place to His Holy Spirit, surrendering each one.

Thank God for His promise to dwell in you forever, to forever be light to you and in you. Picture the light of the candle—symbolizing Christ's light—filling your heart now as you become a light in a dark world.

End your time with God by blowing out the candle and saying the words, "Thank you, God, for your unspeakably good gift. Amen."

Record: How would you describe your time with God this week as you used the candle to broaden your experience of His light in your life?

What did you learn about yourself and God?

Share your experience with a friend you can trust, asking him or her to check in with you next month about how God's indwelling Holy Spirit is transforming your darkness into light.

Write a prayer, committing your steps to the Lord (see Psalm 37:5).

Week 2

Read: God has given us five senses with which to experience Him and the world around us. Even though God is Spirit, we can utilize our senses to connect with Him, as Christians have done throughout the centuries.

Reflect: How often do you use your sense of sight, sound, taste, touch, or smell in worshipping God?

Why do you think that is true about you?

How interested are you in broadening your scope of worship?

Respond: Practice using your senses as you take an "awareness prayer walk."[2] As you walk, combine your awareness of your body moving through the environment with a heightened sense of God surrounding you—so that even the common things you see, hear, smell, taste, and touch become objects that speak to you of Him.

Start by walking as you would ordinarily—in your yard, neighborhood, park, or around the city. It can be as brief as a few minutes or as extensive as a daylong hike.

Focus on your body as it moves and how it does this extraordinary activity called walking. Be aware of lifting your foot, moving your leg forward, placing the heel and then the toe on the ground as you shift the weight in your body with each step. Thank the Lord for how He has intricately made you and knit you together in your mother's womb (see Psalm 139:13).

Next notice your breathing as you walk. Perhaps pray a breath prayer, such as, "Lord Jesus, come. Fill me, release me" as you walk. If there is a slight incline, be aware of the subtle change in your breathing as more is demanded of you. Thank the Lord that He gives you life and breath (see Acts 17:25), that His Word is God-breathed (see 2 Timothy 3:16), and that His Spirit is called the breath of God (see John 20:22).

As you breathe in the air around you, focus on the specific smells, pleasant or not: countryside, earth, vegetation, smog, flowers, grass, something cooking, smoke, etc. Thank God for the gift of smell and that He makes you a sweet fragrance of Jesus wherever you go (see 2 Corinthians 2:15).

Be aware of the sun and wind on your face and the ground beneath your feet. Touch as many things as you can with your fingers. Feel the textures, the hardness or softness in things you find: bark, leaves, stones, wood, seeds, paper, metal, etc. Thank God that He has come near to touch you, and that as He did with Thomas, He invites you to touch Him (see John 20:27).

Look at the shapes of the trees, the curves in the road, the vivid colors of flowers and gardens, and the lines of the buildings. See the contrasts: the light and shadow, the order and chaos, the beauty and need for beautification. Thank God for your eyes and that you can see His world and look into the faces of those you love.

Continue walking, taking it all in.

Notice this week how much you are allowing your senses to connect you to God. Practice this exercise as many times as possible.

Record: How did you use your senses this week to help you connect with God?

What did you learn about yourself and the Lord?

What was helpful about this exercise?

What was challenging?

Share this exercise with a friend you can trust, asking him or her to check in with you next month about how you are using your senses to connect with God.

Write a prayer, committing your steps to the Lord (see Psalm 37:5).

Week 3

Read: Clay is an important medium in the Bible. We read in Scripture that human beings were formed out of clay (see Job 33:6), that God likens Israel to clay in the potter's hand (see Jeremiah 18:6), and that Jesus even used clay to heal a blind man's eyes (see John 9:6-15, NASB).

Reflect: Think about clay. What are the characteristics of clay that might cause God to select this medium to symbolize how He works with us?

Respond: Purchase a lump of clay or Play-Doh at a craft store and begin to knead it with your hands until it becomes soft. As you do this, meditate on these passages:

> O Israel, can I not do to you as this potter has done to his clay? As the clay is in the potter's hand, so are you in my hand.
>
> *Jeremiah 18:6 (NLT)*

> If you only look at us, you might well miss the brightness. We carry this precious Message around in the unadorned clay pots of our ordinary lives. That's to prevent anyone from confusing God's incomparable power with us.   *2 Corinthians 4:7 (THE MESSAGE)*

As you continue to work the clay with your hands, say or sing the words of this chorus:

> *Change my heart, oh God*
> *Make it ever true*

Change my heart, oh God
May I be like You
You are the Potter, I am the clay
Mold me and make me, this is what I pray.[3]

Make a symbol that speaks of your life right now—what God is doing in and with you. Perhaps you feel broken; if so, make your object and then break it. Maybe your life is full of joy; if so, create a symbol to express that joy. As you feel the clay between your fingers, pray and allow God to show you your life.

After you make the symbol, talk with the Lord and offer it to Him. Put it in the sun where it can harden, and as you do, surrender yourself afresh to the Potter, asking God to accomplish the work of grace that only He can do.

Record: What was your experience with the clay this week?

What did you create from molding the clay with your hands?

What did you learn about yourself?

What did you learn about the Lord?

As you surrender yourself afresh to the Potter, write your prayer of consecration in your journal.

Share your prayer with a friend you can trust, asking him or her to check in with you next month about your life with God.

Write a prayer, committing your steps to the Lord (see Psalm 37:5).

Week 4

Integration: Review the last few weeks. What has God taught you?

How will you integrate what you have learned into your life?

If there are ways you need to take action in the future, write them in your journal.

Go to www.ChristianBookGuides.com for intermediate and advanced-level exercises.

16

THE TRADITIONALIST

Loving God through Ritual and Symbol

Record your temperament score for the Traditionalist from page 158. _____
Is it high, medium, or low? _____

Record your practice score for the Traditionalist. _____
Is it high, medium, or low? _____

In spiritual development, repetition is one way the Lord brings growth and transformation. Through repetition, God's Spirit can deal with us at ever-deepening levels and in more detail, which is why we will be focusing on one exercise for an entire week. It will be helpful for you to read and review the weekly activity each day, asking God to increase your capacity to know and love Him each time you revisit the exercise.

SPIRITUAL PRACTICES FOR THE BEGINNING TRADITIONALIST

Week 1

Read: The word *tradition* comes from the Latin word *traditio*, meaning "the action of handing over." A tradition is an inherited, established, customary pattern of thought, action, or behavior. We all have traditions in our lives: the singing of songs and the giving of gifts on birthdays, the ways we observe holidays, or the celebrating of anniversaries and other special occasions. These rituals can be significant, especially to children, because they offer a sense of stability as well as excitement and anticipation of what's coming next.

Reflect: To some, the word *traditionalist* sounds stale and confining. Ponder traditions that are important to you.

What personal and family traditions do you most enjoy and why?

Are there any national holidays that you believe are important? Reflect on their meaning to you.

Do you have personal and family traditions that flow into your life with the Lord?

What established patterns do you enjoy most with Him?

Respond: Make a list of all the customary patterns or traditions you enjoy and the reasons you enjoy them:

Personal Traditions	Meanings
Family Traditions	Meanings
National Traditions	Meanings
Spiritual Traditions	Meanings
Others	Meanings

Begin to plan one traditional event, and schedule the celebration on
your calendar.

Record: What tradition did you begin to plan for this week?

What did you learn about your attitude toward tradition?

How will you allow spiritual tradition—established patterns of thought
or behavior—to enhance your love for God?

Share your discovery with a friend you can trust, asking him or her to
check in with you next month about this insight and the action you
took.

Write a prayer, committing your steps to the Lord (see Psalm 37:5).

Week 2

Read: Gertrud Mueller Nelson, a contemporary artist and writer,
captures well the beauty of the Traditionalist spiritual temperament
when she says that age-old rituals and symbols of the faith move us into
the timeless stream of God.

> God proceeded to create a world of order with space, matter,
> time, life, and humans in his own image. Through ritual and
> ceremonies we people in turn make order out of chaos. In endless
> space, we create a fixed point to orient ourselves: a sacred space.
> To timelessness we impose rhythmic repetitions: the recurrent
> feast. . . . What is too vast and shapeless, we deal with in smaller,
> manageable pieces. We do this for practicality but we also do
> this for high purpose: to relate safely to the mysterious, to
> communicate with the transcendent.[1]

Reflect: Consider the rituals and ceremonies in your life that make
"order out of chaos."

What "rhythmic repetitions" do you impose upon your life that anchor
you in time—for example, eating breakfast in a customary place in the
house, where and when you open your mail, or how you begin and end
your day?

Reflect upon the tools you use to help you relate spiritually to the mysterious and communicate with the transcendent.

Respond: Find a copy of the *Book of Common Prayer*.[2] If you are unfamiliar with this book, ask the staff at your local Christian bookstore for help in finding and using it. Be sure you get one that has a Psalter in the back, as it will give you instructions on which psalm to read in the morning and which psalm to read in the evening.

According to today's date, find the section in the Psalter that corresponds with the calendar. For example, if today's date is May 22, read Psalm 107 for morning prayer and Psalms 108 and 109 for evening prayer. As you read, realize that all those people around the world who use the *Book of Common Prayer* daily are reading the same psalms you are. Allow yourself to feel solidarity with the saints. Continue this practice for the week. If you choose to continue reading for the month, you will read through the entire Psalter.

Ask the Lord to make His Word alive to you as you read, to speak to you every morning and evening as you come to be with Him.

Practice this exercise as many times as possible this week.

Record: How has reading through the *Book of Common Prayer* enhanced your relationship with the Lord this week?

What follow-up do you need to do in the future?

Share about the *Book of Common Prayer* with a friend you can trust, asking him or her to check in with you next month about your reading and how the traditions are stimulating your love for God.

Write a prayer, committing your steps to the Lord (see Psalm 37:5).

Week 3

Read: Our God is a God of history. His acts have been recorded so that we can look back and remember what He has done for us and for His people throughout time (see Psalm 105:5; 143:5). The Bible tells us 175 times to look back and remember, because the record of God's deeds in the past is meant to anchor our faith in the present and the future.

Interestingly, the Lord says that we are not the only ones for whom remembering is critical; He also remembers us—He has tattooed our names on His palms (see Isaiah 49:16), and He stores our tears in His bottle (see Psalm 56:8, NKJV). The Lord remembers those who deeply love Him:

> Those who feared the LORD spoke with each other, and the LORD listened to what they said. In his presence, a scroll of remembrance was written to record the names of those who feared him and always thought about the honor of his name.   *Malachi 3:16 (NLT)*

Reflect: Whom do you know and talk with who fears the Lord, and what do you say about Him to one another?

THE MESSAGE translates Malachi 3:16 this way:

> A book was opened in God's presence and minutes were taken of the meeting.

What do you think the minutes would say about the meetings you have with friends?

What would you want the minutes of your meetings to say?

Respond: This week, be mindful of your conversations. Plan a time to talk with the people you know who fear the Lord and share the truth found in Malachi 3:16.

With your family or some close friends, create your own book of remembrance using a three-ring binder. Give each person at least one page on which to draw a picture of his or her faith journey, including times and people who have helped along the way. Gather pictures of these people to include in your book.

Plan a time to review your book once or twice a year with your family and friends, adding new pages each year as your journey continues. Perhaps you want to make this a regular part of celebrating

Thanksgiving, Easter, or New Year's Day. On your calendar, mark the dates you've set aside to review your book and *remember* together.

Record: Did you enjoy making a book of remembrance with your family or friends this week?

What did you learn?

What was the most helpful part of this exercise? What was the most challenging?

What will you do the same or different next time?

Share your experience with a friend you can trust, asking him or her to check in with you later about how your book of remembrance is impacting your family's life with God.

Write a prayer, committing your steps to the Lord (see Psalm 37:5).

Week 4

Integration: Review the last few weeks. What has God taught you?

How will you integrate what you have learned into your life?

If there are ways you need to take action in the future, write them in your journal.

Go to www.ChristianBookGuides.com for intermediate and advanced-level exercises.

NOTES

PREFACE

1 Bill Bright, "The Four Spiritual Laws" (Canby, Ore.: Christian Literature International, 1969), 9.

2 Richard Foster, *Celebration of Discipline* (San Francisco: Harper, 1978), 1.

3 Myra Boone, "Uniquely Wired: Spiritual Temperaments as Authentic Pathways to Intimacy with God" (DMin dissertation, Azusa Pacific University, 2004).

4 Henri Nouwen, *Life of the Beloved: Spiritual Living in a Secular World* (New York: Crossroad Publishing Co., 1992).

INTRODUCTION

1 Told by Patty Cepin at "The Sanctuary" in Tucson, Ariz.

2 Calvin Miller, *The Table of Inwardness* (Downers Grove, Ill.: InterVarsity Press, 1984), 9.

3 George Cladis, *Leading the Team-Based Church* (San Francisco: Josey-Bass Publishers, 1998), 4.

4 Dallas Willard, *The Divine Conspiracy* (San Francisco: Harper, 1996), 11.

5 "I Hope You Dance" by Mark D. Sanders. Copyright 2000 MCA Music Publishing and Soda Creek Songs. All rights administered by Universal Music Corp./ASCAP. Used by permission. All rights reserved.

CHAPTER 1

1 Timothy John Colborne, "Renewal and Temperament: Spiritual Formation in the Context of Personality Type" (DMin dissertation, Gordon-Conwell Theological Seminary, 1997), 2.

2 This quotation is from Sam Metcalf's "Monday Morning Memo," written to the staff of Church Resource Ministries, November 3, 2003, 4.

3 Kenneth Boa, *Conformed to His Image: Biblical and Practical Approaches to Spiritual Formation* (Grand Rapids, Mich.: Zondervan, 2001).

4 Bill Hybels, *Courageous Leadership* (Grand Rapids, Mich.: Zondervan, 2002), 216-217.

5 See, for example, Chester Michael and Marie Norrisey, *Prayer and Temperament* (Charlottesville, Va.: Open Door, 1984).

6   Gary Thomas, *Sacred Pathways* (Nashville: Thomas Nelson, 1982), 16.

7   Henri Nouwen, *The Road to Daybreak* (New York: Doubleday, 1988), 8.

8   Ken Gire, *Windows of the Soul* (Grand Rapids, Mich.: Zondervan, 1996), 16.

9   Gary Chapman, *The Love Languages of God* (Grand Rapids, Mich.: Zondervan, 2002).

10 As a spiritual director, James Houston gave this feedback to his directee Paul Rhoads in a face-to-face spiritual direction appointment. Paul, a friend and colleague, gave me permission to share this information. Houston was the founding principal and chancellor of Regent College in Vancouver, British Columbia. One of his classic works is called *The Transforming Power of Prayer* (Colorado Springs: NavPress, 1996).

11 Colborne, "Renewal and Temperament," 2.

12 Thomas, *Sacred Pathways*, 34.

13 Ibid.

14 Thanks to Tom Ashbrook and Church Resource Ministries' Imago Christi spiritual formation team, 2003, for this definition.

CHAPTER 2

1   Thomas, *Sacred Pathways*, 16.

2   Adele Ahlberg Calhoun, *Spiritual Disciplines Handbook* (Downers Grove, Ill.: InterVarsity Press, 2005), 15–16.

CHAPTER 3

1   Hybels, *Courageous Leadership*, 215–216.

2   Ibid., 223.

3   Richard Foster, *Streams of Living Water* (San Francisco: HarperSanFrancisco, 2000), 137–144.

4   Hybels, *Courageous Leadership*, 244.

5   Ibid.

6   Roger D. Sorrell, *St. Francis of Assisi and Nature* (New York: Oxford University Press, 1988), 20.

7   Philip Rousseau, *Ascetics, Authority, and the Church in the Age of Jerome and Cassian* (London: Oxford University Press, 1978), 48.

8   Thomas, *Sacred Pathways*, 120.

9   Ibid., 133.

10 Ibid., 136–137.

11 M. Basil Pennington, *A Place Apart: Monastic Prayer and Practice for Everyone* (New York: Doubleday, 1983), 111.

12 Felix Duffey, *Psychiatry and Asceticism* (London: B. Herder Book Co., 1950), 60.

13 Thomas, *Sacred Pathways*, 123.

14 Hybels, *Courageous Leadership*, 221.

15 Thomas, *Sacred Pathways*, 164.

16 Hybels, *Courageous Leadership*, 221–222.

17 Thomas, *Sacred Pathways*, 210.

18 Ibid.

19 Hybels, 221.

20 Richard Foster, *Prayer: Finding the Heart's True Home* (San Francisco: HarperSanFrancisco, 1992), 1–2, 4.

21 Hybels, *Courageous Leadership*, 222–223.

22 Thomas Merton, *Contemplation in a World of Action* (Notre Dame, Ind.: University of Notre Dame Press, 1998), 6, 9.

23 M. Basil Pennington, *Daily We Touch Him* (Garden City, N.Y.: Doubleday & Co., 1977), 51–52.

24 Thomas, *Sacred Pathways*, 182.

25 Ibid.

26 Ibid., 187.

27 Hybels, *Courageous Leadership*, 225–226.

28 Ibid.

29 Ibid., 219.

30 Ibid.

31 Ibid., 234.

32 Ibid, 219.

33 Ibid., 224.

34 Ibid., 225.

35 Thomas, *Sacred Pathways*, 41.

36 Annie Dillard, *Pilgrim at Tinker Creek* (New York: Harper & Row, 1974), 33.

37 Ibid., 16, 30.

38 Loren Wilkinson, *Earthkeeping in the Nineties: Stewardship of Creation* (Grand Rapids, Mich.: Eerdmans, 1991); *Caring for Creation in Your Own Backyard*, with Mary Ruth Wilkinson (Ann Arbor, Mich.: Servant Publications, 1992).

39 Anne Morrow Lindbergh, *Gift from the Sea* (New York: Random House, 1997).

40 Kate White, "The Salmon Creek Trail," used with permission.

41 Hybels, *Courageous Leadership*, 225.

42 Thomas, *Sacred Pathways*, 63.

43 Daniel Clendenin, "From the Verbal to the Visual: Orthodox Icons and the Sanctification of Sight," *Christian Scholar's Review 25* (September 1995): 1, 30.

44 Thomas, *Sacred Pathways*, 61.

45 Ibid., 66.

46 Ibid., 70.

47 Ibid., 71–72.

48 John and Stasi Eldredge, *Captivating: Unveiling the Mystery of a Woman's Soul* (Nashville: Nelson Books, 2005), 22.

49 Philip Whitfield and Mike Stoddart, *Hearing, Taste, and Smell: Pathways of Perception* (New York: Torstar Books, 1985), 153.

50 Thomas, *Sacred Pathways*, 66–67.

51 Gertrud Mueller Nelson, To Dance with God: Family Ritual and Community Celebration (Mahway, N.J.: Paulist Press, 1986), 25.

52 Ibid., 26.

53 Thomas, *Sacred Pathways*, 88.

54 Ibid., 85.

55 Sidney Heath, *Romance of Symbolism* (London: Francis Griffiths, 1909), 57–61.

56 Ibid.

CHAPTER 4

1 Thomas, *Sacred Pathways*, 259–260.

2 Calhoun, *Spiritual Disciplines Handbook*, 17.

3 Thomas, *Sacred Pathways*, 16.

4 As a spiritual director, James Houston gave this feedback to his directee Paul Rhoads in a face-to-face spiritual direction appointment. Paul, a friend and colleague, gave me permission to share this information. Houston was the founding principal and chancellor of Regent College in Vancouver, British Columbia. One of his classic works is called *The Transforming Power of Prayer* (Colorado Springs: NavPress, 1996).

5 James Houston, *The Transforming Power of Prayer* (Colorado Springs: NavPress, 1996), 134–135.

6 Thomas, *Sacred Pathways*, 263.

7 Calhoun, *Spiritual Disciplines Handbook*, 17, 19.

8 Foster, *Celebration of Discipline*, 7.

9 Dallas Willard, *The Spirit of the Disciplines: Understanding How God Changes Lives* (San Francisco: Harper & Row, 1988), 353.

10 Marjorie Thompson, *Soul Feast: An Invitation to the Christian Spiritual Life* (Louisville: Westminster John Knox Press, 1995), 138.

11 Eugene H. Peterson, *Five Smooth Stones for Pastoral Work* (Grand Rapids, Mich.: Eerdmans, 1992), 110.

12 Boa, *Conformed to His Image*, 480.

13 M. Robert Mulholland Jr., *Invitation to a Journey*, 12.

14 Dallas Willard, *Renovation of the Heart* (Colorado Springs: NavPress, 2002).

CHAPTER 5

1 Christian Schwarz, *Natural Church Development* (Carol Stream, Ill.: ChurchSmart Resources, 1996), 63.

2 Christian Schwarz, *The ABC's of Natural Church Development* (Carol Stream, Ill.: ChurchSmart Resources, 1998), 14.

3 Mike Yaconelli, *Messy Spirituality* (Grand Rapids, Mich.: Zondervan, 2002), 13, 17.

4 Ibid., 13.

5 Thanks to Tom Ashbrook and the Church Resource Ministries' Spiritual Formation Team, 2003, for this definition.

CHAPTER 6

1 MercyMe, "I Can Only Imagine," *Almost There* (INO Records, 1999).

2 Anders Nygren, *Agape and Eros* (Chicago: University of Chicago Press, 1982), ix.

3 Brennan Manning, from a message entitled, "Healing Our Image of God and Ourselves", March 10, 2006, Pasadena Covenant Church.

4 A. W. Tozer, *Knowledge of the Holy* (San Francisco: Harper & Row, 1978), 77.

5 Saint John of the Cross, *Spiritual Canticle of the Soul and the Bridegroom of Christ* (Washington, D.C.: ICS Publications, 1991).

6 Manning, "Healing Our Image of God and Ourselves."

7 Leon Morris, *Testaments of Love* (Grand Rapids, Mich.: Eerdmans, 1981), 65–75.

8 Excerpted from *TrueFaced: Trust God and Others with Who You Really Are* by Bill Thrall, Bruce McNicol, and John Lynch, copyright 2004. Used by permission of NavPress, www.navpress.com. All rights reserved.

9 Manning, "Healing Our Image of God and Ourselves."

CHAPTER 7

1 I received this as a handout in the Spiritual Foundations class Richard Foster taught in January 2001 at Azusa Pacific University, Azusa, Calif.

CHAPTER 8

1 *Merriam-Webster's Collegiate Dictionary* (Springfield, Mass.: Merriam-Webster, 2003).

2 Willard, *The Divine Conspiracy*, 22.

3 Ibid.

CHAPTER 9

1 Thomas R. Kelly, *A Testament of Devotion* (San Francisco: Harper, 1992), 3–4, 26.

2 Thomas Crum, *Journey to Center* (New York: Fireside, 1997), 5.

3 Dillard, *Pilgrim at Tinker Creek*, 32–33.

4 Henri Nouwen, *The Dance of Life* (London: Darton, Longman and Todd, 2005), 49.

5 Parts of his meditation are available daily at www.sacredspace.ie, produced by the Irish Jesuits.

6 Timothy Fry, ed., *Rule of Saint Benedict* (Collegeville, Mich.: Liturgical Press, 1981), 313.

7 Brent Peery, "Benedictine Spirituality Contextualized for Evangelical Christians" (DMin dissertation., Azusa Pacific University, 2002), 43.

CHAPTER 10

1 DeWaal, *Seeking God*, 120.

2 Lonni Collins Pratt and Father Daniel Homan, *Benedict's Way: An Ancient Monk's Insights for a Balanced Life* (Chicago: Loyola Press, 2000), 69.

3 DeWaal, *Seeking God*, 120–121.

4 Harald Schützeichel, "The Rule of Benedict as a Guide for Christian Living, Part 2," translated by Sebastian Samay, *American Benedictine Review* 39:3 (September 1988), 255.

5 Peery, 81.

CHAPTER 11

1 Miller, *The Table of Inwardness,* 35–36.

2 Ibid., 30.

3 Ibid., 29.

4 Kelly, *A Testament of Devotion,* viii.

CHAPTER 12

1 Helen H. Lemmel, "Turn Your Eyes upon Jesus" (Singspiration 1922).

CHAPTER 13

1 Harry James Cargas, *Exploring Your Inner Space* (Cincinnati: St. Anthony Messenger Press, 1991).

2 Exercise inspired by Floyd W. Churn, "Nourishment for Peculiar Pilgrims on the Journey of Faith: A Workshop for Mapping Our Spiritual Path Using a Deeper Knowledge of Our Gifts of Personality Type," DMin dissertation, Princeton Theological Seminary, 1995, 184–185.

CHAPTER 14

1 Minucius Felix was a third-century Latin apologist; quotation from an unknown source.

2 C. Austin Miles, "In the Garden," Hall-Mack Co., 1912.

CHAPTER 15

1 Exercise adapted from Churn, 176.

2 Adapted from Henry Morgan, *Approaches to Prayer: A Resource Book for Groups and Individuals* (Harrisburg, Penn.: Morehouse Publishing, 1991), 16–17, 117.

3 "Change My Heart Oh God," written by Eddie Espinosa ©1982 Mercy/Vineyard Publishing (ASCAP). Admin. worldwide by Vineyard Music. Used by permission.

CHAPTER 16

1 Nelson, *To Dance with God,* 25.

2 Charles Mortimer Guilbert, *The Standard Book of Common Prayer* (New York: Oxford University Press, 1990).

ABOUT THE AUTHOR

Dr. Myra Perrine has a passion for intimacy with God and has been speaking and teaching on this subject for more than thirty-five years. She has authored several workbooks to help others draw near to Jesus, and as a Transformational LIFE Coach, Myra is gifted in helping people "think outside the box." With a doctor of ministry degree in spiritual formation, Myra is currently on staff with Church Resource Ministries, a missions organization that develops leaders to start and strengthen churches worldwide, where Myra offers pastoral care and spiritual guidance to some of CRM's three hundred missionaries in twenty-two nations. As an adjunct professor at Azusa Pacific University, she teaches a variety of classes, including spiritual growth and leadership. She also speaks to churches and organizations on topics such as intimacy with God, leadership, and spiritual formation.

Myra and her husband, Dan, have one son and live in Upland, California. They also have two dogs, Nicholas and Ginger.

CRM (Church Resource Ministries) is a movement committed to developing leaders to strengthen and multiply the church worldwide.

More than three hundred CRM missionaries live and minister in nations on every continent, coaching, mentoring, and apprenticing those called to lead and serve the Christian movement in an array of diverse cultural settings. This results in the multiplication of godly leaders who have a passion for their world and who are empowered to reproduce their lives and ministry. Through them, CRM stimulates movements of fresh, authentic churches, holistic in nature, so that the name of God is renowned among the nations.

Those serving with CRM believe that such leadership development is primarily a relational undertaking and, at its core, a process of spiritual formation. Helping leaders go deep in intimacy with God, as Myra Perrine explores in this book, is at the core of what CRM does around the world. CRM believes that leadership is *the* critical issue for the health of Christianity in any era and that spiritual passion is the nonnegotiable essential for such vitality.

CRM EMPOWERING LEADERS

More information about CRM can be found at
www.crmleaders.org

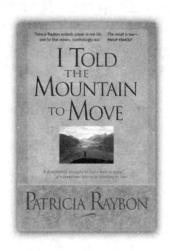

"Imagine a place between seashore and sea, earth and sky, here and now and heaven to come—a place where the veil between this life and the next is so thin you can almost touch the very hand of God."

Have you ever needed to feel the tangible presence of God? The ancients believed there were physical locations, thin places, where the physical and spiritual worlds almost intersected, but what if any place could become a thin place?

In *So Close I Can Feel God's Breath*, Beverly Rose reveals a God who breathes into our lives and hearts in miraculous ways, beckoning us to reach out to and grasp true intimacy with our Creator. She opens our eyes to that which is unseen and alerts our ears to his silent call. You can see him and touch him for yourself today—if you know where to look.

So Close, I Can Feel
God's Breath
experiencing his nearness in thin places
Dr. Beverly Rose

SALT**RIVER**®

CP0057

Discover Your Soul's Path to God

In *Sacred Pathways* (Zondervan, 2002), Gary Thomas strips away the frustration of a one-size-fits-all spirituality and guides you toward a path of worship that frees you to be you.

This book unfolds the traits, strengths, and pitfalls of nine distinct spiritual temperaments. In one or more, you will see yourself and the ways you most naturally express your relationship with Jesus Christ. Whatever temperament or blend of temperaments best describes you, rest assured it's not by accident. It's by the design of a Creator who knew what he was doing when he made you according to his own unique specifications.

Sacred Pathways will show you the route you were made to travel, marked by growth and filled with the riches of a close walk with God.

CP0088